Communications
in Computer and Information

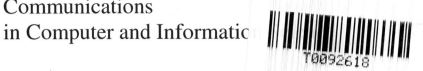

T0092618

Changhoon Lee   Jean-Marc Seigneur
James J. Park   Roland R. Wagner (Eds.)

Secure and Trust Computing, Data Management, and Applications

STA 2011 Workshops: IWCS 2011 and STAVE 2011
Loutraki, Greece, June 28-30, 2011
Proceedings

 Springer

Volume Editors

Changhoon Lee
Hanshin University, School of Computer Engineering, Suwon, South Korea
E-mail: chlee@hs.ac.kr

Jean-Marc Seigneur
University of Geneva, CUI, Geneva, Switzerland
E-mail: jean-marc.seigneur@trustcomp.org

James J. Park
Seoul National University of Science and Technology
Department of Computer Science and Engineering, Seoul, South Korea
E-mail: parkjonghyuk1@hotmail.com

Roland R. Wagner
University of Linz, Institute of FAW, Linz, Austria
E-mail: rwagner@faw.uni-linz.ac.at

ISSN 1865-0929   e-ISSN 1865-0937
ISBN 978-3-642-22364-8   e-ISBN 978-3-642-22365-5
DOI 10.1007/978-3-642-22365-5
Springer Heidelberg Dordrecht London New York

Library of Congress Control Number: Applied for

CR Subject Classification (1998): C.2, H.4, H.3, I.2, K.6.5, D.4.6

Typesetting: Camera-ready by author, data conversion by Scientific Publishing Services, Chennai, India

Printed on acid-free paper

Springer is part of Springer Science+Business Media (www.springer.com)

Preface

STA 2011 was the eighth in a conference series that provides a forum for researchers and practitioners in all areas of security and data management. In conjunction with STA 2011, a series of workshops were held. They were meant to facilitate the exchange of ideas and experiences between active researchers, and to stimulate discussions on new and emerging topics in line with the conference topics. We see the workshops as a necessary extension of the main conference. STA has established itself rapidly as a high-quality conference with a highly competitive selection process. The following workshops were approved and accepted for inclusion in the STA 2011 program:

- International Workshop on Convergence Security in Pervasive Environments, (IWCS 2011)
- International Workshop on Security and Trust for Applications in Virtualized Environments, (STAVE 2011)

The program of each of these workshops was developed by a separate dedicated organizing team and Program Committee. The organization of these workshops was made possible by the voluntary dedicated efforts of many individuals. We thank all the workshop organizers, the members of the Program Committees, and the additional reviewers for their excellent service to the community. We thank the authors for submitting papers to these workshops.

June 2011

Changhoon Lee
Jean-Marc Seigneur
James J. (Jong Hyuk) Park
Roland R. Wagner

International Workshop on Convergence Security in Pervasive Environments

(IWCS 2011)

Preface

On behalf of the Organizing Committees, it is our pleasure to welcome you to the first FTRA International Workshop on Convergence Security in Pervasive Environments (IWCS 2011), which was held in Loutraki, Greece, June 28–30, 2011.

A recent emerging issue in information technology is the convergence of different kinds of applications. Convergence brings a user-centric environment to provide computing and communication services. In order to realize IT advantages, we need the integration of security and data management to be suitable for pervasive computing environments. However, there are still many problems and major challenges waiting for us to solve such as the security risks in convergence applications, which could appear when devices interact with different kinds of applications. Therefore, we need to explore convergence security in pervasive environments.

IWCS 2011 addressed the various theories and practical applications of convergence security in pervasive environments. It presented important results for improving application services and solving various problems within the scope of IWCS 2011. In addition, we believe it triggered further related research and technology developments that will improve our lives in the future.

We sincerely thank all our Chairs and Committees that are listed on the following pages. Without theirhard work, the success of IWCS 2011 would not have been possible.We hope you find the proceedings of IWCS 2011 enjoyable and we would welcome any suggestions for improvement.

Jose A. Onieva
Charalabos Skianis

Conference Organization

General Chairs

Jose A. Onieva   University of Málaga, Spain
Charalabos Skianis   University of the Aegean, Greece

Program Chairs

Kyusuk Han   KAIST, Korea
Rodrigo Roman Castro   University of Málaga, Spain

Publicity Co-chairs

Christos Xenakis   University of Piraeus, Greece
Eleni Darra   University of Piraeus, Greece
Evangelos Rekleitis   University of the Aegean, Greece

IWCS 2011 Program Committee

Alexander De Luca	Ludwig-Maximilians-Universität, Germany
Anthony H.M. Chung	University of Lancaster, UK
Antonio Jara	University of Murcia, Spain
Chan Yeun Yeob	Khalifa University of Science Technology and Research, UAE
Damien Sauveron	XLIM, University of Limoges, France
Deok Gyu Lee	ETRI, Korea
Fabio Martinelli	Information Security Group, IIT-CNR, Italy
Fernando Ferri	Institute for Research on Population and Social Policies, Italy
Florian Michahelles	ETH Zurich, Switzerland
Florina Almenárez	University Carlos III of Madrid, Spain
Han-You Jeong	Pusan University, Korea
Hyohyun Choi	Inha Technical College, Korea
Isaac Agudo	Universidad de Málaga, Spain
Jae-il Lee	KISA, Korea
Javier Lopez	University of Málaga, Spain
Jeong Hyun Yi	Soongsil University, Korea
Jongsub Moon	Korea University, Korea

Jordi Herrera Joancomartí	Universitat Autònoma de Barcelona, Spain
Jose A. Montes	Universidad de Málaga, Spain
Juan Hernández Serrano	Universitat Politècnica de Catalunya, Spain
Magdalena Payeras-Capellà	University of the Balearic Islands, Spain
Manik Lal Das	Dhirubhai Ambani Inst. of Information and Communication Tech., India
Marc Lacoste	France Telecom R&D/Orange Labs, France
María Francisca Hinarejos	University of the Balearic Islands, Spain
Masoom Alam	Institute of Management Sciences, Pakistan
Nicolas Sklavos	Tech. Educational Institute of Patras, Greece
Olivier Markowitch	Université Libre de Bruxelles, Belgium
Panagiotis Rizomiliotis	University of the Aegean, Greece
Pierangela Samarati	University of Milan, Italy
Rodrigo Roman Castro	University of Málaga, Spain
Ruben Rios del Pozo	University of Málaga, Spain
Sokratis Katsikas	University of Piraeus, Greece
Stefanos Gritzalis	Info-Sec-Lab, University of the Aegean, Greece
Sunwoong Choi	Kookmin University, Korea
Thomas Strang	German Aerospace Center (DLR), Germany
Thomas Wook Choi	Hankuk University of Foreign Studies, Korea
Vishal Kher	VMware, USA
Won Joo Lee	Inha Technical College, Korea
Yong Lee	ChungJu University, Korea

International Workshop on Security and Trust for Applications in Virtualized Environments

(STAVE 2011)

Preface

Virtualisation technologies offer many benefits to IT organisations today and into the future. These technologies allow organisations to increase the utilisation of their IT infrastructure while lowering the overall costs of ownership and accelerating the return on investment.

As virtualisation increases the sharing of compute, network and I/O resources with multiple users and applications in order to drive higher utilisation rates, it replaces the traditional physical isolation boundaries with virtual ones. This fundamental change in isolation boundaries introduces new risk vectors for data leakage, cross-contamination as well as new requirements for the auditing and monitoring of such virtualised systems.

In order to allow the deployment of e-Government, e-Health or other application services that use, store, and process highly sensitive data, there are a number of significant, common, complex issues which must be addressed by virtualisation technologies and solutions which have particular relevance:

- Compliance with legal frameworks for data protection and privacy
- Identity management between different governmental services
- Security and trust aspects of using virtualisation in a distributed environment
- Policy mapping (existing security and trust systems with virtualisation solutions)
- Management of risks and policy compliance verification.

The First International Workshop on Security and Trust for Applications in Virtualised Environments (STAVE 2011) brought together industry executives, seasoned managers, agency representatives, expert researchers and senior subject matter experts from a broad array of application and technical areas, as well as government officials who are concerned with security and trust in virtualised environments. It drew out common themes, problems and issues that are encountered, and the solutions that have been devised to deal with the problems of securing virtualised environments and compliance with government regulations. It aimed to provide the basis for a common understanding and common approaches to security and trust that synthesises the insights and best of breed solutions being developed in the diverse areas in which these problems are encountered.

The Workshop Chairs wish to thank the authors of presented papers and speakers for their fine and interesting contributions. Finally, our warmest thanks to the Organizing Committee of STA 2011 and in particular to the Program Chairs of the Security and Trust Computing Track, Taeshik Shon and Costas Lambrinoudakis, for making STAVE 2011 possible.

June 2011

Charalabos Skianis
Panagiotis Rizomiliotis
Isaac Agudo
Barry P. Mulcahy
Eamonn Power
Patrick Phelan

Conference Organization

General Chair

Charalabos Skianis   University of the Aegean, Greece

TPC Chairs

Panagiotis Rizomiliotis   University of the Aegean, Greece
Isaac Agudo   University of Málaga, Spain

Core Organizing Committee

Barry P. Mulcahy   Waterford Institute of Technology, Ireland
Eamonn Power   Waterford Institute of Technology, Ireland
Patrick Phelan   Waterford Institute of Technology, Ireland

STAVE 2011 Program Committee

Enrico Angori   Datamat, Italy
Pascal Bisson   Thales Research & Technology, France
Alexander Boettcher   Technische Universitat Dresden, Germany
Caspar Bowden   Microsoft, EMEA
Pete Bramhall   Hewlett Packard Laboritories, UK
Jan Camenisch   IBM, Switzerland
Gregory Chockler   IBM, Israel
Paolo Collimedaglia   Selex Communications, Italy
Herve Debar   Télécom Research and Development, France
Danny De Cock   Katholieke Universiteit Leuven, Belgium
Hermann de Meer   University of Passau, Germany
Shane Dempsey   Waterford Institute of Technology, Ireland
Rodriguez Diaz   Rodrigo ATOS Origin, Spain
Zeta Dooly   Waterford Institute of Technology, Ireland
Guerrero Fernandez   Daniel ATOS Origin, Spain
Brian Foley   Waterford Institute of Technology, Ireland
Frederic Gittler   Hewlett Packard Laboratories, UK
Marit Hansen   Independent Centre for Privacy Protection, Germany

Table of Contents

Analysis of the Similarities in Malicious DNS Domain Names 1
  Krzysztof Lasota and Adam Kozakiewicz

Time Validity in Role-Based Trust Management Inference System 7
  Anna Felkner and Adam Kozakiewicz

Vaudenay's Privacy Model in the Universal Composability Framework:
A Case Study 16
  Hervé Chabanne and Céline Chevalier

Mining Frequent Items in OLAP 25
  Ling Jin, Ji Yeon Lim, Iee Joon Kim, Kyung Soo Cho,
  Seung Kwan Kim, and Ung Mo Kim

Trust Building and Management for Online File Storage Service 31
  Huiying Duan

Digital Trails Discovering of a GPS Embedded Smart Phone – Take
Nokia N78 Running Symbian S60 Ver 3.2 for Example 41
  Hai-Cheng Chu, Li-Wei Wu, Hsiang-Ming Yu, and Jong Hyuk Park

Opinion Mining in MapReduce Framework 50
  Kyung Soo Cho, Ji Yeon Lim, Jae Yeol Yoon, Young Hee Kim,
  Seung Kwan Kim, and Ung Mo Kim

Towards an Open Framework for Mobile Digital Identity Management
through Strong Authentication Methods 56
  Brahim En-Nasry and Mohamed Dafir Ech-Cherif El Kettani

Deterministic Data Binding for Dynamic Service Compositions 64
  Eunjung Lee, Hyung-Ju Joo, and Kyong-Jin Seo

Integration Retrieval of History Data and Sensing Information Using
SGLN Code in Extended RFID Application 71
  Seungwoo Jeon, Gihong Kim, Bonghee Hong, and Joonho Kwon

Real-Time Quantity Inspection Method for Moving Tags in RFID
Middleware 77
  Goo Kim, Wooseok Ryu, Bonghee Hong, and Joonho Kwon

An Improved Active Learning in Unbalanced Data Classification 84
  Woon Jeung Park

A Study on Aircraft Position Calculation Algorithm in Compliance
with the Wind Parameter 94
    Dong-Hwa Park and Hyo-Dal Park

For Aviation Security Using Surveillance System 103
    Deok Gyu Lee and Jong Wook Han

An Efficient Intrusion Detection Scheme for Wireless Sensor
Networks 116
    Chunming Rong, Skjalg Eggen, and Hongbing Cheng

Policy Based Management for Security in Cloud Computing 130
    Adrian Waller, Ian Sandy, Eamonn Power, Efthimia Aivaloglou,
    Charalampos Skianis, Antonio Muñoz, and Antonio Maña

Management of Integrity-Enforced Virtual Applications 138
    Michael Gissing, Ronald Toegl, and Martin Pirker

Enhancing Accountability in the Cloud via Sticky Policies 146
    Siani Pearson, Marco Casassa Mont, and Gina Kounga

Enhancement of Critical Financial Infrastructure Protection Using
Trust Management 156
    Hisain Elshaafi, Jimmy McGibney, Barry Mulcahy, and
    Dmitri Botvich

Towards Natural-Language Understanding and Automated
Enforcement of Privacy Rules and Regulations in the Cloud: Survey and
Bibliography 166
    Nick Papanikolaou, Siani Pearson, and Marco Casassa Mont

Secure Workstation for Special Applications 174
    Adam Kozakiewicz, Anna Felkner, Janusz Furtak,
    Zbigniew Zieliński, Marek Brudka, and Marek Małowidzki

Dynamic Security Monitoring and Accounting for Virtualized
Environments 182
    Antonio Muñoz, Rajesh Harjani, Antonio Maña, and Rodrigo Díaz

Cryptography Goes to the Cloud 190
    Isaac Agudo, David Nuñez, Gabriele Giammatteo,
    Panagiotis Rizomiliotis, and Costas Lambrinoudakis

Identity Management Challenges for Intercloud Applications 198
    David Núñez, Isaac Agudo, Prokopios Drogkaris, and
    Stefanos Gritzalis

Author Index 205

Analysis of the Similarities in Malicious DNS Domain Names

Krzysztof Lasota[1] and Adam Kozakiewicz[1,2]

[1] NASK - Research and Academic Computer Network, Wąwozowa 18,
02-796 Warsaw, Poland
[2] Institute of Control and Computation Engineering,
Warsaw University of Technology,
Nowowiejska 15/19,00-665 Warsaw, Poland
{adam.kozakiewicz,krzysztof.lasota}@nask.pl

Abstract. This paper presents results of studies on similarities in the construction of malicious DNS domain names. Based on sets of malicious domain names (or URLs, where only mnemonic host names are taken into account) a prototype tool searches for formulated similarities in the construction of malicious domains. A key research task was to find features of similarity which could be useful in the detection of malicious behavior. Research results can be used as an additional characteristic of existing heuristic methods for determining the malicious character of domains or websites. They could also be used as a hint for specialists to take a closer look at domains which are similar to other malicious domains.

Keywords: malicious domains, heuristic detection methods, phishing detection.

1 Introduction

The Internet is quickly becoming a universal communication infrastructure, popular regardless of age, social status or geographic location. Available around the world, with billions of users, it is a rich and relatively safe hunting ground for malicious groups. In the recent years there is a clear trend in one type of malicious behaviors: web threats are becoming more and more common, including phishing and malware distribution. Depending on the type of attack the goal may be taking control of the victim's computer or just stealing personal data for identity theft or other purposes.

This paper presents results of studies on similarities in the construction of malicious DNS names. Next section of this paper contains a description of existing threat detection tools and heuristic methods which were considered during the conceptual work on a prototype tool. Sets of malicious domains and also their selected features were described in Section 3. Chapter 4 presents a brief overview of the tool implemented to perform the analyses. The main value is contained in chapter 5 which describe the formulated similarities between malicious domains, and obtained results. The last part contains a brief summary.

C. Lee et al. (Eds.): STA 2011 Workshops, CCIS 187, pp. 1–6, 2011.

2 Existing Solutions

During state-of-the-art analysis a number of existing threat detection tools and heuristic methods were identified. Apart from functionally similar solutions, other interesting initiatives were analyzed, sharing the goal of increasing security and the same general field of interest.

Google Safe Browsing [3] service enables its clients (usually web browsers) to alert users about the threats presented by malicious WWW sites. The service publishes lists of hashes generated from malicious URLs and their fragments (without query, path or lowest level sub-domain).

DNS Blackholing [2] project's goal is to create and maintain lists of domain names used by sites involved in malicious activity. Several implementations of the mechanism exist, but all of them in fact simply analyze requests to the local DNS server implementing the mechanism and redirect the filtered domains to a predefined address (usually localhost – 127.0.0.1, but redirection to a honeypot is also practiced).

Client honeypots [6,11] are a family of tools designed to actively search for malicious behavior. Most of them specialize in detection of dangerous websites. Different kinds of analyses are used to determine the potential threat associated with visiting a given site. The common property of this group of tools (low- interaction, high-interaction, hybrid) is that – unlike the previously described tools – they use heuristic methods to analyze the actual content of web pages or/and behavior occurring in the operating system while visiting the web pages. Also, they can act as an automatic source of blacklists for the other tools.

Heuristic methods, even though not always one hundred percent correct, ease and accelerate the detection process by limiting the amount of input data to the point where effective in depth processing is possible. The family of heuristic methods which are used to detect malicious domain names (mainly phishing sites) can be divided into two groups: the ones using additional information available from public services (DNS, WHOIS, geolocation), and the ones based on lexical features. Some of lexical properties used as criteria in heuristic methods dealing with mnemonic names are [9,10]:

- the length of the domain name – the average length of malicious domain name is shorter than of a typical non-malicious domain name,
- the number of dots in Fully Qualified Domain Name (without the trailing dot) – statistically the structure of a malicious domain name is more complex than that of a typical non-malicious one,
- the occurrence of a keyword – describes whether a specified string is a part of the domain name (used mainly to detect phishing sites),
- the probability of occurrence of a specific characters – just as different languages using the same alphabet differ in this aspect, we can calculate and compare the probability of occurrence of specific characters in domain names from malicious and benign groups,
- the number of different characters – statistically the number of different characters forming a malicious domain name is lower than in a typical domain name.

The large number of already known threats, their polymorphic capabilities and constantly arising new ones, force the use of heuristic methods for the monitoring and detection purposes. Often they are used as a filtering mechanism for more complex systems, e.g. client honeypots. The vast amounts of input data (e.g. SPAM links) and limited processing capabilities reduce the effectives of typical monitoring systems, necessitating the use of heuristic methods to aid in their work.

The proposed research aims at developing a new lexical feature based on similarities between malicious domain names.

3 Preliminary Analysis of Datasets

For the purpose of our research we used three publicly available data sources: DNS-BH lists [2], DNS-BH2 lists [2] and the ranking of most popular URLs (Top URL) [1]. The first two are assumed to consist only of malicious data. DNS-BH contained about 10 thousand domain names (October 2010), and DNS-BH2 lists about 5 thousand distinct domain names (added after October 2010). The last source contained 1 million URLs, assumed to be almost exclusively benign, and was used as a reference describing trends in global naming schemes. Additionally, the third set needed to be preprocessed to extract distinct domain names.

In the classic terminology the last part of the domain name is known as the TLD – top level domain. The list of available TLDs is controlled by ICANN. However, registrars of sub-domains in different TLDs have their own naming schemes, often reserving second (or more, even up to the fourth) level sub-domains as regional or functional. These rules differ between registrars. Because of that we introduced two additional definitions: real domain and real TLD. The real TLD consists of all sub-domains reserved by the registrar and the real domain is the highest-level sub-domain the registrant is able to register. For example, in name "exam.ple.com.pl" the TLD is "pl", but the real TLD is "com.pl" and the real domain name is "ple". Determining the real domain and real TLD is done by using a specially prepared database containing information about possible registration options for each TLD. The database uses mainly the data made available by the Public Suffix List [14] project.

The first of the analyses was performed to determine the similarities between domain names. Data analysis made by hand and based on common patterns found in the structures of domain names allowed us to propose the terms of domain names similarity. The domain name X is similar to domain name Y when:

- Domain names X and Y are registered under the same real TLD and the Levenshtein distance [4] between real domain names is less than the threshold value. For preliminary analysis we proposed to use value of floor function of square root of the number of characters of the domain name X as the threshold value. Other threshold values and distance functions (e.g. Hamming, LCS, Damerau- Levenshtein) may be proposed.
- The real domain names are the same but were registered under different real TLD.

Table 1. shows how many distinct domain names from the first data set have at least one similar domain name in the second set. First row shows averaged results for

5000 domain names taken randomly from the Top URL, compared with 1 million most popular domains. Second row presents results of analysis of 15 thousand domains taken randomly from the Top URL list. The results show similarities between domains in the same set. Another analysis of this kind was performed on the domain names from the DNS-BH list. The research confirmed our presumptions that the similarity is a very general characteristic common in large datasets. However results for smaller sets of URLs clearly show that malicious domains tend to be more similar to each other than randomly taken non-malicious ones.

Table 1. Similarities between sets of domain names

Set of data I	Distinct domains	Set of data II	Distinct domains	Similarities
Random Top URL	5000	Top URL	1000000	52%
Random Top URL	15000	Random Top URL	15000	4%
DNS-BH	10000	DNS-BH	10000	16%

4 Prototype Tool

The prototype tool implements several analyses, including the ones described in this paper, on one or two lists of domain names. The main function of the tool is to compare two sets of domain names (plain text files). The lists are preprocessed to extract real domains and real TLDs. The names from the first list are compared with the ones from the second lists (exact matches are ignored, so both lists can be the same file). If two domains are similar, then a regular expression matching both names is generated – this is called a similarity schema. Two scheme types are searched for. The first one searches for the same real domain names in different real TLDs. The second one assumes that the Levenshtein mismatch measure cannot exceed the boundary value when comparing real domain names registered under the same real TLD. The amount of necessary comparisons is limited by the length relations of real domain names. The first analysis is only performed if they are equal (only exact matches matter anyway). The second analysis is only performed if the lengths are sufficiently close (the difference cannot be greater than the similarity threshold). Finally, the similarity schemes are tested on the second set again – if more than one match is found, then the scheme is marked as verified.

5 Results

To better present properties of the proposed feature we compare it with a feature based on the probability of occurrence of a character in the benign and malicious sets of URLs. We researched three cases and calculated probabilities of occurrence of single characters (P1), pairs (P2) and threes (P3) of characters in domain names from benign and malicious sets. Classification of a domain depends on whether it's likelihood, computed as the sum of probabilities of all its characters (pairs, threes) is higher using probabilities computed from the malicious or benign set.

We propose two variants of a feature based on similarity measure. The first one assumes that the mismatch measure cannot exceed 1 and the similarity found between two domain names must have been confirmed with a third matching domain name that also was caught with the construed regular expression (SC1). The other case was that we did not require confirmation with the third domain name (SN1).

Table 2. Percentage of domain names classified as malicious

Set of data	P1	P2	P3	SN1	SC1
DNS-BH	8 %	24%	52%	12%	8 %
Random Top URL	6 %	14 %	20 %	0,07 %	0,01 %

Table 2. presents results as produced by the two discussed features. The first row shows the percentage of detected malicious real domain names from the DNS-BH list, which was used to train both features. The second row presents results for the randomly chosen 40 thousand domain name addresses from the Alexa top 1 million list also used to train the feature based on similarities. It is noticeable that the similarity feature has low rate of false positive results on the random set.

Table 3. Percentage of domain names classified as malicious

Set of data	SN1	SC1	SN2	SC2	SN3	SC3
DNS-BH2	0,16 %	0,04 %	0,31 %	0,18 %	0,38 %	0,24 %
Random Top URL	0,07 %	0,01 %	0,07 %	0,01%	0,07 %	0,01 %

Table 3. presents results of the feature based on similarities with the boundary of the mismatch measure set to higher values. The comparison is made on two sets of domain names which are not used to train the similarity feature. The SC2 and SN2 are extended versions of SC1 and SN1 with additional probability schemes that set the mismatch measure boundary value to 2 for real domain names which are longer than 8 characters. Likewise, the SC3 and SN3 extensions are equipped with additional probability schemes that set the mismatch measure boundary value to 3 for the domain names longer than 15 characters, effectively implementing the proposal "floor of square root" rule.

As can be observed, although the detection factor of the presented feature is improved, a small amount of false positives still appear when applied to the benign set of URLs.

6 Summary

The proposed feature has a relatively low degree of false positives but is able to detect only a small amount of yet unknown threats. Having such characteristics, it is not usable as an independent detection mechanism but can be used as a detection assisting mechanism filtering input data for more complex systems. It is especially important considering the nature of malicious domains which have a very short life span. The feature can be applied quickly and extract interesting domain names from large datasets for the more complex systems to process before the domain name stops being active.

A closer look at the results shows that one in two and a half hundred domain names is similar to our small knowledge-base of only 10 thousand domain names classified as malicious. It confirms our assumptions that there is a direct correlation between malicious domain names.

The future work of the project is directed towards researching an optimal boundary function for the mismatch measure for the domains registered under the same or different TLDs and real TLDs. Also research in other types of similarities is to be conducted, e.g. what characters are most commonly exchanged between similarly looking domain names. This should lead to new and interesting results.

References

1. Alexa, Top million sites, http://http://www.alexa.com/
2. DNS Blackholing, http://www.malwaredomains.com/
3. Google Safe Browning,
   http://code.google.com/p/google-safe-browsing/
4. Gusfield, D.: Algorithms on strings, trees, and sequences: computer science and computational biology. Cambridge University Press, New York (1997)
5. ITU Study on the Financial Aspects of Network Security: Malware and Spam, Final Report (2008)
6. Kijewski, P., Overes, C., Spoor, R.: The HoneySpider Network – fighting client side threats. In: 20th Annual, First Conference on Computer Security Incident Handling, Vancouver, Canada (June 2008)
7. Kolari, P., Finin, T., Joshi, A.: SVMs for the Blogosphere: Blog Identification and Splog Detection. In: Proceedings of the AAAI Spring Symposium on Computational Approaches to Analysing Weblogs, Stanford (2006)
8. Kozakiewicz A., Lasota K.: Monitoring of malicious URLs in HTTP traffic (in polish). In: KSTiT 2010, Wrocław (2010); Przegląd Telekomunikacyjny (ISSN 1230-3496), nr.(September 8, 2010), str.1325-1332
9. Ma, J., Saul, L.K., Savage, S., Voelker, G.M.: Beyond Blacklists: Learning to Detect Malicious Web Sites from Suspicious URLs. In: Proceedings of the SIGKDD Conference, Paris (2009)
10. McGrath, D.K., Gupta, M.: Behind Phishing: An Examination of Phisher Modi Operandi. In: Proc. of the USENIX Workshop on Large-Scale Exploits and Emergent Threats (LEET), San Francisco (2008)
11. Nazario, J.: PhoneyC: A Virtual Client Honeypot. In: Proceeding of the 2nd USENIX Workshop on Large-Scale Exploits and Emergent Threats, LEET 2009 (2009)
12. PhishTank, http://www.phishtank.com
13. Provos, N., Mavrommatis, P., Abu, M., Monrose, R.F.: All your iframes point to us. In: Google Inc. (2008)
14. Public Suffix List, http://publicsuffix.org/
15. Stokes, J., Andersen, R., Seifert C., Chellapilla K.: WebCop: locating neighborhoods of malware on the web. In: Proceedings of the 3rd USENIX Conference on Large-Scale Exploits and Emergent Threats LEET 2010 (2010)

Time Validity in Role-Based Trust Management Inference System

Anna Felkner[1] and Adam Kozakiewicz[1,2]

[1] NASK - Research and Academic Computer Network, Wąwozowa 18,
02-796 Warsaw, Poland
[2] Institute of Control and Computation Engineering, Warsaw University of Technology,
Nowowiejska 15/19, 00-665 Warsaw, Poland
{Anna.Felkner,Adam.Kozakiewicz}@nask.pl

Abstract. The topic of this paper is RT^T, a language from the family of Role-based Trust management (RT) languages, which is used for representing security policies and credentials in distributed large scale access control systems. A credential provides information about the privileges of users and the security policies issued by one or more trusted authorities. RT languages combine trust management and Role Based Access Control features. RT^T provides manifold roles to express threshold and separation of duties policies. A manifold role defines sets of entities whose cooperation satisfies the manifold role. The goal of this paper is introduction of time validity constraints to show how that can make RT^T language more realistic. The core part of the paper describes a sound and complete inference system, in which credentials can be derived from an initial set of credentials using a set of inference rules.

Keywords: trust management, Role-based Trust management, inference system.

1 Introduction

The problem of guaranteeing that confidential data and services offered by a computer system are not disclosed to unauthorized users is increasingly significant. It is a challenging issue, which must be solved by reliable software technologies that are used for building high-integrity applications. A traditional solution to this problem is an implementation of some access control techniques, which fits well into closed and centralized environments, in which the identity of users is known in advance. Quite new challenges arise in decentralized, distributed open systems, where the identity of the users is not known in advance and the set of users can change in time.

To overcome the drawbacks of traditional access control schemes, trust management models have been proposed [1], [2], [3], [4], [5], [11]. Trust management is a specific kind of access control, in which decisions are based on credentials issued by multiple principals. A credential is an attestation of qualification or authority, issued to an individual by a third party. The potential and flexibility of trust management approach stems from the possibility of delegation: a principal may transfer limited authority over a resource to other principals. Such a delegation is implemented by

C. Lee et al. (Eds.): STA 2011 Workshops, CCIS 187, pp. 7–15, 2011.

means of an appropriate credential. This way, a set of credentials defines the access control strategy and allows deciding on who is authorized to access a resource, and who is not.

To define a trust management system, a language is needed for describing entities, credentials and roles, which the entities play in the system. Responding to this need, a family of Role-based Trust management languages has been introduced in [9], [10], [12]. The family consists of five languages: RT_0, RT_1, RT_2, RT^T, RT^D, with increasing expressive power and complexity. This paper focuses on RT^T, as it provides useful capabilities not found on RT_0, RT_1 or RT_2: manifold roles, threshold and separation of duties policies. A *manifold role* defines a set of principal sets, each of which is a set of principals whose cooperation satisfies the manifold role. A *threshold* policy requires a specified minimum number of entities to agree on some fact. *Separation of duties* policy requires a set of entities, each of which fulfills a specific role, to agree before access is granted. A set-theoretic semantics has been defined for RT^T in [6].

2   The RT^T Language

Basic elements of RT languages are entities, role names, roles and credentials. *Entities* represent principals that can define roles and issue credentials, and requesters that can make requests to access resources *Role names* represent permissions that can be issued by entities to other entities or groups of entities. *Roles* represent sets of entities that have particular permissions granted according to the access control policy. A role is described as a pair composed of an entity and a role name. *Credentials* define roles by appointing a new member of the role or by delegating authority to the members of other roles.

2.1   The Syntax of RT^T Language

We use capital letters or nouns beginning with a capital letter to denote entities and sets of entities. Role names are denoted as identifiers beginning with a small letter or just small letters. Roles take the form of an entity (the issuer of this role) followed by a role name separated by a dot. Credentials are statements in the language. A credential consists of a role, left arrow symbol and a valid role expression. There are six types of credentials in RT^T, which are interpreted in the following way:

$A.r \leftarrow B$ - entity B is a member of role $A.r$.

$A.r \leftarrow B.s$ - role $A.r$ includes (all members of) role $B.s$.

$A.r \leftarrow B.s.t$ - role $A.r$ includes role $C.t$ for each C, which is a member of role $B.s$.

$A.r \leftarrow B.s \cap C.t$ - role $A.r$ includes all the entities who are members of both roles $B.s$ and $C.t$.

$A.r \leftarrow B.s \odot C.t$ - role $A.r$ can be satisfied by a union set of one member of role $B.s$ and one member of role $C.t$. A set consisting of a single entity satisfying the intersection role $B.s \cap C.t$ is also valid.

$A.r \leftarrow B.s \otimes C.t$ - role $A.r$ includes one member of role $B.s$ and one member of role $C.t$, but those members of roles have to be different entities.

Example 1. The following example has been adapted from [9]. A bank B has three roles: *manager, cashier* and *auditor*. Security policy of the bank requires an *approval* of certain transactions from a *manager*, two *cashiers*, and an *auditor*. The two *cashiers* must be different. However, a *manager* who is also a *cashier* can serve as one of the two cashiers. The *auditor* must be different from the other parties in the transaction. Such a policy can be described using the following credentials:

$$B.twoCashiers \leftarrow B.cashier \otimes B.cashier \tag{1}$$

$$B.managerCashiers \leftarrow B.manager \odot B.twoCashiers \tag{2}$$

$$B.approval \leftarrow B.auditor \otimes B.managerCashiers \tag{3}$$

Now, assume that the following credentials have been added:

$$B.cashier \leftarrow \{Alice\} \tag{4}$$

$$B.cashier \leftarrow \{Doris\} \tag{5}$$

$$B.manager \leftarrow \{Alice\} \tag{6}$$

$$B.auditor \leftarrow \{Kate\} \tag{7}$$

Then one can conclude that, according to the policy of B, the following set of entities can cooperatively approve a transaction: {Alice, Doris, Kate}.

2.2 Inference System over RT^T Credentials

RT^T credentials are used to define roles and roles are used to represent permissions. The semantics of a given set $\mathcal{P}$ of RT^T credentials defines for each role $A.r$ the set of entities which are members of this role. The member sets of roles can also be calculated in a more convenient way using an inference system, which defines an operational semantics of RT^T language. An inference system consists of an initial set of formulae that are considered to be true, and a set of inference rules, that can be used to derive new formulae from the known ones.

Let $\mathcal{P}$ be a given set of RT^T credentials. The application of inference rules of the inference system will create new credentials, derived from credentials of the set $\mathcal{P}$. A derived credential c will be denoted using a formula $\mathcal{P} \succ c$, which should be read: credential c can be derived from a set of credentials $\mathcal{P}$. The definition of inference system for RT^T consisting of six rules (W_1-W_6) was given in [7]. There could be a number of inference systems defined over a given language. To be useful for practical purposes an inference system must exhibit two properties. First, it should be *sound*, which means that the inference rules could derive only formulae that are valid with respect to the semantics of the language. Second, it should be *complete*, which means that each formula, which is valid according to the semantics, should be derivable in the system. Both properties have been shown in [7], proving that the inference system provides an alternative way of presenting the semantics of RT^T.

Example 2. We use the inference system to formally derive a set of entities which can cooperatively approve a transaction.

Using credentials (1)-(7) according to the rule (W_1) we can infer:

$$\frac{B.twoCashiers\leftarrow B.cashier\otimes B.cashier \in \mathcal{P}}{\mathcal{P}\succ B.twoCashiers\leftarrow B.cashier\otimes B.cashier}$$

$$\frac{B.managerCashiers\leftarrow B.manager\odot B.twoCashiers \in \mathcal{P}}{\mathcal{P}\succ B.managerCashiers\leftarrow B.manager\odot B.twoCashiers}$$

$$\frac{B.approval\leftarrow B.auditor\otimes B.managerCashiers \in \mathcal{P}}{\mathcal{P}\succ B.approval\leftarrow B.auditor\otimes B.managerCashiers}$$

$$\frac{B.cashier\leftarrow\{Alice\} \in \mathcal{P}}{\mathcal{P}\succ B.cashier\leftarrow\{Alice\}} \qquad \frac{B.manager\leftarrow\{Alice\} \in \mathcal{P}}{\mathcal{P}\succ B.manager\leftarrow\{Alice\}}$$

$$\frac{B.cashier\leftarrow\{Doris\} \in \mathcal{P}}{\mathcal{P}\succ B.cashier\leftarrow\{Doris\}} \qquad \frac{B.auditor\leftarrow\{Kate\} \in \mathcal{P}}{\mathcal{P}\succ B.auditor\leftarrow\{Kate\}}$$

Then using credentials (1), (4), (5) and rule (W_6) we infer:

$$\frac{\mathcal{P}\succ B.twoCashiers\leftarrow B.cashier\otimes B.cashier \qquad \mathcal{P}\succ B.cashier\leftarrow\{Alice\}}{\mathcal{P}\succ B.cashier\leftarrow\{Doris\} \qquad \{Alice\}\cap\{Doris\}=\varnothing}$$
$$\mathcal{P}\succ B.twoCashiers\leftarrow\{Alice, Doris\}$$

In next step we use it and additionally credentials (2), (6) and rule (W_5):

$$\frac{\mathcal{P}\succ B.managerCashiers\leftarrow B.manager\odot B.twoCashiers \qquad \mathcal{P}\succ B.manager\leftarrow\{Alice\}}{\mathcal{P}\succ B.twoCashiers\leftarrow\{Alice, Doris\}}$$
$$\mathcal{P}\succ B.managerCashiers\leftarrow\{Alice, Doris\}$$

Then we use that credential and add (3) and (7) and using rule (W_6) we can infer:

$$\frac{\mathcal{P}\succ B.approval\leftarrow B.auditor\otimes B.managerCashiers \qquad \mathcal{P}\succ B.auditor\leftarrow\{Kate\}}{\mathcal{P}\succ B.managerCashiers\leftarrow\{Alice, Doris\} \qquad \{Kate\}\cap\{Alice, Doris\}=\varnothing}$$
$$\mathcal{P}\succ B.approval\leftarrow\{Alice; Doris; Kate\}$$

showing that the set of entities that can cooperatively approve a transaction is: $\{Alice, Doris, Kate\}$.

3   Time Validity in RT^T

Inference rules with time validity for RT_0 were originally introduced in a slightly different way in [8]. In this paper we will try to extend the potential of RT^T language by putting time validity constraints into this language. In this case credentials are given to entities just for some fixed period of time. Time dependent credentials take the form: c *in* v, meaning "the credential c is available during the time v". Finite sets of time dependent credentials are denoted by CP and the new language is denoted as RT^T_+. To make notation lighter we write c to denote "c **in** $(-\infty, +\infty)$". Time validity can be denoted as follows: $[\tau_1, \tau_2]$; $[\tau_1, \tau_2)$; $(\tau_1, \tau_2]$; (τ_1, τ_2); $(-\infty,\tau]$; $(-\infty,\tau)$; $[\tau, +\infty)$; $(\tau, +\infty)$; $(-\infty, +\infty)$; $v_1\cup v_2$; $v_1\cap v_2$; $v_1 \setminus v_2$ with τ ranging over time constants and v_1, v_2 of any form in this list.

Example 3. In our scenario, it is quite natural to assume that *Alice* and *Doris* are cashiers only for a fixed period of time. The same with *Alice* as a manager and *Kate* as an auditor. Thus, credentials (4)-(7) should be generalised to:

$$B.cashier \leftarrow \{Alice\} \text{ in } v_1 \tag{8}$$

$$B.cashier \leftarrow \{Doris\} \text{ in } v_2 \tag{9}$$

$$B.manager \leftarrow \{Alice\} \text{ in } v_3 \tag{10}$$

$$B.auditor \leftarrow \{Kate\} \text{ in } v_4 \tag{11}$$

stating that (4), (5), (6), and (7) are only available during v_1, v_2, v_3, v_4, respectively. On the other hand, credentials (1) - (3) are always valid, as they express some time-independent facts. Now, by using (1)-(3) and (8)-(11), we want to be able to derive that the set {Alice, Doris, Kate} can cooperatively approve a transaction during all of the period: $v_1 \cap v_2 \cap v_3 \cap v_4$.

Our set-theoretic semantics of RT^T language has been adapted to the new form of credentials. Because it is not a subject of this paper, it will be omitted due to space constrains.

3.1 Time Validity for Inference System over RT^T_+ Credentials

Now, we can adapt inference system over RT^T credentials to take time validity into account. Let CP be a given set of RT^T_+ credentials. The application of inference rules of the inference system will create new credentials, derived from credentials of the set CP. A derived credential c valid in time τ will be denoted using a formula $CP \succ_\tau c$, which should be read: credential c can be derived from a set of credentials CP during the time τ.

Definition 1. The initial set of formulae of an inference system over a set CP of RT^T_+ credentials are all the form: c ***in*** $v \in$ CP for each credential c valid in time v in CP. The inference rules of the system are the following:

(CW_1)
$$\frac{c \text{ } \textit{in} \text{ } v \in CP \qquad \tau \in v}{CP \succ_\tau c}$$

(CW_2)
$$\frac{CP \succ_\tau A.r \leftarrow B.s \qquad CP \succ_\tau B.s \leftarrow X}{CP \succ_\tau A.r \leftarrow X}$$

(CW_3)
$$\frac{CP \succ_\tau A.r \leftarrow B.s.t \qquad CP \succ_\tau B.s \leftarrow C \qquad CP \succ_\tau C.t \leftarrow X}{CP \succ_\tau A.r \leftarrow X}$$

(CW_4)
$$\frac{CP \succ_\tau A.r \leftarrow B.s \cap C.t \qquad CP \succ_\tau B.s \leftarrow X \qquad CP \succ_\tau C.t \leftarrow X}{CP \succ_\tau A.r \leftarrow X}$$

(CW_5)
$$\frac{CP \succ_\tau A.r \leftarrow B.s \odot C.t \qquad CP \succ_\tau B.s \leftarrow X \qquad CP \succ_\tau C.t \leftarrow Y}{CP \succ_\tau A.r \leftarrow X \cup Y}$$

(CW_6)
$$\frac{CP \succ_\tau A.r \leftarrow B.s \otimes C.t \qquad CP \succ_\tau B.s \leftarrow X \qquad CP \succ_\tau C.t \leftarrow Y \qquad X \cap Y = \emptyset}{CP \succ_\tau A.r \leftarrow X \cup Y}$$

All the credentials, which can be derived in the system, either belong to set CP (rule CW_1) or are of the type: $CP \succ_\tau A.r \leftarrow X$ (rules CW_2 - CW_6). This new inference system mainly extends the inference rules from [7], by replacing rules (W_i) with (CW_i) and considering only valid time-dependent credentials from CP.

To prove the soundness of the inference system we must prove that for each new formula $CP \succ_\tau A.r \leftarrow X$, the triple (A, r, X) belongs to the semantics S_{CP} of the set CP. The proof will be omitted due to space constrains. It is simple adaptation of the proof for RT^T shown in [7].

3.2 Inferring Credentials Time Validity

This inference system evaluates maximal time validity, when it is possible to derive the credential c from CP. It enhances formula $CP \succ_\tau c$ to $CP \succ\succ_v c$, specifying that at any time $\tau \in v$ in which CP has a semantics, it is possible to infer the credential c from CP. To make notation lighter we write $\succ\succ$ to denote $\succ\succ_{(-\infty, +\infty)}$. The inference rules of the system are the following:

(CWP₁) $\dfrac{c \ \textit{in} \ v \in CP}{CP \succ\succ_v c}$

(CWP₂) $\dfrac{CP \succ\succ_{v1} A.r \leftarrow B.s \qquad CP \succ\succ_{v2} B.s \leftarrow X}{CP \succ\succ_{v1 \cap v2} A.r \leftarrow X}$

(CWP₃) $\dfrac{CP \succ\succ_{v1} A.r \leftarrow B.s.t \qquad CP \succ\succ_{v2} B.s \leftarrow C \qquad CP \succ\succ_{v3} C.t \leftarrow X}{CP \succ\succ_{v1 \cap v2 \cap v3} A.r \leftarrow X}$

(CWP₄) $\dfrac{CP \succ\succ_{v1} A.r \leftarrow B.s \cap C.t \qquad CP \succ\succ_{v2} B.s \leftarrow X \qquad CP \succ\succ_{v3} C.t \leftarrow X}{CP \succ\succ_{v1 \cap v2 \cap v3} A.r \leftarrow X}$

(CWP₅) $\dfrac{CP \succ\succ_{v1} A.r \leftarrow B.s \oslash C.t \qquad CP \succ\succ_{v2} B.s \leftarrow X \qquad CP \succ\succ_{v3} C.t \leftarrow Y}{CP \succ\succ_{v1 \cap v2 \cap v3} A.r \leftarrow X \cup Y}$

(CWP₆) $\dfrac{CP \succ\succ_{v1} A.r \leftarrow B.s \otimes C.t \qquad CP \succ\succ_{v2} B.s \leftarrow X \quad CP \succ\succ_{v3} C.t \leftarrow Y \qquad X \cap Y = \varnothing}{CP \succ\succ_{v1 \cap v2 \cap v3} A.r \leftarrow X \cup Y}$

(CWP₇) $\dfrac{CP \succ\succ_{v1} c \qquad CP \succ\succ_{v2} c}{CP \succ\succ_{v1 \cup v2} c}$

The key rule is (CWP_1). It claims that CP can be used whenever it is valid. Rules (CWP_2)-(CWP_6) simply claim that an inference rule can be used only when all its premises are true and that the validity of the resulting credentials is the intersection of validity periods of all premises. Finally, the rule (CWP_7) claims that if a credential c can be inferred both with validity v_1 and v_2, then c can be inferred with validity $v_1 \cup v_2$.

Because several possible ways may exist to infer a certain c from CP, all providing a different period of validity, the rule (CWP_7) can be used several times to broaden c's validity.

Definition 2. An inference terminating in $CP \succ\succ_v c$ is called maximal if and only if:

1. there exists no $v' \supset v$ such that $CP \succ\succ_{v'} c$, and
2. every sub-inference terminating in $CP \succ\succ_{v''} c'$ for $c' \neq c$, which does not use c in its premises, is maximal.

The first condition ensures that the rule (CWP₇) has been used as much as possible to infer the validity of c. The second condition ensures that this property is propagated through the whole inference tree. Maximal inferences guarantee that v in (CWP₁) is the maximal time validity for $A.r \leftarrow X$. For these inferences we can prove soundness and completeness of $CP \succ\succ_v$ but the proof will be omitted due to space constrains.

Example 4. Let us get back to our example and use credentials: (1)-(3) and (8)-(11). According to rule (CWP₁) we can infer:

$$\frac{B.twoCashiers \leftarrow B.cashier \otimes B.cashier \in CP}{CP \succ\succ B.twoCashiers \leftarrow B.cashier \otimes B.cashier}$$

$$\frac{B.managerCashiers \leftarrow B.manager \odot B.twoCashiers \in CP}{CP \succ\succ B.managerCashiers \leftarrow B.manager \odot B.twoCashiers}$$

$$\frac{B.approval \leftarrow B.auditor \otimes B.managerCashiers \in CP}{CP \succ\succ B.approval \leftarrow B.auditor \otimes B.managerCashiers}$$

$$\frac{B.cashier \leftarrow \{Alice\} \text{ in } v_1 \in \mathcal{P}}{CP \succ\succ_{v1} B.cashier \leftarrow \{Alice\}} \qquad \frac{B.manager \leftarrow \{Alice\} \text{ in } v_3 \in CP}{CP \succ\succ_{v3} B.manager \leftarrow \{Alice\}}$$

$$\frac{B.cashier \leftarrow \{Doris\} \text{ in } v_2 \in \mathcal{P}}{CP \succ\succ_{v2} B.cashier \leftarrow \{Doris\}} \qquad \frac{B.auditor \leftarrow \{Kate\} \text{ in } v_4 \in CP}{CP \succ\succ_{v4} B.auditor \leftarrow \{Kate\}}$$

When we want to check when two different cashiers can cooperate, from credentials (1), (8), (9) and rule (CWP₆) we infer:

$$\frac{CP \succ\succ B.twoCashiers \leftarrow B.cashier \otimes B.cashier \quad CP \succ\succ_{v1} B.cashier \leftarrow \{Alice\}}{CP \succ\succ_{v2} B.cashier \leftarrow \{Doris\} \qquad \{Alice\} \cap \{Doris\} = \varnothing}{CP \succ\succ_{v1 \cap v2} B.twoCashiers \leftarrow \{Alice, Doris\}}$$

In next step we use it and additionally credentials (2), (10) and rule (CWP·):

$$\frac{CP \succ\succ B.managerCashiers \leftarrow B.manager \odot B.twoCashiers}{CP \succ\succ_{v3} B.manager \leftarrow \{Alice\} \qquad CP \succ\succ_{v1 \cap v2} B.twoCashiers \leftarrow \{Alice, Doris\}}{CP \succ\succ_{v1 \cap v2 \cap v3} B.managerCashiers \leftarrow \{Alice, Doris\}}$$

Then we use that credential and add credentials (3) and (11) and using rule (CWP·) we can infer:

$$\frac{CP \succ\succ B.approval \leftarrow B.auditor \otimes B.managerCashiers \quad CP \succ\succ_{v4} B.auditor \leftarrow \{Kate\}}{CP \succ\succ_{v1 \cap v2 \cap v3} B.managerCashiers \leftarrow \{Alice, Doris\} \qquad \{Kate\} \cap \{Alice, Doris\} = \varnothing}{CP \succ\succ_{v1 \cap v2 \cap v3 \cap v4} B.approval \leftarrow \{Alice; Doris; Kate\}}$$

showing that the set of entities that can cooperatively approve a transaction is: {$Alice$, $Doris$, $Kate$} during the time: $v_1 \cap v_2 \cap v_3 \cap v_4$.

4 Conclusions

This paper deals with modelling of trust management systems in decentralized and distributed environments. The modelling framework is a RT^T language from a family of Role-based Trust management. The core part of the paper is a formal definition of a sound and complete inference system, in which credentials can be derived from an initial set of credentials using a set of inference rules. The semantics is given by the set of resulting credentials of the type $A.r{\leftarrow}X$, which explicitly show a mapping between roles and sets of entities. Using RT^T one can define credentials, which state that an action is allowed if it gets approval from members of more than one role. This improves the possibility of defining complex trust management models in a real environment. The goal of this paper is introduction of time validity constraints to show how that can make RT^T language more realistic. The new language is denoted as RT^T_+. The properties of soundness and completeness of the inference system with respect to the semantics still hold in RT^T_+ however is not presented in this paper. Inference systems presented in this paper are simple, but well-founded theoretically. It turns out to be fundamental mainly in large-scale distributed systems, where users have only partial view of their execution context.

Acknowledgments. This work is partially funded by the Polish Ministry of Science and Higher Education as part of project "Secure workstation for special applications", grant number OR00014011.

References

1. Blaze, M., Feigenbaum, J., Lacy, J.: Decentralized Trust Management. In: 17th IEEE Symposium on Security and Privacy, Oakland, CA, pp. 164–173 (1996)
2. Chadwick, D., Otenko, A., Ball, E.: Role-Based Access Control with X.509 Attribute Certificates. IEEE Internet Comput. 2, 62–69 (2003)
3. Chapin, P., Skalka, C., Wang, X.S.: Authorization in Trust Management: Features and Foundations. ACM Comput. Surv. 3, 1–48 (2008)
4. Czenko, M., Etalle, S., Li, D., Winsborough, W.H.: An introduction to the role based trust management framework RT. Foundations of Security Analysis and Design IV. Springer, Heidelberg (2007)
5. Felkner, A.: Modeling Trust Management in Computer Systems. In: Proc. 9th International PhD Workshop OWD 2007, PTETiS, vol. 23, pp. 65–70 (2007)
6. Felkner, A., Sacha, K.: The Semantics of Role-Based Trust Management Languages. In: CEE-SET 2009, pp. 195–206 (2009) (preprints)
7. Felkner, A., Sacha, K.: Deriving RT^T Credentials for Role-Based Trust Management. e-Informatica Software Engineering Journal 4(1), 9–19 (2010)
8. Gorla, D., Hennessy, M., Sassone, V.: Inferring Dynamic Credentials for Role-Based Trust Management. In: Proc. 8th ACM SIGPLAN Conference on Principles and Practice of Declarative Programming, pp. 213–224. ACM, New York (2006)
9. Li, N., Mitchell, J.: RT: A Role-Based Trust-Management Framework. In: Proc. 3rd DARPA Information Survivability Conference and Exposition, pp. 201–212. IEEE Computer Society Press, Oakland (2003)

10. Li, N., Mitchell, J., Winsborough, W.: Design of a Role-Based Trust-Management Framework. In: Proc. IEEE Symposium on Security and Privacy, pp. 114–130. IEEE Computer Society Press, Oakland (2002)
11. Li, N., Winsborough, W., Mitchell, J.: Beyond proof-of-Compliance: Safety and Availability Analysis in Trust Management. In: Proc. IEEE Symposium on Security and Privacy, pp. 123–139. IEEE Computer Society Press, Oakland (2003)
12. Li, N., Winsborough, W., Mitchell, J.: Distributed Credential Chain Discovery in Trust Management. J. Comput. Secur. 1, 35–86 (2003)

Vaudenay's Privacy Model in the Universal Composability Framework: A Case Study

Hervé Chabanne[1] and Céline Chevalier[2]

[1] Télécom ParisTech and Morpho
[2] LSV – ENS Cachan/CNRS/INRIA
chabanne@telecom-paristech.fr
celine.chevalier@lsv.ens-cachan.fr

Abstract. At ASIACCS'09, Bringer et al. introduced different Zero-Knowledge (ZK) identification protocols which respect privacy. To do so, they give a generic technique to increase the privacy of existing ZK schemes. As an application, they transform the Girault-Poupard-Stern (GPS) scheme to get new protocols. Their proofs rely on the privacy model of Vaudenay. We here want to examine the validity of their results in the more general framework of the Universal Composability (UC). This is relevant considering that Contactless Devices (CLDs) seem to be the first target for implementing these protocols. More precisely, we here transpose Vaudenay's privacy model in the UC framework, and we show how to modify the Randomized Hashed GPS scheme in order to obtain a secure protocol in the UC framework.

Keywords: Zero-Knowledge identification protocols, Privacy, Universal Composability framework.

1 Introduction

This work comes from our interest in the Internet of Things (IoT) (refering to the term invented by the MIT Auto-ID Center in 2001). In this domain, many contactless devices (CLDs) are going to communicate over the internet with a web server. By CLDs, we mean of course RFID tags but, more generally, also contactless smartcards. The first step for the CLDs is naturally to let the server identify them. We thus need a cryptographic protocol which ensures the security of the identification but also its privacy. We do not want an eavesdropper to be able to recover an identity among many connections or even to track a CLD (without knowing its identity) over the internet. A nice attempt was made in [9, 14] with the GPS identification protocol. Indeed, this GPS protocol gathers many assets: from a theoretical point of view, its zero-knowledgeness insures good security features and practically, it can be implemented in some ways requiring very few resources [12]. Unfortunately, [2] shows that this GPS protocol as it is (and generally, many other ZK identification protocols) does not respect privacy as an adversary is able to follow and after to link together the different attempts of a CLD to identify itself. To counteract that, [3] provides a generic framework which increases the privacy of such ZK schemes and applies it to the GPS protocol. It should be noted that the resulting protocols are included in the HIP-tags

C. Lee et al. (Eds.): STA 2011 Workshops, CCIS 187, pp. 16–24, 2011.

privacy architecture [16, 13, 15] as a way for RFID tags to prove their identity. From our point of view, the security analysis of [3] would benefit from a more general model than the one initially considered. In particular, in this context of IoT, it seems important to us that the security of the protocol be analysed in a way that handles different instances of the protocol (e.g. see [17]). This is why we consider in this paper the ZK identification protocols of [3] in the Universal Composability (UC) framework which has been introduced by Canetti in [5] to support this kind of situation where interactions of many executions of the same protocol could become problematic.

Related works. The work of Bringer *et al.* studies ZK protocols in the UC framework but not their respect of privacy. Burmester *et al.* [11, 4] also introduce and then analyze RFID Identification and Authentication Protocols in the UC framework. But their work takes place in a particular context, assuming the existence of anonymous channels, and considering symmetric keys shared between tags and a unique server, which is different from the setting we have in this work. It should be noted that [4] does not consider adversaries compromising RFID tags (*ie* the control of the memory of a tag by an adversary) as a valid threat. Moreover, their proposals are tuned for very low-end tags with scarce resources. This is not the case of our work which could be implemented in cryptographic smartcards.

2 Zero-Knowledge Schemes

As shown in [3], many ZK identification schemes do not respect privacy, which motivated their work; A necessary requirement is to hide identities. We consider here the context in which identifications are made thanks to CLDs and the communication is monitored (and potentially recorded) by the adversary. Among the different classes of identification protocols (ZK or closely related), we restrict ourselves to those based on arithmetic relations. Following [3], we formalize such schemes as follows:

P(public key I, secret key s) parameters: KA_p, V

$\text{COMPUTEA}_{s,KA_p}() = (A, r_A)$ $\xrightarrow{A}$

$\xleftarrow{c}$ pick c

$\text{COMPUTEB}_{s,KA_p}(r_A, c) = B$ $\xrightarrow{B}$ $f(B) \overset{?}{=} A.g_I(c)$

Let P be a three-move identification protocol between a prover and a verifier. Let us denote $[A,c,B]$ a transcript of P with A,B sent by the prover and c by the verifier after reception of A. The protocol is made of several algorithms: $\text{SETUPAUTHORITY}(1^K) \mapsto (KA_s, KA_p)$ polynomially outputs a private/public key pair of an authority. KA_p also defines the underlying group structure. $\text{SETUPPROVER}_{KA_p}(1^K) \mapsto (s,I)$ polynomially outputs a pair private key/public key of a prover. s is the secret linked to the identity I of the prover thanks to a one-way function Id: $Id(s)=I$. $\text{COMPUTEA}_{s,KAP}() \mapsto (A, r_A)$ computes A thanks to a random value r_A. $\text{COMPUTEB}_{s,KAP}(R_A, C) \mapsto B$ computes B. $\text{VERIFY}(I,[A,C,B]) \mapsto x \in \{0,1\}$ checks whether the verifier identifies the prover with I, *ie* if the following equation holds: $f(B)=A\, g_I(c)$ where f and g_I are two deterministic functions that depend on KA_p (note that the identity I of the prover is needed to compute g_I). In the sequel of the paper, we assume that g_I is an exponentiation in base I. A scheme is *sound* if there exists an extractor E which can retrieve a secret of a prover given several transcripts of the form $[A,c_i,B_i]$ (with the same A). This means that an adversary able to identify himself is in possession of a valid secret: a B verifying $f(B)=A$ $g_I(c)$ should be hard to compute without the knowledge of s and r_A. This implies that f is one-way. A scheme is called *Honest-Verifier* Zero-Knowledge (HVZK) if there exists a simulator S able to simulate a protocol instance given the prover's identity I and a challenge c, *ie* such that $S(c,I)$ outputs a pair A and B, where $[A,B,c]$ is a valid transcript identifying I. A scheme is called *Malicious-Verifier* Zero-Knowledge (MVZK) if there exists an S able to simulate protocol instances given the prover's identity I such that outputs are indistinguishable from prover's outputs for an arbitrary c. In HVZK schemes, legitimate verifiers cannot get information on the prover's secret since such a simulator which does not use the prover's secret exists. Furthermore, MVZK schemes reveal no information even to an adversary who impersonates a verifier. The simulation is *perfect* when the distribution of simulated outputs is the same as the distribution of genuine outputs from a legitimate prover, and *statistical* if the distributions are not the same but statistically close.

3 Vaudenay Security Model

We recall in this section the model for privacy, correctness and soundness described in [19] and modified in [3] to capture zero-knowledge properties (in particular the fact that the identities of the provers can be either public or hidden).

Provers are assumed to be CLDs trying to identify themselves by a unique serial number (SN). For sake of privacy, a random virtual serial number (vSN) is used during the identification phase, divided in two steps: First the system is (securely) set up by an authority, and then the protocol is run between the devices and the verifiers.

Setup Algorithms. Note that the setup is done independently for the devices and the verifiers (in particular, the pair is not needed to set up a CLD, and thus leaks no information on the secret of a CLD). SETUPAUTHORITY(1^k) $\mapsto$ (KA_s,KA_p) outputs a private/public key pair of an authority. SETUPVERIFIER$_{KA_p}$() allows to initialize a verifier. It may generate a private/public key pair (KV_s,KV_p), associated to the verifier, which can be used to protect communications between CLDs and verifiers. SETUPCLDSECRET$_{KA_p}$(SN) returns the parameters of the CLD identified by SN. It outputs a couple (s, I) where s is the private key of the CLD, I its public key and identity. SETUPCLDSTATE$_{KV_p}$(SN,s,I) returns S, the initial internal memory of the CLD. SETUPCLD$_{KV_p}$(SN) first uses SETUPCLDSECRET then SETUPCLDSTATE to initialize the CLD. It also stores the pair (I,SN) in a database.

Adversarial Model. The identification protocol between a CLD and a verifier is made of messages sent by the two parties, given a public key . The possible actions of an adversary (interactions or eavesdropping) are modeled by oracles, leading to different privacy levels: CREATECLD(SN) creates a CLD with serial number SN initialized via SETUPCLD. At this point, it is a free CLD, i.e. not yet in the system. DRAWCLD(*distr*) $\mapsto$ ((vSN_1,b_1),...,(vSN_n,b_n)) moves a random subset of CLDs from the set of free CLDs into the set of drawn CLDs in the system. Virtual serial numbers ($vSN_1,...,vSN_n$), used to identify the drawn CLDs, are randomly chosen according to a given distribution. If b_i is one, this indicates whether a CLD is used in the system. This oracle creates and keeps a table of correspondences T where $T(vSN)=SN$.

Adversary has no knowledge of this table T. FREE(vSN) moves the CLD vSN to the set of free CLDs. LAUNCH()$\mapsto \pi$ makes the verifier launch a new protocol instance π. SENDVERIFIER(m, π) $\mapsto m'$ sends the message m to the verifier who responds m' in the protocol instance π. SENDCLD(m', π) $\mapsto m$ sends the message m' to the CLD who responds m in the protocol instance π. RESULT(π) $\mapsto x$ returns, when π is a complete instance of P, 1 if the verifier succeeds in identifying a CLD from π and 0 otherwise. CORRUPT(vSN) $\mapsto S$ returns the internal state S of the CLD vSN.

These oracles lead to six types of adversaries: a *strong* adversary is allowed to use all of the above oracles; a *forward* adversary cannot use any oracle after one CORRUPT query, *ie* he destructs the system when he corrupts a CLD; a *weak* adversary is not allowed to use the CORRUPT oracle. Each of these three types can in addition be *narrow*, which means that the adversary is not allowed to use the RESULT oracle.

Security Notions. This model defines correctness, resistance against impersonation attacks and privacy. A scheme is *correct* if the identification of a legitimate CLD fails only with negligible probability. A scheme is said *resistant against impersonation attacks* if no polynomially bounded *strong* adversary can be identified by a verifier except with a negligible probability. This definition deals with active adversaries, who are able to impersonate verifiers and CLDs and to eavesdrop and modify communications. This security notion is already widely studied for ZK schemes, see for instance [1]. Obviously, a scheme is not resistant against impersonation attacks if an adversary can modify outputs from a prover without changing the identification result (in particular in a replay attack). Finally, there is a *privacy leakage* if the system cannot be simulated without the adversary becoming aware of it (see [19] for details).

As stated in [19], this definition of privacy is more general than anonymity and untraceability. To the six kinds of adversary enumerated above correspond accordingly six different notions of privacy. Note that CORRUPT queries are considered to always leak information on CLDs' identity. For instance, an adversary can systematically open CLDs in order to track them. In this model, such an adversary is considered as a trivial. Strong privacy is defined only to ensure that CLDs cannot be tracked using their outputs even if their secrets are known. Vaudenay shows in [19] that a scheme both secure against impersonation attacks and narrow-weak (*resp.* narrow-forward) private is weak (*resp.* forward) private.

New Types of Adversaries for Zero-Knowledge. A ZK scheme enables to prove the knowledge of a secret without revealing any information on it whereas privacy implies that an adversary gains no advantage over the identity of CLDs.

Since the setup algorithms are defined to ensure that the secret s and are independent, a simulator against an honest verifier is thus authorized to use to simulate CLDs' outputs, as gives him no advantage on s. This remark allows the authors of [3] to show that the definition of *Honest-Verifier* ZK schemes remains unchanged but the use of KV_s will be considered in the security analysis of the schemes.

Thus they define two new adversaries: A hidden-identity (HI) adversary does not have the list of identities chosen during the setup phase initiated by the multiple calls to SETUPCLD. A public-identity (PI) adversary has access to this list. These notions are identical for a strong adversary against privacy since he is able to read the secrets of all CLD's.

4 Vaudenay's Model in the UC Framework

In this section, our aim is to express the Vaudenay's model in a different framework; namely the universal composability one. We assume basic familiarity with this UC framework. See [6, 7] for details. The model considered is the UC framework with joint state proposed by Canetti and Rabin [8].

In a nutshell, an important difference between the "standard" models and the UC model is that the latter models all the security notions and requirements by the means of a simple functionality, capturing all the properties needed, and allows protocols to remain secure when composed arbitrarily. It makes use of session identifiers (*sid*), mentioned in all the messages exchanged in a specific instance of a protocol.

Our goal here is to model private ZK schemes in the UC framework: We thus define the corresponding functionalities, which different variants will exactly capture the different variants of adversaries in Vaudenay's model.

Ideal Functionality for the setup of the Servers. We enhance the model proposed by Vaudenay by allowing several different servers. We thus need to set them up, that is, to generate and give them their pairs of private and public keys. This is the aim of the functionality, which interacts with an adversary S and a set of servers S_1, ..., S_p via the following query:

PUBLIC KEY GENERATION. Upon receiving a message (*KeyGen,sid,S$_i$*) from a server S_i, hand (*KeyGen,sid,S$_i$*) to the adversary S. Upon receiving a value (*Keys,sid,sk,pk*) from S, where *sk* and *pk* are random, output (*PublicKey,sid,pk*) to S_i and record (*sid,S$_i$,pk*). Ignore any subsequent values (*KeyGen,sid,**).

F_{init} is strongly inspired by the work of Canetti [6] for modeling CCA-secure public-key encryption in the way it lets the adversary determine the value of the encryption key. This reflects the fact that the intuitive notion of security for encryption does not make any requirements on this value.

Ideal Functionality for Private ZK Schemes. The functionality $\mathcal{F}$ is parameterized by a relation R. It interacts with an adversary S and a set of tags P_1, ..., P_n and servers S_1, ..., S_p via the following queries:

PROOF. Upon receiving a value (*Prove,sid,P$_i$,S$_j$,pk$_j$,p,w*), ignore it if $\neg R(p,w)$. Otherwise send the output (*Prove,sid,p*) to S. As soon as S allows the delivery, send (*Proven,sid,P$_i$,p*) to S_j and (*Proven,sid,p*) to S if *pk$_j$* is equal to the public key stored by F_{init}, and (*Proven,sid,P$_i$,p*) to S_j otherwise.

CORRUPTION. Upon receiving a message (*Corrupt,sid,P$_i$*) from the adversary, send w to the adversary. Furthermore, if the adversary now provides a value (*Prove,sid,P$_i$,S$_j$,pk$_j$,p',w'*) such that the relation $R(p',w')$ holds, the public key corresponds and no output was yet given to $\underline{S_j}$, then output (*Proven,sid,P$_i$,p*) to $\underline{S_j}$.

Waiting for S to allow the delivery is a usual requirement of the UC framework, allowing him to decide the exact moment when corruptions should occur. The message sent by the prover needs to contain his name (P_i), the server targetted (S_j), the assumed public key of the latter (*pk$_j$*), the proof p and the witness (secret) w.

F checks whether the proof is correct (*ie R(p,w)*) and the prover knows the public key of the server it is talking to. If so, the proof is accepted. Otherwise, it is rejected.

The above functionality guarantees security against strong adversaries in the sense *S* is notified whether the proof succeeded. To restrict to narrow-strong adversaries, one has to get rid of the output (*Proven,sid,p*) to *S* if the proof is accepted. To restrict to weak adversaries, one has to get rid of the *Corrupt* query. To model forward adversaries, any new *Prove* query with this tag is ignored.

Furthermore, this functionality directly models the public identity adversary. To model a hidden identity adversary, one would have to complete the query (*KeyGen,sid,S$_i$*) of *F*$_{init}$ with a list of identities only known to *S$_i$*. Finally, note that only the provers can be corrupted, and not the servers. Otherwise, the latter could recover all the secret values trivially, which does not have much sense.

Recall that no communication is allowed in the ideal world between the adversary and the players so that the former only obtains the information given by the functionality. The privacy is thus directly obtained from the fact that *A* never gains the identity of the prover in his outputs from the functionality.

5   The Enhanced UC-Secure GPS Scheme

Computational Assumptions. Let *G* be a cyclic group of order *q*. The Discrete Logarithm (DL) problem can be defined as: Given *g* and *g^a* in *G* with *a* randomly chosen in [0,*q*-1], compute *a*. The DL with Short Exponent (DLSE(*S*)) problem [18] is the usual DL problem but with short exponents instead of normal ones (*a≤S*). Let us recall the Decisional Diffie-Hellman (DDH) problem: Given *g*, *g^a*, *g^b* with *a*, *b* randomly chosen in [0,*q*-1], given *g^c=g^{ab}* with probability 1/2 and *g^c=g^d* with probability 1/2 with *d* randomly chosen in [0,*q*-1], decide whether *g^{ab}* equals *g^c*. [10] introduces a similar problem where the exponents are short, called the Short Exponent DDH (SEDDH) problem and hard if and only if DDH and DLSE problems are hard.

Scheme. Our protocol builds upon the randomized hashed GPS protocol defined in [3]. Our aim is to enhance it in order that it remains secure in the UC framework. The main difference in the UC framework is that we have to construct a simulator able to extract the secret *s* from a corrupted tag trying to identify itself. To this end, an easy solution is to add to the randomized hashed GPS protocol an extractable commitment of *s* in the first round: as soon as the simulated server receives it, he can recover *s*, as required in the model. A classical way to build such a commitment is to use an encryption scheme, which parameters will be stored into a CRS (common reference string): This will allow the simulator to program this string in order to know the trapdoor of the scheme, decrypt the message sent, and thus extract the secret *s*.

Of course, this commitment would be useless if the adversary changed its mind and used another value of *s* on behalf of the prover in the following rounds. This commitment thus has to be linked to the following messages in order to forbid this to happen and to engage the corrupted tag on the value of *s* chosen at the beginning.

An easy way to link the commitment in the first round of the protocol to the following messages is to take advantage of some homomorphic properties of the encryption scheme. We here chose to use ElGamal encryption scheme with parameters

$(g,h=g^a)$ (a being the secret key), in its additive version: $EG^+(m)=(g^r,h^r g^m)$. A drawback of this version is that the extraction of the value encrypted requires the computation of a discrete logarithm in base g, which is a hard problem. To overcome this difficulty, one simply has to imagine that the encryption of s is done bit per bit: $EG^+_{bit}(m)= (EG^+(m_1), ..., EG^+(m_n))$ where $m=m_1...m_n$. For sake of simplicity, we did not show these details in the figure describing the protocol.

In a first step, the prover randomly chooses r_1,r_2 in $[0,A-1]$ as before, and also R, R_1 and R_2 which will be the random values used in the encryptions (commitments). Then, instead of sending directly $A_1=g^{r_1}$ and $A_2=(g^v)^{r_2}$, he computes an encryption C of s with randomness R, C_1 of r_1 with randomness R_1 and C_2 of r_2 with randomness R_2 and sends them, along with a hash of A_1 and A_2 to the verifier (the latter value ensures that only the verifier can make the verification). The verifier sends a challenge c randomly chosen in $[0,B-1]$. The prover responds with $y=r_1+r_2+s_c$, with r_1+r_2 hiding the secret, making the scheme remaining ZK: This computation is made without any modular reduction, this is one of the main differences with the Schnorr scheme. He also sends A_1 and A_2, making the verifier able to check the hash value sent in the first place. He also sends an encryption of y with randomness $R_c+R_1+R_2$. When the server receives the encryption of y, he is thus able to check if it corresponds to the product of the encryptions of s, r_1 and r_2 (thanks to the homomorphic property). The verifier computes $I=(g^{vy}A_1^{-v}A_2^{-1})^{1/cv}$ and finally checks whether $I \in L$ and $0 \leq y \leq 2A-2 + (B-1)(S-1)$. If these four conditions are verified, the prover is identified.

We consider static adversaries, which have to choose which user to corrupt prior to the execution of the considered instance of the protocol. We have the following security result, which proof is given in the full version:

Theorem 1: Assume the hardness of the SEDDH problem, assume H is preimage and collision resistant, assume BS/A is negligible then this variant of the GPS scheme UC-emulates functionality F (in its version public identity, strong private and statistically ZK) and is secure against impersonation attacks by static adversaries.

P secret key $s \in [0, S-1]$ parameters : g, g^v, A, B, S	V secret key v
public key $I = g^s$	public key g^v

pick r_1, r_2, R, R_1, R_2 in $[0, A-1]$	$C = (g^R, g^s h^R),$ $C_1 = (g^{R_1}, g^{r_1} h^{R_1}),$ $C_2 = (g^{R_2}, g^{r_2} h^{R_2})$	
	$\xrightarrow{\quad z=H(g^{r_1},(g^v)^{r_2}) \quad}$	pick $c \in [0, B-1]$
$y = r_1 + r_2 + sc$ $R' = Rc + R_1 + R_2$	$\xleftarrow{\quad c \quad}$	
$D = (g^{R'}, g^y h^{R'})$	$\xrightarrow{\quad A_1=g^{r_1}, A_2=(g^v)^{r_2}, y, D \quad}$	Compute $I = (g^{vy} A_1^{-v} A_2^{-1})^{1/cv}$ Check whether $I \in L$ and $z = H(A_1, A_2)$ and $D = C^c C_1 C_2$ and whether $0 \leq y,$ $y \leq 2A - 2 + (B-1)(S-1)$

An important element is that all the computations can be made offline and do not reveal information on the secret of the prover. As already claimed, this scheme is perfectly scalable as a verifier only has to compute a constant number of operations to identify a device. Also, since it is public-identity forward private, it could be used in common applications where identities are public. Furthermore, no list has to be stored on the verifier side since it suffices to check that the identity that it computes from the protocol transcript is the same as the identity read on the document.

References

[1] Bellare, M., Palacio, A.: GQ and Schnorr Identification Schemes: Proofs of Security against Impersonation under Active and Concurrent Attacks. In: Yung, M. (ed.) CRYPTO 2002. LNCS, vol. 2442, pp. 162–177. Springer, Heidelberg (2002)

[2] Bringer, J., Chabanne, H., Icart, T.: Cryptanalysis of EC-RAC, a RFID Identification Protocol. In: Franklin, M.K., Hui, L.C.K., Wong, D.S. (eds.) CANS 2008. LNCS, vol. 5339, pp. 149–161. Springer, Heidelberg (2008)

[3] Bringer, J., Chabanne, H., Icart, T.: Efficient zero-knowledge identification schemes which respect privacy. In: ASIACCS 2009, pp. 195–205. ACM Press, New York (2009)

[4] Burmester, M., Van Le, T., de Medeiros, B., Tsudik, G.: Universally composable rfid identification and authentication protocols. ACM Trans. Inf. Syst. Secur. 12(4) (2009)

[5] Canetti, R.: Security and composition of multiparty cryptographic protocols. Journal of Cryptology 13(1), 143–202 (2000)

[6] Canetti, R.: Universally composable security: A new paradigm for cryptographic protocols. In: 42nd FOCS, pp. 136–145. IEEE Computer Society Press, Los Alamitos (2001)

[7] Canetti, R., Halevi, S., Katz, J., Lindell, Y., MacKenzie, P.D.: Universally Composable Password-Based Key Exchange. In: Cramer, R. (ed.) EUROCRYPT 2005. LNCS, vol. 3494, pp. 404–421. Springer, Heidelberg (2005)

[8] Canetti, R., Rabin, T.: Universal Composition with Joint State. In: Boneh, D. (ed.) CRYPTO 2003. LNCS, vol. 2729, pp. 265–281. Springer, Heidelberg (2003)

[9] Girault, M.: Self-certified public keys. In: Davies, D.W. (ed.) EUROCRYPT 1991. LNCS, vol. 547, pp. 490–497. Springer, Heidelberg (1991)

[10] Koshiba, T., Kurosawa, K.: Short Exponent Diffie-Hellman Problems. In: Bao, F., Deng, R., Zhou, J. (eds.) PKC 2004. LNCS, vol. 2947, pp. 173–186. Springer, Heidelberg (2004)

[11] Van Le, T., Burmester, M., de Medeiros, B.: Universally composable and forward-secure RFID authentication and authenticated key exchange. In: ASIACCS 2007, pp. 242–252. ACM Press, New York (2007)

[12] McLoone, M., Robshaw, M.J.B.: Public key cryptography and RFID tags. In: Abe, M. (ed.) CT-RSA 2007. LNCS, vol. 4377, pp. 372–384. Springer, Heidelberg (2006)

[13] Nyamy, D.D., Elrharbi, S., Urien, P., Chabanne, H., Icart, T., Pépin, C., Bouet, M., De Oliveira Cunha, D., Guyot, V., Krzanik, P., Susini, J.-F.: HIP tags, a new paradigm for the Internet of Things. In: Proceedings of the 1st IFIP Wireless Days Conference – IFIP 2008, Dubai, United Arab Emirates (November 2008)

[14] Poupard, G., Stern, J.: Security Analysis of a Practical "On the Fly" Authentication and Signature Generation. In: Nyberg, K. (ed.) EUROCRYPT 1998. LNCS, vol. 1403, pp. 422–436. Springer, Heidelberg (1998)

[15] Urien, P., Lee, G.M., Pujolle G.: Hip support for rfids,
http://tools.ietf.org/html/draft-irtf-hiprg-rfid-00

[16] Urien, P., Nyami, D., Elrharbi, S., Chabanne, H., Icart, T., Pépin, C., Bouet, M., De Oliveira Cunha, D., Guyot, V., Pujolle, G., Gressier-Soudan, E., Susini, J.-F.: HIP Tags Privacy Architecture. In: Proceedings of the 3rd International Conference on Systems and Networks Communications – ICSNC 2008, pp. 179–184. IEEE, IEEE Computer Society, Sliema, Malta (2008)

[17] van Deursen, T., Radomirovic, S.: Untraceable rfid protocols are not trivially composable: Attacks on the revision of ec-rac. Cryptology ePrint Archive: Report 2009/332

[18] van Oorschot, P.C., Wiener, M.J.: On Diffie-Hellman Key Agreement with Short Exponents. In: Maurer, U.M. (ed.) EUROCRYPT 1996. LNCS, vol. 1070, pp. 332–343. Springer, Heidelberg (1996)

[19] Vaudenay, S.: On privacy models for RFID. In: Kurosawa, K. (ed.) ASIACRYPT 2007. LNCS, vol. 4833, pp. 68–87. Springer, Heidelberg (2007)

[20] Yao, A.C.-C., Yao, F.F., Zhao, Y.: A note on universal composable zero-knowledge in the common reference string model. Theor. Comput. Sci. 410(11), 1099–1108 (2009)

Mining Frequent Items in OLAP

Ling Jin, Ji Yeon Lim, Iee Joon Kim, Kyung Soo Cho,
Seung Kwan Kim, and Ung Mo Kim

Database Laboratory, Information and Communication Engineering, SungKyunKwan
University, 440-746 Suwon, Korea
jinlingchao@gmail.com, revolutiony@cyworld.com,
uk3080789@naver.com, kisschks@hotmail.com, libertas@korea.kr,
umkim@ece.skku.ac.kr

Abstract. On-line analytical (OLAP) is a data summarization and aggregation tool that helps simplify data analyzing where containing in the data warehouse. However, OLAP is some different with data mining tools, which discover the implicit patterns and interesting knowledge in large amount of databases. In this study, we propose to translate the frequent pattern tree structure into the 3-D multidimensional data structure. The frequent pattern tree is used for generating compact set of frequent patterns, so the 3-D multidimensional data structure, which is converted by FP-tree is only storage the frequent patterns. And then import the multidimensional data structure into the OLAP tool to discover the interesting knowledge. The efficiency is in three aspects: (1) because the frequent pattern tree is mining the complete set of frequent patterns that helps only analyzing the meaningful patterns in data warehouse. (2) It integrates OLAP with data mining and mining knowledge in multidimensional databases.

Keywords: OLAP, FP-tree, multidimensional data structure, data warehouse, data mining.

1 Introduction

As multidimensional data sets [1] have grown in size and complexity, direct hands on data analysis has increasingly become important. A developer cannot use all of the data in data sets, so appropriately filtering out the useless data items is useful for data analysis. In this paper, we import the frequent pattern tree approach to extract the frequent items in data warehouse and translate the frequent pattern tree structure to the multidimensional data array structure. The FP-tree is mainly responsible for extracting frequent patterns from data warehousing [2]. And translate the FP-tree to the multidimensional data array is order to manipulate the frequent patterns in on-line analytical processing. This, together with data visualization [3] and data analysis approach, will greatly enhance the power and flexibility of exploratory data mining [4].

This paper is composed as follows. In the section 2, we discuss the theoretical related work. In section 3, we describe our framework of constructing cube array structure. In section 4, we talk about how the association cubes can be derived from our framework. In section 5, we finish the paper with a conclusion and our future work.

C. Lee et al. (Eds.): STA 2011 Workshops, CCIS 187, pp. 25–30, 2011.
© Springer-Verlag Berlin Heidelberg 2011

2 Related Work

2.1 Frequent Pattern Tree

The FP-tree [5] is an extended prefix-tree structure storing crucial, quantitative information about frequent patterns. To insure the tree structure is compact and informative, only frequent length-1 items will have nodes in the tree, and the tree nodes are arranged in such a way that more frequently occurring nodes will have better chances of node sharing than less frequently occurring ones. Most efficiency is according to the FP-tree constructed methodology to be achieved. It is constructed by reading the data set one transaction at one time and mapping each transaction into a path of the FP-tree. First, perform one scan of transaction database to identify the set of frequent items by an obtained *minimum support threshold* value. Second, the set of frequent items of each transaction should be stored in some compact structure that in order to avoid repeatedly scanning the original transaction database. Third, with the accepted transaction database construct a frequent pattern tree, which is to speak of that the each path of a tree will follow their frequency descending order. Based on above steps, the complete set of frequent items of transactions in the database can be derived from FP-tree. Therefore, mining frequent patterns using the FP-tree is efficiency in mining process.

2.2 Multi-dimensional Data Cube Structure

An multi-dimensional data cube [6] is that stores the group-by aggregation of all possible combinations of the n dimensions, and a data cube can be viewed as a lattice of cuboids. The n-D space or n-D layer (the base cuboids) consists of all data cells, each of the cell represent its meaning for x-axis, y-axis and z-axis. The (n-1)-D space consists of the sum cells storing the count information for each (n-1)-D combination of the dimensions, and so on. Furthermore, the data cube structure, which is multi-dimensional array-based model, can be stored in chunk [7]. Each chunk is partitioned according to dimension hierarchies, chunking forms a semantically meaningful cuboids and its computation is equivalent to computing an interesting and meaningful cuboids. And what is the most important that each chunk and its summary layers are small enough to fit in main memory. Based on chunking efficiency, we can do mining operations in partitioned cuboids and then aggregation the results by metadata.

2.3 On-Line Analytical Processing

OLAP [8] can be performed in data warehouse and marts using the multidimensional data model. Typical OLAP operations include *roll-up, drill-(down, across, through)*, *slice-and-dice, pivot(rotate)*, as well as statistical operations such as ranking and computing moving averages and growth rates. In our study, we talk about how to manipulate the relational data cube by the OLAP operation. First, construct the frequent items into the cube array structure. Second, manipulate the frequent items through analyzing the cube array structure by the on-line analytical processing. So as the same time, it is making from the on-line analytical processing translate to the on-line analytical mining (OLAM) [9].

3 Construct the Cube Array Framework

3.1 Construct FP-Tree Structure

In order to explain our framework, using an example of constructed FP-tree. Let the transaction database be the first two columns of Table 1, and the minimum support threshold be 3(i.e., $\xi = 3$).

Table 1. A transaction database

TID	Items bought	(Ordered)frequent items
100	f , a , c , d , g , i , m , p	f , a , m , p
200	a , b , f , l , m , o	f , a , b , m
300	b , f , h , j , o , a	f , a , b
400	b , f , s , p	f , b , p
500	a , c , e , l , p , m , n	a , m , p

Based on this example, according to FP-tree construction algorithm [5], a frequent pattern tree can be designed. To facilitate tree traversal, an item header table is built in which each item points to its first occurrence in the tree via a node-link. Nodes with the same item-name are linked in sequence via such node-links. After scanning all the transactions, the tree, together with the associated node-links, is built such as shown in figure 1.

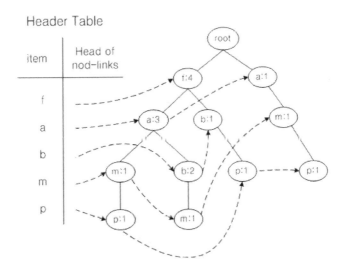

Fig. 1. Frequent Pattern tree constructed based on our example

3.2 Create Multidimensional Data Array Algorithm

In order to design a compact data cube array structure [10], let us based on following steps.

Step1. Create an array structure to initialize cube[i][j][k].
    1)   i = x-axis; // record parent node.
    2)   j = y-axis; //record child node, always record the left child.
    3)   k= z-axis; //record item_name;
Step2. Generate the coordinates by the header table shown in figure 1.
    1)   x-axis starts with "null" and ends with most infrequent item. Because root node haven`t parent node.
    2)   y-axis starts with the most frequent item and ends with "null". Because leaf node haven`t any nodes.
    3)   z-axis starts with root item and end with most infrequent item.
Step3. Load the FP-tree items to the cube structure by top down way and start with root node. Until there is no items could be loaded.
    1)   x-axis = node-link.parent_link;
    2)   y-axis = node-link.child_link;
    3)   z-axis = item_name;
Step4. If the location cell has values in the cube projected by coordinates, then evaluate cube[i][j][k] = n // n is the count that registers the number of path reaching this node;
    else cube[i][j][k] = 0;
Step5. Delete all of the cell which cube[i][j][k] = 0;

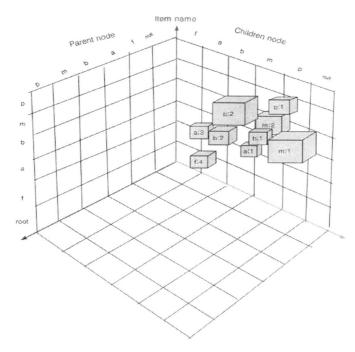

Fig. 2. The cube based on our example

With the above steps, a data cube array can be constructed as follows. It consists of three coordinates: *item*, *parent node*, and *child node*, where item represents each of the item's name and the *parent node* represents the each of the item's parent node as also the *child node* represents the each of the item's child nodes. Every space cell counts the number of transactions reaching this position.

Compare the number of the nodes in this cube with the number of the nodes in this example FP-tree; it is easily to be found that the number of nodes in the cube is less than the number of nodes in the FP-tree. Because some duplicate items, which is the same of *parent node* and *child node*, are represented by one position.

4 Manipulate the Association Cubes On-Line

In practice, not all the cubes in the data warehouse should be computed. There are some associations among cubes. For example, if someone want to manipulate the hierarchy of *b* in this cube array, then it can slice for *item name* = "*b*" and the result is *b:1* and *b:2*. (1) *b:1* is associated with parent node *f:4*, child node *p:1*. (2) *b:2* is associated with parent node *a:3*, child node *m:1*. Moreover, the frequent patterns also can be generated by this cube. Let's generate the frequent patterns for *b*. (1) *item name* = "*b*", the result is *b:1* and *b:2*. (2) Traverse the parent of *b:1* and super parent of *b:1* until *parent node* = "*null*", the result is{ *f:4, b:1*}. (3) Traverse the parent of *b:2* and super parent of *b:2* until *parent node* = "*null*", the result is{ *f:4, a:3, b:2*}. So the last result, the frequent pattern generated for *b* is {*f:3, b:3*}. Based on such relations among the cubes in the cube array structure, it is efficiently that compute the a few associated fragment cubes by on-line analytical processing.

5 Conclusion and Future Work

This paper presents the study of precomputing the cubes in data warehouse. We focus on the association cubes in the cube array structure. The cube array structure is constructed based on the frequent pattern tree structure, so the infrequent cubes are filtered out by the *minimum support threshold*. These methods enable us to obtain a set of frequent cubes in cube array structure and integrate the on-line analytical processing with data mining knowledge in multidimensional databases.

Future work we would include the more detailed working process to get the more strongly evident on our search that make the on-line analytical processing with data mining Synchronized.

References

1. Pedersen, T.B., Jensen, C.S.: Multidimensional Data Modeling for Complex Data. In: Proceedings of ICDE (1999)
2. Surajit, C., Umeshwar, D.: An Overview of Data Warehousing and OLAP Technology. Newsletter ACM SIGMOD Record Homepage Archive (1997)
3. Keim, D.A.: Information Visualization and visual data mining. IEEE Transactions on Visualization and Computer Graphics (2002)
4. Yu, G., Chen, J., Zhu, L.: Data mining techniques for materials informatics: datasets preparing and applications. In: 2009 Second International Symposium on Knowledge Acquisition and Modeling (2004)

5. Han, J.W., Pei, J., Yin, Y.W., Mao, R.Y.: Mining Frequent Patterns without Candidate Generation: A Frequent-Pattern Tree Approach. Data Mining and Knowledge Discovery (2004)
6. Gray, J., et al.: Data Cube: A Relational Aggregation Operator Generalizing Group-By, Cross-Tab and Sub-Totals. In: Proc. of ICDE, pp. 152–159 (1996)
7. Sawires, A.S., El Makky, N.M., Ahmed, K.M.: Multilevel Chunking of Multidimensional Arrays. In: IEEE International Conference on Computer Systems and Applications (2005)
8. Pourabbas, E., Shoshani, A.: The composite OLAP-Object Data Model: Removing an unnecessary Barrier. In: International Conference on Scientific and Statistical Database Management (2006)
9. Zheng, H.Z., Liu, G.Z., Zhan, D.C.: In: International Conference on Machine Learning and Cybernetics (2004)
10. Ge, T.j., Zdonik, S.: A*-tree: A Structure for Storage and Modeling of Uncertain Multidimensional Arrays. In: Proceedings of the VLDB Endowment (2010)

Trust Building and Management for Online File Storage Service

Huiying Duan

Department of Computer Science, University of Kaiserslautern
D-67653 Kaiserslautern, Germany
duan@informatik.uni-kl.de

Abstract. This paper introduces a series of methodologies not only to evaluate, monitor and predict the performance of Online File Storage Service but also to advance robustness of trust management system. Firstly, the approaches of evaluating attributes of Online File Storage Service are proposed. Afterwards, in order to reduce vulnerability of the basic trust model, a novel detection mechanism named Baseline Sampling is proposed. Finally, a simulation is designed to assess the vulnerability of the basic model and evaluate the efficiency of the detection technique. Results indicate that with the assistance of Baseline Sampling the deviation of trust value caused by malicious behavior is controlled in a reasonable range.

Keywords: trust and reputation management system, online file storage service, malicious behavior detection and mitigation, QoS monitoring.

1 Introduction

Recently great attention has been drawn upon trust and reputation in terms of construction of interactive systems and applications, such as P2P information systems, recommender systems, e-commerce, MANET, Semantic Web, etc. They play a crucial role in the current research procedures due to the fact that with the increasing involvement of human factor into software systems, trust and reputation are regarded as a life-saving straw for enhancing the dependability of the system. In order to decrease the number of downloads of inauthentic files in a peer-to-peer file-sharing network, eigentrust [1] is introduced to evaluate the trustworthiness of each peer. Amazon is one of the best online stores who successfully integrate the advantage of reputation systems into recommender systems, in order to provide the most suitable product to the client. Trust is imported into research on Semantic Web with the purpose of addressing the issue that to what degree each information source is trustworthy. Although it exists a lot of research on trust and reputation management in different application domains, few of them focus on the online service with seemingly simple but intangible characters such as Online File Storage Service.

Online File Storage Service (OFSS) refers to an Internet hosting service specifically designed to store static content such as music tracks, movies, software, etc. There are a great number of providers out there, for instance Amazon.com, box.net, mozy.com, Azure, etc. Our research attempts to answer a seemingly simple question: which

C. Lee et al. (Eds.): STA 2011 Workshops, CCIS 187, pp. 31–40, 2011.
© Springer-Verlag Berlin Heidelberg 2011

instance of OFSS is the most suitable one for a particular client? For the first glance, it is an easy question to answer due to the single and plain functionality of service which refers to file transfer and storage. The value of trust should only reflect the expected value for each attribute of service, such as reliability and performance of file transfer. However, answering the question in a client-oriented way is not easy. Considering the service consumer and provider paradigm that a client perceives quality of service via the Internet, due to the heterogeneous character of the Internet, different clients experience quality of service differently. Asking an African client using Amazon S3, he probably holds quite different opinion on quality of service than an American client does. Furthermore, it is not reasonable to provide only one value instead of a series of values over time, since the quality of different attributes of service may vary with different frequency (e.g. per day, per month or per year). Finally, once notion of trust or reputation is imported into system, the robustness of trust management system becomes an inevitable issue. Since no one will use a reputation management system which is quite vulnerable to manipulation and destruction.

2 Related Work

It is effortless to find different definitions and understandings about trust in different research fields such as psychology, economics, sociology and computer science, because this concept contains different implications in different contexts [2]. We are using the most general and operational definition by Gambetta, that trust is the subjective probability by which an individual, A, expects that another individual, B, performs a given action on which its welfare depends. The detailed discussion about this issue can be found in [3].

There exist many approaches for evaluating trust and reputation. The trust evaluation function or model is used to calculate trust value via given different weights on different pieces of historical data. For instance, EigenTrust [1] and powertrust [4] calculate reputation (global trust) score of peers in P2P environment through repeated and iterative multiplication and aggregation of trust scores along transitive chains, until the trust scores for all members of the P2P community converge to stable values. The personalized similarity-based measurement among peers is proposed in peerTrust [5] to weight different peers for the trust calculation with respect to a specific peer. Bayesian system [6] and Dirichlet-multinomial model [7] are the sound theories for trust evaluation on binary and discrete ratings respectively.

Furthermore, few works systematically discuss robustness issue on Trust Management Systems (TMSs) and Reputation Systems (RSs). An analytical framework by which RSs can be decomposed, analyzed and compared using a common set of metrics is proposed in [8]. In this paper, the attacks against RSs are classified and what system components are exploited by each attack category is analyzed. A robust RS [9] in which a Bayesian system plays the core role is introduced. And only second-hand trust information that is not incompatible with the current reputation is accepted. The basic idea of this work is that, only slight change of the trust value is acceptable. In the online trading community, the reputation bias caused by unfair positive ratings is analyzed, and cluster filtering is proposed to reduce or eliminate the effect of attack in [10].

All of these studies enlighten our current work, but none of them provides support to the essence of trust building and managing on service. Since trust or reputation building and management is a subject-oriented topic, different approaches and constraints are derived from different research areas. OFSS, which is a technical level service, requires some new methodologies to achieve a reasonable and robust trust evaluation procedure in terms of customer's point of view.

3 Basic Trust Model for OFSS

People consider a service in terms of different attributes. Taking selection of a restaurant for instance, people balance factors such as cuisine, service and decoration. Following the same idea, firstly we identify the main attributes of OFSS with respect to trust evaluation. Then trust evaluation function for each attribute is proposed. Afterwards, a trust vector for attributes is used to calculate a trust value for a service. In the paper, the service is selected as OFSS. According to the size limit of the paper, we are not going to introduce how to calculate the rational trust value for a service, but discuss how we can compute a trust value for each attribute of OFSS and how the TMS controls influence of malicious behavior.

In the paper, we only consider two attributes which are success rate and average bandwidth. Success Rate (SR) for file upload (download) refers to the probability of uploading (downloading) file successfully and it is a measure of reliability from client's point of view. Moreover, Average Bandwidth (AB) for file transfer is also a large concern from the client's point of view in terms of nonfunctional requirement.

For SR without considering any abuse or attack behavior, the beta-distribution can be applied to evaluate the trust value [6]. Beta-distribution is the natural candidate for SR, because it can be modeled as a binomial distribution, and beta-distribution represents the distribution for its expected value which is exactly the interpretation with respect to trust. The prerequisite of binomial distribution refers to independence of the sequence of n experiments, which is valid in our basic trust model. Furthermore, it is one of the significant facts that TMS interacts with the clients continuously. In the basic model, first of all, trust value is used to create a ranking of instances of a service and to assist clients to determine which instance of a service is more appropriate. Afterwards, clients send ratings of the corresponding instance of service back to system. It is significant to notice that new rating is independent from previous one, but the number of new ratings depends on the previous ones. Since the more positive ratings an instance of a service got, the more ratings it probably will own next.

The basic model for *SR* is a parameterized beta system, in which different weights are given to different observations in terms of time. We consider the previous ratings contribute to trust evaluation less than the recent ones. So ratings are categorized into two classes: long term and short term ratings. The parameters used here are a time window *tw* and weight w_t. The weight given to rating within *tw* corresponds to *st*, otherwise to *lt*, furthermore they fulfill the equation $lt + st = 1$.

In addition, network context influences evaluation of service (e.g. SR and AB). Network context refers to the characterization of clients with respect to service performance such as IP address, Autonomous System number, Internet connection type, geographical location, etc. Given sufficient computing and communication capacity of clients, two clients who locate in the same region probably share similar observations on service performance. It is probably meaningless to aggregate the ratings of a client from South Africa into the trust evaluation which is rendered by American clients, because they have different network performance such as latency, network reliability, and so on. On the one hand, in order to evaluate trust in a reasonable way, we group the clients in terms of network context. The assumption here is the more similar network context, the more similar the network performance they observe. We have done an experiment on PlanetLab [11] to find out the most significant indicators which strongly correlated with network performance. Unsurprisingly it is suggested that IP prefix is the best indicator. It follows the intuitive judge on this statement. Since the same IP prefix usually implies that they belong to the same computer network, share the same ISP provider which results in similar routing choice from local to the OFSS server, or their geographical location is close e.g. in the same building or campus. On the other hand, not considering the rest of clients saves a large number of computing power but with more reasonable result. Considering the above factors, the trust evaluation function (TEF) for SR is defined as:

$$TEF^{SR} = \frac{\sum_{V_{SR}^i=1} w_t^i}{\sum_{V_{SR}^i=1} w_t^i + \sum_{V_{SR}^j=0} w_t^j} \tag{1}$$

Formula (1) represents a trust evaluation function for SR and only the ratings of clients who own a similar network context are considered. In the formula, i and j represent the index of rating whose value for SR is either positive (1) or negative (0). Different from SR, a heuristic approach is proposed to evaluate the trust value (i.e. expected value and deviation) for AB. The basic idea of the approach is to calculate expected value depending on ratings collected within the time window tw. We consider AB is a dynamic value which may change with a higher frequency than success rate, therefore the long-time memory may mislead the evaluation. So we only consider the ratings within a relatively short period of time.

$$TEF^{AB} = \sum_i V_{AB}^i \tag{2}$$

In formula (2), only the ratings within the tw and that of the clients who own a similar network context are considered.

4   Abuse Detection and Filtering Model: Baseline Sampling

TMS collects all ratings from clients, aggregates them and calculates the trust value of a service in a reasonable way. Once a TMS is running as a serious business system and is involved into service-oriented environment, both abuse and attack would swarm towards it. These malicious behaviors are divided into two main classes in terms of the intention of behavior. Attack refers to the behavior leading to destruction of TMS. The real purpose behind the attack could be competitors of this TMS intend to bring it down. Abuse refers to the behavior generated by the purpose of pushing or nuking certain instance of a service. The incentive behind it could be, a service provider itself wants to step up the ranking of his own service, or his competitors are willing to knock it down.

Baseline sampling is the main technique we use in malicious behavior detection and filtering. *Baseline Sampling* (BS) refers to creation of a reference for current performance of each attribute by collecting a certain number of ratings from some "special" clients. The "special" client refers to the client who is absolutely trusted by the TMS, therefore the ratings generated by them are clean. With the creation of baseline sampling, the root of trust is built up and the trust on the providing ratings is derived from it. The basic idea is to create a baseline for the current performance over time. Current performance with respect to an evaluation of trust at certain time is calculated by latest ratings and as the time goes by, current performance is recalculated with a certain frequency. The difference between trust value and corresponding current performance reflects the precision of prediction by trust evaluation. By comparing the baseline with current performance, the malicious force could be identified and we can make an assertion that the corresponding ratings are contaminated. BS seems like creating a secure tunnel for evaluation of current performance. When the procedure of BS is well designed, the real current performance is well protected by the secure tunnel. In other words, if the current performance is deviated from the baseline too far, we assert that TMS is under abuse or attack.

Considering the observation of all honest clients as the population, we can do statistical inference by creating a random sample. In order to guarantee the sample is a random sample (named baseline in the work), a number of "trusted" clients are needed. The basic idea is to create general statistical information from a small trusted part of clients, and compare it to the whole picture generated by ratings from all clients. If the strength of abuse or attack is larger than a certain degree, this malicious behavior is able to be detected by comparing the two kinds of information. There are two possibilities to implement it, either we use only statistical information from baseline, for instance, the mean and deviation and try to build the confidence interval for point estimation, or we consider the difference between the shape of distribution for baseline and that for the whole clients.

Moreover, one time file transfer could be regarded as a binary event, either fail or success. SR of file transfer is supposed to be quite high, hence it implies that failure rate is very low. The big problem here is the failure event occurring in service provisioning is not equivalent to observations clients perceive. For instance, a server is down for a whole day, during the day client A tries to upload a file 100 times and all fail, which doesn't mean it has 100 failure events but should be much less. Otherwise it is unfair to assert that A observes failures 10 times as much as B, if client B only uploads file 10 times on that day and all fail. It is rational to assume that the failure event is a rare event, so the adjacent negative observations in a short interval correspond to only one failure event. After the adjustment, both A and B observe only one failure event.

Under certain condition, repetition of file transfer could be considered as n Bernoulli trials which fulfills binomial distribution $B(n,p)$. Following the definition of failure event above, p is quite close to 1, hence the number of failure in a certain interval could be approximated by poisson distribution $Pois(\lambda)$. Given an interval T (e.g. one month), it could be partitioned into subinterval t_i (e.g. one day) and λ, which is a positive real number, denotes the expected number of failure occurrences that occur during T. The selection of T should not be so large that BS can't reflect the variation of performance with respect to SR. The design of BS aims to finding out the parameter λ in a statistical sense. Assuming there are m trusted clients who share the similar network context and n file transfer (e.g. upload and download) for each trusted client in T. And the success rate p is the same for each client, therefore, it is an m-time experiment of n Bernoulli trials which fulfills binomial distribution $B(n,q)$ where q (failure rate) is equal to $1 - p$. According to the law of rare events, the binomial distribution could be approximated by a poisson distribution $Pois(nq)$ with the condition that n is sufficiently large, q is sufficiently small and nq is a constant. Following the rule of thumb, we can end it up with excellent approximation if n is larger than or equal to 100. In the design of BS we have already defined a random sample with size m in which the set of observation is $\{X_1, X_2, X_3, ..., X_m\}$. Then λ is estimated by formula (3).

$$\hat{\lambda} = E(x) = \overline{X} = \frac{\sum_{i=1}^{m} X_i}{m} \tag{3}$$

In accordance with the central limit theorem and rule of thumb, if m is larger than or equal to 30, then normal approximation Z will be satisfactory to model the distribution of estimated λ regardless of the shape of the population, which is a poisson distribution in this case. Then the confidence interval of λ is given by formula (4) where t denotes t-distribution and α stands for the significance level of a test.

$$\hat{\lambda} - t_{\alpha/2, m-1} * (S/\sqrt{m}) \leq \lambda \leq \hat{\lambda} + t_{\alpha/2, m-1} * (S/\sqrt{m}) \tag{4}$$

TMS has M clients (M $>> m$), who share the similar network context, and n_i trials for each client in T. It is reasonable to assume that when all the n_i are sufficiently large and q_i sufficiently small, then all the X_i, where i is a natural number between 1 and M, can be regarded as an observation of the same poisson distribution. Since, we consider the expected number of failure occurring in T as a constant for every client, who shares the similar network context. The explanation for this assumption is that a service provider treats all the clients in an unbiased way, and influence of the Internet is considered as the main oscillating impact on each client in terms of SR and AB. If we group clients in a certain way (e.g. with similar network context) such that for different groups they still have different expected failure rate in T, but within the group there exists relatively small variation, then our assumption makes sense.

The similarity-based grouping implies the distribution of AB is a normal distribution. Assuming the size of the baseline clients in the group is m. Then the estimation of mean and its confidence interval can be generated as we have done for SR.

Once the baseline information is known and the previous assumptions are fulfilled, the graph of Probability Density Function (PDF) or Probability Mass Function (PMF) with respect to baseline can be drawn. Then compare it to the corresponding graph of PDF or PMF generated by the whole data afterwards. In practice, the latter is really difficult to fit by any class of distribution, because it contains dirty ratings. Therefore, we prefer to compare the baseline graph to the histogram generated by the whole data instead. Graph based BS is superior than confidence interval based BS, since once confidence interval is created, the influence of two types of abuse (push and nuke) are merged into one. It is impossible to detect the case that both push and nuke perform at the same time using confidence interval based BS.

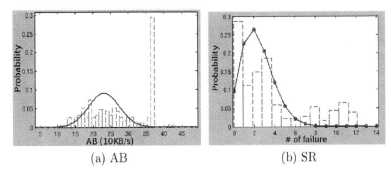

(a) AB   (b) SR

Fig. 1. Abuse Patterns Represented by Graph based BS

Table 1. Primary Parameters of Simulation

Parameter Name	Value
PUSH	
Percentage of Dishonest Client (% of DC)	10%, 30%, 50%, 70%
Times of file Transfer Frequency (TTF)	2x, 4x, 6x
Average Bandwidth Offset (ABO)	30%, 50%, 70%, 90%
NUKE	
% of DC	10%, 30%, 50%, 70%
Offset to Number of Failure (O2NF)	0, +1, +2, +3
ABO	30%, 50%, 70%, 90%
BOTH	
% of DC	30%, 50%, 70%
ratio of Pusher to Nuker (P2D)	1:9, 3:7, 5:5, 7:3, 9:1
Average Bandwidth Offset (ABO)	90%
Combination of TTF and O2NF	(2x,1), (2x,2), (4x,1), (4x,2)

Fig. 1 demonstrates two typical cases for patterns of abuse. For AB, horizontal axis stands for the value of attribute whose measure unit is 10 KB/s, and vertical one for its corresponding probability. Taking subfigure (a) for instance, comparing with the corresponding probability of normal distribution generated from baseline, the extremely high probability at value 370 KB/s is the very evidence of pushing a instance of OFSS. Subfigure (b) represents that both operations of pushing and nuking are performing on Attribute SR. We also propose two algorithms BSA_Normal and BSA_Poiss for detecting abuse on AB and SR respectively [12].

5 Experiment Design and Simulation Result

The purpose of the simulation is to evaluate vulnerability of our trust model, and efficiency of detection mechanisms such as graph-based BS and confidence interval based BS. The simulation platform is designed as a highly flexible and parameterized one in which every key feature of the target system is represented by set of parameters, such as number of communities in which all the clients share the similar network context, size of each community, percentage of dishonest clients in each community, the distribution of AB and SR in each community for honest clients and dishonest ones, the frequency of file transfer for each client, etc. Generated data is composed of clean and dirty ones. Especially, distribution of AB and SR in each community with respect to honest clients, are generated by following assumed distributions like normal distribution and poisson distribution. Moreover, we model attack in terms of its types and intensity. Regarding to its categorization, three types of attack, which are push, nuke and both of them, are considered. And in terms of intensity, different dimensions shown in Table 1, are considered depending on the types of attack. For all the types, the percentage of dishonest clients (% of DC) in the community is the necessary parameter to consider. For push attack, the intensity of attack with respect to success rate is simulated by Times of file Transfer Frequency (TTF) which stands for the times of transfer frequency with respect to normal client. And the intensity with respect to average bandwidth is simulated by Average Bandwidth Offset (ABO) which refers to the ratio of mean difference between honest clients and dishonest ones, to the mean of honest ones. For nuke attack, the intensity in terms of SR is characterized by Offset to Number of Failure (O2NF) per week which represents difference of mean of poisson distribution between dishonest clients and honest ones, and for AB the same parameter ABO is used. For the case of both push and nuke attack, we reuse all the parameters above. According to the combination of parameters for each type, we generate 400 test cases without dirty data, 48 for push attack, 64 for nuke attack and 60 for both.

Table 2. Simulation Result

Abuse Type	Maximal Deviation (MD) with BS	MD without BS
Push on SR	4.6%	28.1%
Nuke on SR	-6%	-32.1%
Both on SR	0% - 8.21%	-15.9% - 13.4%
Push on AB	14.5%	68.3%
Nuke on AB	-10%	-46%
Both on AB	-10% - 15%	-24.8% - 59.6%

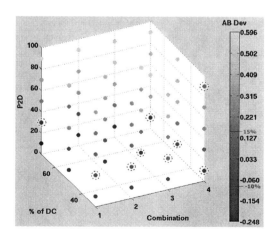

Fig. 2. Both Push and Nuke on AB

Fig. 2 indicates the simulation results for one of the 6 types of abuse in a 4-dimension way. The number 1 - 4 on dimension of Combination denote value (2x,1), (2x,2), (4x,1) and (4x,2) respectively. Each point represents a test case with specific value of parameters, and the difference in color stands for the deviation of trust value on AB in the contaminated system from the trust value calculated without considering abusers. The points with doted circles are the test cases which can't be detected out by BS. By using BS, the deviation of trust value is able to be restricted into the interval of -10% - 15%, instead of the maximal deviation -24.8% - 59.6%. Furthermore, the deviation for all the types of abuse is shown in Table 2, and it is obvious to display that in every type of abuse the Maximal Deviation (MD) using BS is much less than that without using BS. One more point of view to be emphasized is that, the set of test cases is only the small subset of the whole population space, therefore the real MD without using BS is much larger than the number shown in the simulation results. However, the simulation results suggest that, MD using BS is influenced not by the strength of abuse, but the quality of baseline samples and the assumed probability distributions for different attributes of instance of a service. Therefore, the effect of restriction to malicious behavior should be much stronger than the results show in this paper. By the way, none of all the 400 test cases for clean data are misdetected out as malicious behavior.

6 Conclusion

This paper is the first work focusing on evaluation of performance of OFSS using a trust-based approach and considering the quality of service from client's perspective. Our work contributes to the following aspects:

1. The trust evaluation function for each attribute of OFSS such as success rate and average bandwidth is developed.
2. The Baseline Sampling technique for abuse detection is proposed.
3. A simulation platform to assess the vulnerability of TMS and to evaluate the efficiency of detection approaches is built up.

The simulation results indicate that with the application of trust evaluation function on attribute and BS, system deviation of the TMS caused by malicious behavior is controlled in a reasonable range. Further research is needed in order to find the border of deviation in a theoretical way, and to design the baseline management to deal with the dynamics of target system and baseline clients.

References

1. Kamvar, S., Schlosser, M., Garcia-Molina, H.: The eigentrust algorithm for reputation management in p2p networks. In: Proceedings of the 12th International Conference on World Wide Web, WWW 2003, pp. 640–651. ACM, Budapest (2003)
2. Mcknight, D.H., Chervany, N.L.: The meanings of trust. Tech. rep., Management Information Systems Research Center, University of Minnesota (1996)
3. Jøsang, A., Ismail, R., Boyd, C.: A survey of trust and reputation systems for online service provision. Decision Support Systems (2007)

4. Zhou, R., Hwang, K.: Powertrust: A robust and scalable reputation system for trusted peer-to-peer computing. IEEE Transactions on Parallel and Distributed Systems 18, 460–473 (2007)
5. Xiong, L., Liu, L.: Peertrust: supporting reputation-based trust for peer-to-peer electronic communities. IEEE Transactions on Knowledge and Data Engineering 16(7), 843–857 (2004)
6. Jøsang, A., Ismail, R.: The beta reputation system. In: Proceedings of the 15th Bled Electronic Commerce Conference, Bled, Slovenia (2002)
7. Zhang, Y., Fang, Y.: A fine-grained reputation system for reliable service selection in peer-to-peer networks. IEEE Transactions on Parallel and Distributed Systems 18, 1134–1145 (2007)
8. Hoffman, K., Zage, D., Nita-Rotaru, C.: A survey of attack and defense techniques for reputation systems. ACM Comput. Surv. 42, 1:1–1:31 (2009)
9. Buchegger, S., Boudec, J.Y.L.: A robust reputation system for peer-to-peer and mobile ad-hoc networks. In: Proceedings of P2PEcon 2004. Harvard University, Cambridge (2004)
10. Dellarocas, C.: Immunizing online reputation reporting systems against unfair ratings and discriminatory behavior. In: Proceedings of the 2nd ACM Conference on Electronic Commerce, EC 2000, pp. 150–157. ACM, New York (2000)
11. http://www.planet-lab.org
12. Duan, H.: Trust building and management for online file storage service. Tech. rep., Department of Computer Science, University of Kaiserslautern (2010), https://sites.google.com/site/duanhuiying/publications

Digital Trails Discovering of a GPS Embedded Smart Phone – Take Nokia N78 Running Symbian S60 Ver 3.2 for Example

Hai-Cheng Chu[1], Li-Wei Wu[2], Hsiang-Ming Yu[3], and Jong Hyuk Park[4]

[1] Department of International Business
National Taichung University of Education, 140 Min-Shen Road, Taichung 40306 Taiwan ROC
[2,3] Department of International Business
Tunghai University, No.181, Sec. 3, Taichung Port Rd., Taichung 40704, Taiwan ROC
[4] Department of Computer Science and Engineering
Seoul National University of Technology, 172 Gongneung-dong 2, Nowon-gu 139743, Korea
hcchu@mail.ntcu.edu.tw, lwwu@thu.edu.tw, bravedean@gmail.com,
parkjonghyuk1@hotmail.com

Abstract. As mobile computing devices becomes pervasive, more and more civilians deposit precious information in mobile phones than desk top PCs especially for Global Logistics Management operators, who heavily depend on Global Position System in order to effectively and efficiently fulfill just-in-time delivery. In this paper, an embedded Global Position System smart phone was applied to travel along the roads trying to disclose the associate digital evidences concerning the locations that the current user had actually been or wish to go via data mining technology. From digital forensics point of view, digital evidences essentially play a critical and decisive role in some cybercriminal or cyber terrorism cases although the diversities of mobile phones and the corresponding operating systems. The paper provides the generic guides and methodologies for the law enforcement agencies or the digital forensics specialists to ponder when they deal with the similar cases.

Keywords: digital forensics; global position system; geotagging; mobile computing device; non-volatile memory; smart phone.

1   Introduction

In the past few years, the cost down of Global Positioning System (GPS) related technology has stimulated massive civilians to install GPS devices on their computing devices (PC, laptop, PDA, smart phone, or on the dash board of the vehicle) with affordable and competitive prices. The phenomenon has dramatically changed the way in many aspects of our daily lives. Not only does the GPS function facilitate the operations of business, but also becomes the tool for criminals to commit high technology crimes [2, 3, 6, 7]. In this case, the Digital Forensics (DF) of those GPS based communication devices is an urgent and imminent task for law enforcement agencies. Initially, the GPS technology was deployed by the U.S Department of

C. Lee et al. (Eds.): STA 2011 Workshops, CCIS 187, pp. 41–49, 2011.
© Springer-Verlag Berlin Heidelberg 2011

Defense as a tool for military that could assist the soldiers navigate foreign territory and deliver munitions accurately on the targets since 1978 [2].

In this research, the digital trails of *Nokia N78* (with *Symbian S60 Version 3.2* operating system) was collected, analyzed, and documented. The experiment was conducted via two ways: The first experiment is to delete the GPS track files directly from the mobile phone and the second experiment is to delete those files from PC via the micro SD card reader. In this experiment, *Final Data* [11] and *R-Studio* [12] were applied trying to recover the delete entries for the purpose of digging out the digital breadcrumb trail regarding the current mobile communication device–*Nokia N78*. The experiment indicates that whether the user deletes the GPS track files directly from the mobile phone or via PC connections, all the deleted files are able to be recovered via both *Final Data* and *R-Studio*.

The GPS track files could be saved in different places depending upon the mobile communication device. If the GPS track file is stored in the Random Access Memory (RAM), those precious digital trails would be vanished as long as the power of the mobile phone goes down. On the contrary, if the GPS track files are kept in the non-volatile memory (Internal memory, micro SD card), those digital trails would be obtainable even the user purposely deletes those files. The mobile device (*Nokia N78*) being utilized does not have to be always on during the digital evidence collection stage because the digital trails were stored in micro SD card instead of RAM. Furthermore, the procedure of DF evidence acquisition concerning the portable communication device is classified as non-invasive, which means the device is not required to be opened or the internal memory removed [4, 5, 8] in this case.

The GPS track file(s) in the mobile communication device would not display any relevant time information on *Google Maps* or *Google Earth* although *Google Maps* shows the path with small boxes along the node. Regrettably, those marks do not show a record of those metadata. Besides, *KML* GPS track files do not embed the time stamping. However, *Picasa Web Albums* provides additional fascinating services for *Google Map* or *Google Earth* users. End users can upload photos with GPS embedded information to this web album and the associate metadata will be displayed in *Google Maps* or *Google Earth*. The GPS related metadata of the photos include latitude, longitude, and sea level, etc. Moreover, *KUSO EXIF Viewer* can also be utilized to visualize the photos taken by *Nokia N78* with enabling the GPS recording functions for latitude and longitude into photos. Similarly, *Windows Live search Maps*, *Panoramio*, and *Flickr* are also capable of inspecting those metadata with respect to the digital photos. The dates of those recorded photos are based on the time stamp of the *Nokia N78*.

The experiment is conducted based on the hypothesis that the user enables the GPS track recording function and then deletes the tracks directly from the smart phone or through the PC connection running the popular navigation software, *PAPAGO! VR-ONE* [10], respectively. Two representative data recovery software packages, *Final Data* and *R-studio*, were applied trying to disclose the trails that the user had actually been. Other popular data recovery application programs are also available including *File Recovery Pro*, *Handy Recovery* and *Smart Data Recovery*, which will not be discussed in this research. Two GPS track files (*KML* file) were generated in order to carry on the associate DF of the current mobile communication device.

At last, using *PAPAGO! VR-ONE* (regardless of GPS function is turning on or off), will keep recording in the *PPGOINE.DAT* if we input some Point of Interest (POI) to "*My Favorite*". The date of the file will be in accordance with the smart phone date. Using *Hex Workshop* [13] through Unicode encoding, we are capable of can inspecting "*My Favorite*" information within the file.

2   Literature Review

GPS Navigation software packages have been mushrooming on notebooks, PDAs, or smart phones. For example, TomTom GPS navigation devices are one of the most popular kinds of satellite navigation devices in the UK. Like many other gadgets, the TomTom device is operated via a touch-screen and menu-driven interface, which allows the user to enter locations, plan routes or itineraries, save favorites, or look up POIs [1, 9]. The TomTom devices, which are one of the most popular mobile portable navigation gadgets worldwide, incorporate both the internal memory and the SD card into the equipment. The memories on TomTom devices behave just like any other digital memory. Likewise, in Taiwan, *PAPAGO! VR-ONE* is one of the leading navigation software packages. The time stamps on the photo of *Nokia N78* were dating GMT (Greenwich Time) standard. The time difference is 8-hour compared to local time of Taiwan. Satellite detection system has become extremely widespread and most automotive vehicles are fitted with such systems today.

The GPS track file can positively confirm the current user, who was actually been to those places. Unfortunately, based on the items of *My Favorite*, the DF officer can't guarantee that the suspect had actually been to those places. In addition, the time stamps of the photos storing in *Nokia N78* were dating GMT (Greenwich Time) standard. The pervasive GPS navigation software suites provide the user to plan the travelling routes, store favorite geographic locations, and look up Point of Interest (POI).

For *Nokia N78*, if detailed information (like address, phone number, etc.) is founded within the *Recentmp.dat* file, it indicates that the user must have searched first and then clicks the build-in land mark. However, from DF point of view, this information only shows the place where the user searched before, but does not guarantee the user had physically present in that destination during the navigation. Besides, some researchers focus on the utilizing the SIM tools to extract digital evidence present in the file system. Furthermore, most forensic sound SIM tolls support a range of examination and reporting function except data acquisition. Some tools deal exclusively with SIM, while others are part of a complete toolkit that also target on handsets.

Google Maps provides a comprehensive e-map service for global users via common web browsers. Depending on the user's location, the user can view basic, customized e-maps as well as local business data, which includes business locations, contact information, and driving directions. After the user signs into individual's account, user can click "*My Maps*" on the left side of the panel and upload the file(s) to create personalized e-map.

On the other hand, the *Google Earth* is a software package which is capable of executing on the local computer with/without steadily connecting to ubiquitous networks. With the *Google Earth*, a computer becomes a window allowing any user to access global view with high-resolution aerial and satellite images including photos, elevation terrain, street labels, and business listings in most area on the planet. In addition, the user can open *KML* files directly within *Google Earth* on local computer without uploading procedure.

Few researches also pointed out that the forensics acquisition and analysis of the contemporary mobile computing devices is an urgent task to combat the criminals using high technology like GPS to compile information before committing crimes.

3   Design of Experiment

In this research, the experiment is conducted based on the hypothesis that the user was using the navigation software suite, *PAPAGO! VR-ONE* for *Symbian S60 3th* edition, on *Nokia N78* with enabling the recording function. During the experiment, two GPS track files were generated (*99100605.kml* and *99100606.kml*) and securely stored. The scenario of the experiment is divided into two categories: the user deletes the GPS track files directly from the mobile communication device as well as the user erases the GPS track files via PC connection through micro SD card reader. For both cases, *Final Data* and *R-studio* application programs were incorporated in order to recover the GPS trails for the purpose of demonstrating the mobile user had actually been. The memory card (Micro SD 2G) being under examined was formatted as FAT.

Scenario 1: The mobile user deletes two GPS track files directly from Nokia N78.
Part A: Using R-studio to recover the deleted GPS track files
Step 1: Connecting the memory cards (Micro SD 2G) to desktop PC and scanning it as Fig. 1 shown.

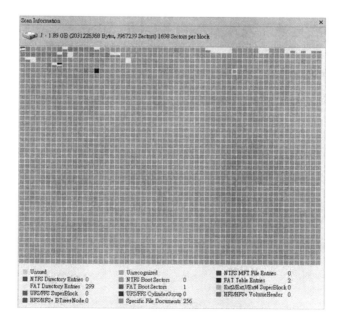

Fig. 1. *R-studio* shows the information during scanning

Step 2: Two deleted KML files were discovered within R-studio as Fig. 2 indicates.

	Name	Size	Created	Modified
☑ 🦊	?9100605.kml	9883 Bytes	2010/11/22···	2010/10/6 上午 08:19:04
☑ 🦊	?9100606.kml	4507 Bytes	2010/11/22···	2010/10/6 上午 08:22:32

Fig. 2. Two deleted files were discovered within R-studio

Step 3: Two deleted KML files were recovered and the log report was generated from R-studio as Fig. 3 depicts.

	Type	Date	Time	
🛈	System	2010/11/22	下午 12:01:12	Enumeration of files for J: started
🛈	System	2010/11/22	下午 12:01:12	Enumeration of files for J: completed
🛈	System	2010/11/22	下午 12:01:35	Recover files started
🛈	Recover	2010/11/22	下午 12:01:41	Successfully restored: 1 files. Failed: 0 files.
🛈	System	2010/11/22	下午 12:01:41	Recover files completed
🛈	System	2010/11/22	下午 12:01:47	Recover files started
🛈	Recover	2010/11/22	下午 12:01:48	Successfully restored: 1 files. Failed: 0 files.
🛈	System	2010/11/22	下午 12:01:48	Recover files completed

Fig. 3. Log report from R-studio concerning two deleted GPS track files

Step 4: The WordPad was applied to check the rescued files and 99100606.kml was recovered perfectly. Unfortunately, the 99100605.kml got some scrambled codes near the beginning of the file as Fig. 4 illustrates.

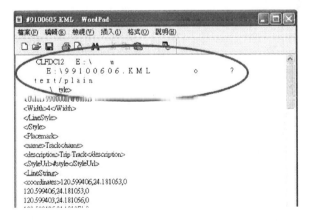

Fig. 4. Some scrambled codes occurred near the beginning of the file, 99100605.kml

Step 5: The WordPad was applied again to remove those scrambled codes and obtained the newly revised GPS track file, 99100605.kml. After taking care of the scrambled code issue, the newly revised 99100605.kml was identical to the original one as Fig. 5a and Fig. 5b shown correspondingly.

46   H.-C. Chu et al.

Step 6: The newly revised *99100605.kml* and the recovered 99100606 were uploaded to *Google Maps*. They reflected the real paths that the user had actually been as Fig. 6 and Fig. 7 displayed separately.

Part B: Using Final Data to recover the deleted GPS track files

The experiment was conducted and obtained similar results by *Final Data*. In other words, the two deleted GPS track files were successfully recovered and demonstrated the same paths as the previous section.

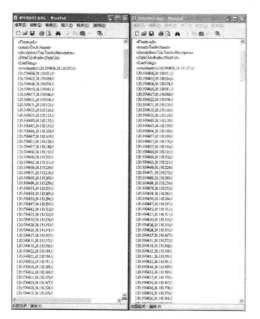

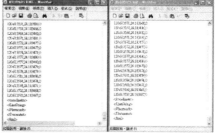

Fig. 5a. The newly revised 99100605.kml was identical to the original one

Fig. 5b. The newly revised 99100605.kml was identical to the original one

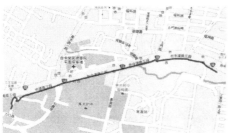

Fig. 6. The path of the newly revised 99100605.kml file is the same as the original file

Fig. 7. The path of the recovered 99100606.kml file is the same as the original file

Scenario 2: The mobile user deletes two GPS track files through PC connection via micro SD card reader.
The memory card of the mobile phone was removed and connecting to the desktop PC by means of micro SD card reader. Two GPS track files, *99100605.kml* and *99100606.kml*, were both successfully recovered/rescued via both *R-studio and Final Data*. All procedures were carried on similar to *Scenario 1*. The recovered GPS track files were uploaded to *Google Maps* or *Google Earth* and demonstrated the same results as in *Scenario 1*.

Furthermore, the experiment was also conducted by formatting the micro SD card to NTFS format. However, the result proved that the Nokia N78 smart phone is not able to read the memory card in this condition. Consequently, we construct a valuable table (Table 1) to summarize and illustrate the essence of the undergoing experiment.

Table 1. Summary of the undergoing experiment

Micro SD	Memory card format	Directly delete on the phone		Delete by PC connection	
		Final Data	*R-studio*	*Final Data*	*R-studio*
2G	FAT	All successful	All successful	All successful	All successful
	NTFS	*Nokia N78* cannot read NTFS format memory card			

4   Discussion/Data Mining of the Hidden Message

During the experiment, if the user sets some Point of Interest (POI) to *My Favorite* of the current navigation application program (*PAPAGO! VR-ONE*), the information will be saved into the file, *PPGOINE.DAT*. Hence, from DF point of view, if the file is saved first before any possible intrusive forensics procedure might take place, the digital evidence will be strongly probative. For instance, Fig. 8 indicates that the user saves three POIs into *My Favorite*. Fig 9 points out that the items of *My Favorite* could be interpreted by *Hex Workshop* via Unicode setting while inspecting the file. The arrow labeled #1 is one of the user's *My Favorite* and it would be diagnosed via *Hex Workshop* as arrow #1 indicates in Fig. 9.

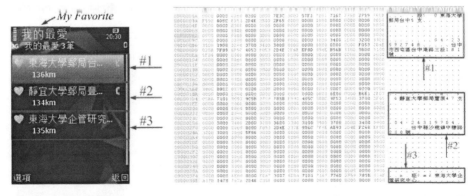

Fig. 8. The user saves three POIs into My Favorite

Fig. 9. Hex Workshop via unicode setting to inspect the file (PPGOINE.DAT)

As long as the user clicks/selects any land mark from the search results, the selected target will be saved in *RECENTMP.DAT*. However, from DF point of view, the information being mined from the files only indicates the intention of the user. In reality, there is no guarantee that the user had really been to those POIs. The research also identifies that if the user does not key in any words and just directly clicks/selects on some landmarks on the e-map for navigation, the search record will only display self-starting and self-built destination.

5 Conclusion

PAPAGO! VR-ONE navigation data is stored in the memory card rather than the internal memory nor RAM of the smart phone, *Nokia N78*. Hence, any generated *KML* track file will be saved in the memory card. Consequently, turning off the phone or low battery will not cause data loss for the GPS track files. Using *PAPAGO! VR-ONE* (regardless of GPS function turning on or off), if any POI has been added to "*My Favorite*", it will be recorded into *PPGOINE.DAT*. Also, the time stamps of the files will be in accordance with the date of the smart phone. Using *Hex Workshop* through Unicode encoding, the information in "*My Favorite*" could be spotted. If the user does not key in any word or directly clicks on the landmark on the e-map, there will be only 'self-starting' and 'self-built' destination displayed within *RECENTMP.DAT*. The information being disclosed within *RECENTMP.DAT* can only identify that the user has searched certain landmark first and then clicks the build-in one. However, from DF point of view, this information does not guarantee that the user had physically presented in those destinations during the navigation. Lastly, the GPS track files being recovered can prove that the current user has actually been to those geographic locations.

Acknowledgment

The author would like to acknowledge the funding support of NSC (National Science Council) of Taiwan concerning the grant of Project NSC 99-2221-E-142-009.

References

1. Nutter, B.: Pinpointing TomTom location records: A forensic analysis. Digital Investigation 5, 10–18 (2008)
2. Strawn, C.: Expanding The Potential for GPS Evidence Acquisition. Small Scale Digital Device Forensics Journal 3(1), 1–12 (2009)
3. Weaver, A.C., Morrison, B.B.: Social Networking. Computer 41, 97–100 (2008)
4. Iqbal, M.U., Samsung, L.: Legal and ethical implications of GPS vulnerabilities. Journal of International Commercial Law and Technology 3(3), 17–187 (2008)
5. Danker, S., Ayers, R., Mislan, R.P.: Hashing Techniques for Mobile Device Forensics. Small Scale Digital Device Forensics Journal 3(1), 1–6 (2009)

6. Fusco, S.J., Michael, K., Michael, M.G.: Using a social informatics framework to study the effects of location-based social networking on relationships between people: A review of literature. In: 2010 IEEE International Symposium on Technology and Society, ISTAS, pp. 157–171, 7–9 (2010)
7. Counts, S., Fisher, K.E.: Mobile Social Networking: An Information Grounds Perspective. In: Hawaii International Conference on System Sciences, HICSS (2008)
8. Ćosić, J., Bača, M.: A Framework to (Im)Prove Chain of Custody in Digital Investigation Process. In: Proceedings of the 21st Central European Conference on Information and Intelligent Systems (CECIIS), pp. 43–438 (2010)
9. LeMere, B., Sayers, A.: TomTom gps device forensics, http://www.forensicfocus.com/tomtom-gps-device-forensics (retrieved November 21, 2010)
10. http://www.mactiontech.com/
11. http://www.finaldata.com/
12. http://www.r-studio.com/
13. http://www.hexworkshop.com/

Opinion Mining in MapReduce Framework

Kyung Soo Cho, Ji Yeon Lim, Jae Yeol Yoon, Young Hee Kim,
Seung Kwan Kim, and Ung Mo Kim

School of Information and Communication Engineering SungKyunKwan University,
2nd Engineering Building 27039 CheonCheon-Dong, JangAn-Gu,
Suwon 440-746, Republic of Korea
kisschks@hotmail.com, {01039374479,vntlffl}@naver.com,
younghees@gmail.com, libertas@korea.kr, umkim@ece.skku.ac.kr

Abstract. Presently, many researching fields are crossed and mashed up to each fields, however, some of computer science fields cannot be solved by technique only. Opinion mining sometimes needs a solution from other fields, too. For example, we use a method from psychology to gain information from text about users. Likewise, we suggested a new method of opinion mining which is using MapReduce before, and this method also uses a WordMap which is dictionary-like. WordMap just has information of category and value of word. If we use a novel method of Opinion mining, it could be mining opinion from web more powerful than before. Therefore, for stronger opinion mining, we suggest a framework of Opinion mining in MapReduce.

Keywords: Framework, Opinion mining, WordMap, POS tagging, MapReduce.

1 Introduction

Opinion mining and Semantic web techniques are fascinating domain of searching engine. Between them, Opinion Mining is one of the mining techniques, extracts estimation from the internet, analyzes it, and puts out the results. These results are usable and useful in many areas like marketing or product reviews. Nonetheless, current methods are inefficient and use time too much for huge data because they run on a single node to process. To settle this problematic, cloud computing, which is the center of attention for next computing environment, is appropriate. MapReduce, which is one of cloud computing methods, already be used in Google file system. Therefore, this paper suggests Opinion Mining in MapReduce framework to this novel trial for designing under a cloud computing environment, and we look forward to the framework showing performance moderately. This framework is able to be utilized when a developer who has wanted for some object and expectations about performance makes Opinion mining tools in MapReduce.

This paper is composed as follows: in the section 2, we explain a technique of opinion mining and existing representative research which has relation with the framework. In the section 3, we present the framework of opinion mining in MapReduce function. In the section 4, we finish the paper with a conclusion and our future work.

C. Lee et al. (Eds.): STA 2011 Workshops, CCIS 187, pp. 50–55, 2011.
© Springer-Verlag Berlin Heidelberg 2011

2 Related Work

2.1 Opinion Mining Methods

Opinion mining study has been gradually growing since the late 90s. Known as sentiment classification, Opinion Mining focuses not on the topic, but a user's mental attitude that topic. In late years, opinion mining has been applied to product reviews, or other commercial things. [1] WY. Kim and others suggest a method for opinion mining of product reviews using association rules. [2] Opinion mining field also includes featured-based opinion mining, summarization, comparative sentence, relation mining, opinion searching, opinion spamming, and the linguistic resource defining & constructing. [3] [4]

In a case of sentiment classification, reading text and analyzing make a result like <word I value>, and <word I value> is similarly to MapReduce's [5] data structure. So sentiment classification has a lot possibility of well-matching within MapReduce. In addition, some rules for analysis, which is like the POS tagging technique [6] [7], or dictionary information are usable, too.

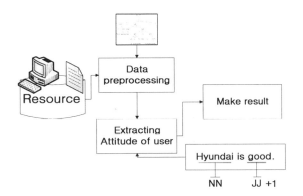

Fig. 1. Example of sentiment classification

Figure 1 shows sentiment classification. Sentiment classification is simple concept. It selects the sentiment of a portion of a document set Positive or Negative. If a blog user write "Hyundai is good", it will calculate and make a result positive on Hyundai.

A topic associated word is realized as important in a technique of Topic-based classification; however, it is as insignificant in sentiment classification. The late research on sentiment classification is mainly performed in a document level, which can find a detailed attribute. Sentence-level studies are also being done. B Pang, and L Lee introduce the ways of discovering sentiment in mining. [8] SM Kim and E Hovy suggest the way of recognizing opinion and sentiment of each opinion in a given topic using sentiment classification of sentence level, [9] It describes that opinions are categorized by the technique of POS tagging(Part-of-speech tagging). Some academics have focused on comments with emoticons. For instance, Potthast and S. Becker give a method of opinion summarization of web comments [10], and J. Read introduces a relationship between emoticons and sentiment classification, and recognizes an emoticon-trained classifiers. [11] "Opinion holder" means a person or a group who makes an opinion in analyzed resource. A considering of opinion holder is central in opinion mining. Thus, SM Kim, and E Hovy submit a paper of a technique of mining opinions generated by an opinion holder on topics in online news media texts also. [12] Along with sentiment classification research, methods of weight for sentiment information also have studied. We suggest reader weight and method of using LIWC[13], before.

2.2 MapReduce

Google suggest MapReduce for analyzing large data, and they use it in their BigTable [8]. MapReduce is very simple and strong for huge size data like terabytes or petabytes, and it is able to customize to each systems efficiently. For these reason, MapReduce is paid attention from many researchers.

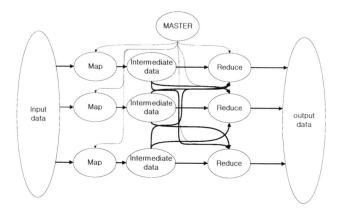

Fig. 2. MapReduce

Figure 2 shows how MapReduce implements. A master node controls all of Worker nodes which are called by Map or Reduce nodes, and Map nodes make intermediate data which structure is <key, value>, and Reduce nodes collect intermediate data and transform <key, value> to <key, listed value>. It is just general fact, and it will change for each systems.

Some researchers in field of mining have attention to this function. They consider that it will make methods of mining stronger. Kelvin Cardona, Jimmy Secretan, Michael Georgiopoulos and Georgios Anagnostopoulos suggest a grid based system for data mining using MapReduce. [15] In addition, Bayir, M.A, Toroslu, I.H, Cosar, A, and Fidan, G suggest a smart miner: a new framework for mining large scale web usage data. [16] They suggest novel methods using data mining and MapReduce. Xia, T suggest SMS mining with MapReduce which is Large-scale sms messages mining based on map-reduce in a "Computational Intelligence and Design". [17] In their thesis, performance of mining methods improves because of MapReduce. This mean is MapReduce is suitable for Mining technique, and it is also adoptable to opinion mining. We suggest a method of Using WordMap and Score-based weight in opinion mining with Mapreduce before. [18]

3 Opinion Mining in MapReduce Framework

3.1 WordMap

A paper of Using WordMap and Score-based weight in opinion mining with Mapreduce gives a structure of WordMap. It is multidimensional indexing, dictionary data, and usable to any systems flexibly. It is possible that a developer uses this concept on his system, and changes its element like mean or value of words. Also, it can use additional weight policy. For example, LIWC or leader weight can use in connected WordMap. WordMap is able to choose two ways, and the first is that the WordMap includes supplementary weight information, and the second is linking weight information externally. Including weight information is faster than an external way, however, adding weight information to completed WordMap will require a lot of time and data space.

3.2 RuleBox

RuleBox is a part to classify sentiment and analyze in the opinion mining in MapReduce framework. It can connected additional component like as POS tagging technique. It defines a sentence or document with using WordMap part. A system developer is always able to choose and customize reasonable rules in RuleBox for appropriate his systems; however, RuleBox must have one or more rules like a natural language processing method. The POS tagging, we mentioned, is a representative natural language processing method.

3.3 Framework

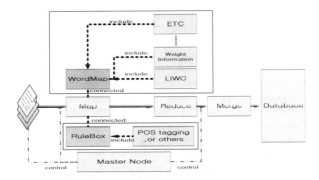

Fig. 3. Opinion mining in MapReduce framework

Figure 3 shows Opinion mining in MapReduce framework. This framework has three parts: MapReduce, WordMap, and RuleBox. The MapReduce part is membrane of the framework, the RuleBox part is brain, and the WordMap part is resource for the framework.

The WordMap and RuleBox influence to accuracy of opinion mining, and MapReduce improves time performance of the framework. [16][18] The Opinion mining in MapReduce framework can use for searching engines and it will make searching results wealthier. Also it is able to use strong marketing analyzing tools in companies for collecting their product reviews, and government is able to utilize this framework for their information gathering and analysis. For example, In case of America, Google and CIA make co-financing investment company which called recorded futures. This company uses mining methods with a technique of huge data processing. This fact is issued in several newspapers.

4 Conclusion and Future Work

We suggest an opinion mining in MapReduce framwork. It is novel method of opinion mining technique and using MapReduce. This framework is useful to someone who wants to develop opinion mining in MapReduce, however, it is unsuitable for small size data because the construction of WordMap part spends a lot of time cost, and it is inefficient that several nodes analyze small size data. Nonetheless, it is powerful for large scale data, and has a strong point of flexibility. Today, many companies want to know opinion of their products in the internet, therefore, opinion mining which analyze huge resource is interesting research topic. Next task is to improve performance and accuracy of opinion mining technique in MapReduce.

Acknowledgments. This work was supported by the Korea Science and Engineering Foundation (KOSEF) grant funded by the Korea government (MEST) (No. 2009-0075771).

References

1. Conrad, J.G., Schilder, F.: Opinion mining in legal blogs. In: Proceedings of the 11th International Conference on Artificial Intelligence and Law, pp. 231–236. ACM, New York (2007)
2. Kim, W.Y., Ryu, J.S., Kim, K.I., Kim, U.M.: A Method for Opinion Mining of Product Reviews using Association Rules. In: Proceedings of the 2nd International Conference on Interaction Sciences: Information Technology, Culture and Human (ICIS 2009), Seoul, Korea, November 24-26, pp. 270–274 (2009)
3. Esuli, A., Sebastiani, F.: SENTIWORDNET: A Publicly Available Lexical Resource for Opinion Mining. In: Proceedings of the 5th Conference on Language Resources and Evaluation (LREC 2006), Citeseer (2006)
4. Esuli, A., Sebastiani, F.: PageRanking WordNet synsets: An application to opinion mining. In: Proceedings of the 45th Annual Meeting of the Association for Computational Linguistics (ACL 2007), Citeseer (2007)
5. Dean, J., Ghemawat, S.: MapReduce: Simplified data processing on large clusters. Communications of the ACM 51(1), 107–113 (2008)
6. Stanford Tagger Version 1.6 (2008), http://www.nlp.staford.edu/software/tagger.shtml
7. Stanford Parser Version 1.6 (2008), http://nlp.stanford.edu/software/lex-parser.shtml
8. Pang, B., Lee, L.: Opinion mining and sentiment analysis. Foundations and Trends in Information Retrieval 2(1-2), 1–135 (2008)
9. Kim, S.M., Hovy, E.: Determining the sentiment of opinions. In: Proceedings of the 20th International Conference on Computational Linguistics (2004)

10. Potthast, M., Becker, S.: Opinion Summarization of Web Comments. Advances in Information Retrieval, 668–669 (2010)
11. Read, J.: Using emoticons to reduce dependency in machine learning techniques for sentiment classification. In: Proceedings of the ACL Student Research Workshop, pp. 43–48. Association for Computational Linguistics (2005)
12. Kim, S.M., Hovy, E.: Extracting opinions, opinion holders, and topics expressed in online news media text. In: Proceedings of ACL/COLING Workshop on Sentiment and Subjectivity in Text, Sydney, Australia (2006)
13. Cho, K.S., Ryu, J.S., Jeong, J.H., Kim, Y.H., Kim, U.M.: Credibility Evaluation and Results with Leader Weight in Opinion Mining. In: The 2nd International Conference on Cyber-Enabled Distributed Computing and Knowledge Discovery, Huangshan, China, October 10-12 (2010)
14. Chang, F., Dean, J., Ghemawat, S., Hsieh, W.C., Wallach, D.A., Burrows, M., Chandra, T., Fikes, A., Gruber, R.E.: Bigtable: A distributed storage system for structured data. ACM Transactions on Computer Systems (TOCS) 26(2), 4 (2008)
15. Cardona, K., Secretan, J., Georgiopoulos, M., Anagnostopoulos, G.: A grid based system for data mining using MapReduce. Technical Report TR-2007-02, AMALTHEA (2007)
16. Bayir, M.A., Toroslu, I.H., Cosar, A., Fidan, G.: Smart miner: a new framework for mining large scale web usage data. In: Proceedings of the 18th International Conference on World Wide Web, pp. 161–170. ACM, New York (2009)
17. Xia, T.: Large-scale sms messages mining based on map-reduce. In: International Symposium on Computational Intelligence and Design, ISCID2008, pp. 7–12. IEEE, Los Alamitos (2008)
18. Cho, K.S., Jung, N.R., Kim, U.M.: Using WordMap and Score-based Weight in Opinion mining with MapReduce. In: IEEE International Conference on Service-Oriented Computing and Applications (2010)

Towards an Open Framework for Mobile Digital Identity Management through Strong Authentication Methods

Brahim En-Nasry and Mohamed Dafir Ech-Cherif El Kettani

Information Security Research Team - ISeRT,
Ecole Nationale Supérieure d'Informatique et d'Analyse des Systèmes - ENSIAS,
University Mohammed V-Souissi, Rabat, Morocco
{ennasri,dafir}@ensias.ma

Abstract. Mobile computing becoming a widespread working tool, and a large scale deployed technology, it should be strong enough to meet basic security expectations. Privacy in a mobile environment should be driven by the choice of appropriate identity management mechanisms, that will have a large impact on different aspects of daily life. But people being unable to spend all their time administering their digital identities, the implementation of mobile identity management technologies has become a top priority for involved companies, in order to protect their customers against fraudsters. Today, identity management and strong authentication are converging, since provided solutions encompass user access, signing and verification of users and transactions, through strong authentication. Although, simply using strong authentication will not resolve all mobile digital identity requirements from a security viewpoint; our objective is to propose an extensible protocol based on an independent architectural model that provides a foundation for user-centric identity management.

Keywords: Identity management, mobile identity, strong authentication, identification, trust, interoperability.

1 Introduction

With the prevalence of electronic transactions throughout our world today, provisioning and monitoring credentials for secure access to online services is of utmost importance. Breaking down borders, organizations are increasingly relying on internet infrastructure to communicate and conduct business, exchanging and sharing digital files containing sensitive data with an extended network of collaborators. As identity is about humans and process, efficient and comprehensive identity management not only covers technical aspects of securing access to assets but also should consider economic, cultural, social and legal implications of new approaches to identity management. Mobile IDM can be analysed at different levels and from 3 perspectives, such as pure identity paradigm (multiple identities without affecting security), user access paradigm, and service paradigm.

Each initiative is a specific case implementation, requiring adaptation of existing infrastructure to deal only with a single method. Thus, an open universal scalable

C. Lee et al. (Eds.): STA 2011 Workshops, CCIS 187, pp. 56–63, 2011.

framework that enables easy integration of all methods and taking into consideration all dimensions of mobile digital identity (context and profile) is required.

This paper is organized in 5 sections. after this introduction, section 2 defines the global context of our contribution in terms of the preparation of the groundwork for an open universal authentication framework for mobile digital identity to access online services. Section 3 presents current approaches related to mobile IDM. Section 4 proposes the model, consisting in a Middleware that will play the role of an entry point to online services in a way that ensures flexibility, transparency, security and commodity. Section 5 is a conclusion.

2   Global Context

2.1   Mobility and Identity

Mobility: We can distinguish at least three kinds of mobility, in terms of identity management, which are not isolated, since they often interact and can be concurrently modified, creating thus complex situations : Device mobility (a person uses the same identity through different devices), Location mobility (a person uses the same device through different locations) and Context mobility (a person receives services based on different societal roles)

Identity: Identity is both a "real-world" concept and a digital construct. Identity is built on Identifier, Attribute and Profile. The full Digital Identity has legal as well as technical implications [3]. Digital identity management (IDM) is the management of the life cycle of an identity, focusing essentially on maintaining asserted characteristics of subjects, which are created, used, and deleted [4], primarily used for two purposes: inventory and access control [5]. When combined with strong authentication and access control, an effective IDM framework should be built.

Mobile Identity and Mobile Identity Management: Mobile identity and mobile IDM respectively are extensions of the digital identity and IDM. The term "mobile digital identity" implies these identities to be portable. This involves device and user mobility, meaning that the service can be accessed with a device while moving as well as that service can be used independently from device and location [6].

2.2   Requirements Fulfilled by Identity 2.0 Technologies

Mobile Identity Digital Management requirements will be proposed within the context of «Identity 2.0 » technologies, through the following criteria :

- Total control of users over their privacy and Usability
- Consistent user experience due to uniformity of identity interface
- Maximum protection against identity attacks (phishing), and reachability (spam)
- Policy review on both sides, Huge scalability and Secure conditions assurance
- Digital identity decoupled from applications and Open environment

3 Current Approaches to Mobile Identity Management

3.1 Evolution of Mobile Identity

Whereas static identity has already been implemented by Web 2.0, many aspects of dynamic identity still can not be easily implemented, such as user's position or temporal context, which gains increasing importance for new kinds of mobile applications. For example, Subscriber Identity Module (SIM) identities are used as a kind of mobile IDM, without meeting all requirements for a complete mobile IDM.

Current mobile identity infrastructure solutions can be classified into 3 categories:

- **Category 1:** inspired from wired solutions, it is limited to the users of mobile devices running the same operating system.
- **Category 2:** they include connected or unconnected mobile devices, considered as personal authentication devices.
- **Category 3:** based on implantable radio-frequency identifier (RFID) devices, it is expected to increase rapidly.

3.2 Types of Strong Authentication Associated to Mobile IDM

Without authentication, no attribute related to Digital Identity can be meaningful. Authentication factors are knowledge, possession and biometrics. Today, identity management and strong authentication are converging, since provided solutions encompass user access, signing and verification of users and transactions, through strong authentication. Strong authentication attracts all businesses that would like to deploy dual-channel authentication but worry about cost and usability.

In a mobile network, 3 methods specify the core set of authentication credentials: SIM-based authentication, PKI-based authentication, and OTP-based authentication. 802.1x already defined EAP methods for each of proposed authentication methods.

Although, simply using strong authentication will not resolve all mobile digital identity requirements from a security viewpoint; our objective is to propose an extensible protocol based on an independent architectural model.

3.3 Mobile IDM Available Solutions

Mobile IDM available solutions are generally associated to eGov applications. Indeed, mobile device usage is ever increasing along multiple dimensions end most government credentials contain embedded smartcards with access control mechanisms, cryptographic capabilities and biometrics records. So far, the vast majority of cards is still -until today- not used for on-line transactions. With suitable card readers, smartcards may be recognized and used as a token support into back-end government databases for identity verification. Another promised mobile identity use allows public elections vote, empowering citizen's right for better governance. A research conducted by ENISA outlines that all mobile eID implementations are based on similar technologies based on mobile phones and PKI [1].

The management of identity could be performed with federated identity management models. Such models can be identity management "meta-systems", such as Windows CardSpace [7] or OpenID. Solutions are readily available or have been used in e-government environments, such as Austria (A server-based signature solution), Estonia (A WPKI recently being launched), Norway (Telenor started to deploy crypto-SIMs), Sweden (Common WPKI specifications), The Netherlands (Digital authentication of citizens using the mobile phone as additional authentication factor), Turkey (Turkcell launched a mobile signature service), and Finland (In order to create a common identification and payment service, based on PKI..

We can present some Mobile IDM standardization and research projects: Many organizations work to develop standards for mobile communication primarily for mobile eIDs (ETSI, ESI, 3GPP, OMA and FIDIS etc.). Meanwhile, IEEE, IETF, WECA, and ITU participate in major standardization efforts to promote adoption of wireless technologies. Many research projects, such as SWIFT, have been launched to help people to protect their autonomy and retain control over personal information.

3.4 Discussion on Authentication Methods versus Mobile IDM

Digital identity, as a strategic innovation for crime prevention and detection, requires disclosing personal information and the applicability of contextual information as well as allowing users to be in control of their identities." [2]. In this perspective, authentication methods, in particular, the IEEE 802.1x standard, along with the Protected EAP protocol, provides much more secure authentication both to users and service providers but, still suffer from significant drawbacks, for example: Difficulty to juggling different accounts and credentials, Data duplication, Cost of implementation, Interoperability, Handling credentials, Deployment and extensibility, Utility, usability and Transparency, Poor user interface and trustworthy of interface.

4 Open Mobile IDM Proposed Framework

4.1 Context and Profile Management

Mobile identity is a more complex object than current SIM-centric identities. Personal information about users, collected in profiles, and more generally mobile context, should be used to determine the mobile identity of users. Mobile context can be defined as the set of facts, events, circumstances, and information that surrounds the mobile user at a given point in time and their interactions: type of user identified, social context, device capabilities, transactions, accountability, law enforcement and custom, location, presence, activity, privacy and access filters for tracking [8].

To exploit mobile context, concepts have to be correctly defined. But we have to discuss first arising questions on how and where to store user's profile and what are appropriate ways to aggregate and exchange these data in a secure channel. Context and Profile management also have to address the issue of privacy by using Privacy Enhancing Technologies, such as: Flexibility and user consent, Lack of support, Identification, Security issue, and Complex architecture.

Concepts such as middleware, mobile context, profile management, centralized registries and so on already do exist in the literature. In current solutions to identity management, when a user wants to access a service, he directly contacts the service provider. The service provider's authentication system redirects the user to Identity

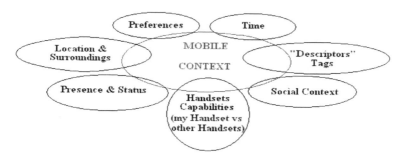

Fig. 1. The elements of the mobile context

Providers login page. The user is authenticated by the Identity Provider. Authentication assertion confirming the user's identity is then sent to service provider. Then, user is redirected back to the service provider's service and can use the service according the access rights granted for their identity.

4.2 Open Mobile IDM Architecture

The model we propose (Fig. 2), aims to reverse the trend by centralizing all processes of accessing online services federated in circle of trust, side IDP. Acting as obligatory passage and initial point to many online services, the middleware rely on this basic first authentication process to use a universal strong identifier to authenticate the user with high confidence when he accesses the main portal of the IDP to truly associate the device with its user. In this stage, a secure encrypted tunnel must be established between the user and IDP and then multiple authentication factors and Knowledge Base System must be integrated in an encrypted manner to reinforce initial authentication process. Once access granted, initial portal must inform authenticated user, in a common user-friendly interface, about available services, trusted information on service providers as well as guidelines, constraints and policies in order to express freely his consent before engaging any transaction. The middleware should integrate all authentication methods, manage profiles and contexts and also discharges user from the actions of remembering different authentication tokens and make easy to select the service needed in a flexible way while trusting the middleware to generate an authentication framework negotiated with service provider to be used in authentication process. Here are some properties of the proposed architecture:

Adaptability of the authentication method: it generates user's frameworks for authentication and service discovery, concerning mobile context and user profile.

Authentication platform: The network architecture designed to support this platform consists in three basic entities: the mobile terminal (TM), the identity provider - the Mobile network operator (MNO) and trusted service provider (TSP).

The mobile user's device allows the user to communicate with identity provider, to access directory service, to discover trusted service providers who offer their services.

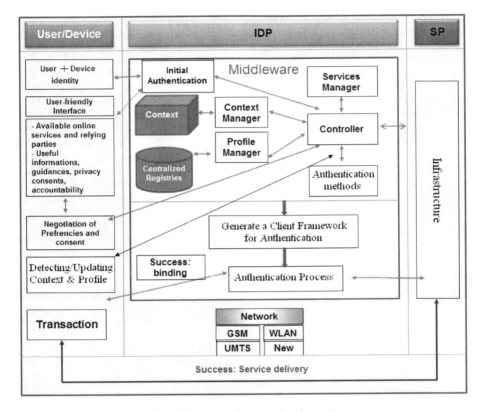

Fig. 2. Proposed framework schematic

As shown in figure 2, the platform consists in the following components:

- **Services Register:** (installed in the Service Provider) manages all trusted services to be offered to mobile users by the service provider.
- **Service Manager:** It manages the coordination of functions required for a trusted and context-sensitive service discovery.
- **Context manager:** we refer in this middleware, minimally, but nevertheless illustrative, to user and his physical environment.
- **Profile manager:** The model is based on profiles, for the **user** to describe his preferences, the **terminal** to describe its capabilities, the **location** to specify terminal location and, **Network Resources** to describe available resources.

4.3 Authentication Process

In the next step, context manager acquires information about mobile context and updates mobile context database, and the profile manager do the same for profiles. In the last step, the system generates a client framework for authentication process, in a negotiation-based protocol with the network access server of the service provider.

The Access Protocol acts between the middleware and the NAS, thus, it should be flexible to envelope standards authentication methods and support negotiation messages. The proposed framework is to be validated by the user. To access the service, the middleware provides credentials, eventually responds to challenges to authenticate user to the service in a transparent way before linking him to the service.

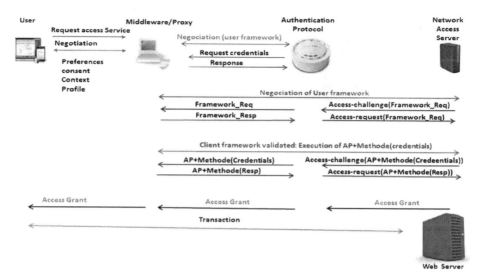

Fig. 3. Authentication process

4.4 Implementation Issues of This Framework

The implementation of an authentication platform for future mobile telecommunications networks to access online services is still a complex problem. Thus, the use of an intermediary have been highlighted as a potential means of achieving authentication for mobile users in a transparent manner.

However, as this problem combines several research areas (mobility, user preferences, QoS management, adaptability, service discovery, user profiles, context awareness), these solutions address only part of the needs that we identified.

The research will now develop all components of the framework and proceed towards the implementation and evaluation of an associated prototype solution. All modules and all interactions between components of the platform have to be implemented and validated successfully.

The investigation will ultimately be conducted to the selection of standards, and candidate components to support all aspects proposed in this article (Fig. 3). To achieve this, we need to focus on adaptation of existent standards and protocols in order to facilitate the transparent way that is desired. All features will be tested to illustrate the discovery mechanism and provision of context sensitive.

Hence, security tokens must be stored in a secure database controlled from the center, rather than user's devices, but such system should leave the user with a margin to express consent and make decision. By separating data and applications through centralized registries, the system easily maintains integrity of multiple user identities: subscriber data, profile accounts, data context, user attributes and preferences, credentials and security tokens.

In this extensible model, it will be easy to add new domains, services and technologies, and graft new methods. As the IDP centralizes authentication process, it will avoid third party authentication provider and enforce trust among relying parties.

Flexibility is granted through negotiation process where the exchange of these data is under the control of the user. The user selects preferences and expresses his agreement on the use of his attributes, credentials and security tokens and then delegates the middleware to run the authentication process.

As the middleware supports context management, it provides background information about the context. Context management will help to better associate the device to its user by accommodating techniques like activity, input frequency, etc.

5 Conclusion

Reinforcing the authentication by an open universal framework flexible, secure and transparent enables best-of-breed solutions. This work is a template; further works have to be developed to enrich each component of this framework. The challenge task is the integration of subscriber profiles in a generic subscriber data model of centralized subscriber register and adaptation of the authentication protocol to carry out different data needed in the authentication process. Current works on NGPR, GAA and ontologies will carry out solutions for the centralized subscriber register and generic wireless authentication [9]. Telecom operators should be elected to act as a core identity provider, acting as MSSP, Registration Authority and Certification authority, and trust must be reinforced between them and all stakeholders. Interoperability and common standards facilitate cooperation and data sharing. To be effective, a specification must be jointly defined and published by stakeholders that share the vision of a universal framework reducing risks and costs and leverage trust by the integration of all strong authentication methods.

References

1. ENISA, "Security Issues in the Context of Authentication Using Mobile Devices (Mobile eID)", http://www.enisa.europa.eu/doc/pdf/deliverables/enisa_pp_mobile_eID.pdf
2. Arabo, A., Shi, Q., Merabti, M.: A Framework for User-Centered and Context-Aware Identity Management in Mobile Ad-hoc Networks (UCIM). School of Computing & Mathematical Sciences, Liverpool. John Moores University, UK
3. Vacca, J.R.: Computer and Information Security Handbook. Morgan Kaufmann Editions, San Francisco (2009), ISBN: 978-0-12-374354-1
4. Windley, P.: Digital Identity. O'Reilly Media, Inc., Sebastopol (2005)
5. Tsui, W.: Digital Identity Management on the Internet (April 28, 2006)
6. Final report, STORK-eID Consortium " STORK Work Item 3.3.6 Mobile eID"
7. Microsoft, "Introducing Windows CardSpace", http://msdn.microsoft.com/en-us/library/aa480189.aspx
8. Hinz, M., Fiala, Z.: Context modeling for device and location-aware mobile web applications. In: PERMID (2005)
9. José, S., et al.: New Architecture for a Centralized Next Generation Profile Register in Future Mobile Telecommunication Networks. In: INC (2006)

Deterministic Data Binding
for Dynamic Service Compositions[*]

Eunjung Lee, Hyung-Ju Joo, and Kyong-Jin Seo

Computer Science Department, Kyonggi University
San 94, Yi-ui Dong, Suwon, South Korea
ejlee@kyonggi.ac.kr, {giantjj,logen0104}@gmail.com

Abstract. Dynamic web service composition is an important issue that needs to be solved to construct a service-oriented computing environment. Although there have been many researches on service compositions on the server side, this paper focuses on developing client systems that support a dynamic service environment and client side service composition. Moreover, we propose the concept of deterministic data binding from repeated output data to the input parameters of another method. For a given set of data mappings between services, we investigate a binding condition from the current context and discuss the generation of user interface-context popup menus. The proposed method allows users to control data and service composition using a simple and convenient interface. We present a historical tourism service using the proposed approach.

Keywords: Service composition, mashup, data mapping, user interface.

1 Introduction

With more and more content and services becoming available as web services, web service composition is becoming one of the most important application development approaches. On the other hand, as services become more dynamic by depending on location and user contexts, user-centered client-side mashup gets more attention [1,2].

In this study, our goal was to determine possible service compositions for a given service specification and data mapping relations and then generate the context menus and user interface for a client web page. In order to support a dynamic service environment, we developed a code generation system that dynamically generates Javascript functions and data structures with no intervention from developers. Moreover, the result page can provide a simple and convenient interface for service composition and navigation with minimal interactions.

In order to request the next composable method, the data element should be bound for the corresponding input parameters. We call this *(parameter) binding* in this paper. We are interested in the deterministic binding condition from the current view and context, which needs no further user interaction to make the request. Moreover, we introduce the condition *repeat binding*, where the current context of the repeated part of the output tree allows deterministic binding.

[*] This work was supported by the GRRC program of Gyeonggi province.

C. Lee et al. (Eds.): STA 2011 Workshops, CCIS 187, pp. 64–70, 2011.
© Springer-Verlag Berlin Heidelberg 2011

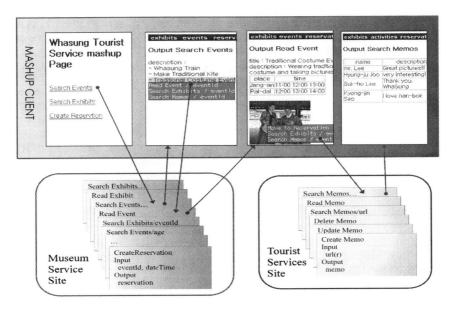

Fig. 1. A mashup page interfacing and navigating multiple service sites

This paper uses historical tourism services as a running example. There are two service sites, one for museum services providing exhibits, events, and reservations and one for user-customized community services such as memos and logins. In Figure 1, the client page navigates views and service calls for a given set of service methods. Using the appropriate composition menus, a user can easily select the next methods; input parameters are transferred from the current view data by data mapping.

Previous studies did not consider parameter binding issues for this kind of composition. Our approach can identify all of the possible compositions for a given client page context. For a repeated part of the data, we use a formal approach to determine the composition menus to be activated as data are selected.

This paper is organized as follows. Section 2 discusses the related studies and background, and Section 3 describes our data mapping model and introduces repeat bindings. Section 4 presents the implementation of the code generation system, along with the generated binding context menus. Section 5 concludes the paper.

2 Background

Service composition involves integrating services by connecting and relaying data. There have been many researches on user-interface development approaches for service compositions. Lecue et al. analyzed the types of data compositions and developed XSL adapter modules to automate data flows [3]. On the other hand, Liu et al. proposed an enterprise mashup concept as a special case of service compositions and proposed hosting-site architecture to provide service mashup [5]. Nestler et al. proposed a model driven approach to developing a user interface for service compositions [6]. The present authors' previous paper presented a code generation approach for client side service navigations [7].

Recently, several client side service composition and execution frameworks have been published. MashArt is a framework intended as a component-based development tool for mashup, integrating all three layers of application, data, and presentation [8]. Pietman et al. presented the CRUISe framework, which is developed as so-called thin server architecture [9].

Our approach was similar to theirs in that it targets a client side composition platform and focuses more on the syntactic information of the service specification. However, the above two frameworks apply traditional software development approaches such as a component-based approach or model-driven design and try to achieve a general framework independent of language and/or platform. In this study, we specified the language and execution platform by selecting Javascript as a target language. By doing so, our solution became more lightweight and, more importantly, ready to use for browsers. Moreover, this more easily allows developers to further update the output codes based on their needs.

3 Data Binding Conditions for Service Compositions

3.1 Model

In this subsection, we introduce the service specification and data mapping. In addition, we introduce the client page model as a service composition platform.

For a client page, a service environment is defined by a set of available services, which is described in a service specification. Usually, a service specification includes the type, URL, and method signatures for service methods. A method signature defines the output data type and a set of input parameter types. This study used WADL (Web Application Description Language), a standard for describing REST style services [10], to specify the available services.

Data mapping refers to the creation of connections between data types of different services and/or domains. In this paper, we use type-based data mapping, including type equivalence, as well as user-defined mappings, denoted as $M = \{(t_1, t_2) \mid t_1, t_2$ are types defined in schemas of given WADL files, $t_1 \neq t_2\}$.

The client page is responsible for communicating with service sites, presenting views for user actions, determining available service compositions from the current output data, and providing user interface menus for transferring data and requesting the next method.

3.2 Parameter Binding from Output Tree

For a set of data mappings M, a mapping (t_1, t_2) refers to the relation where data of type t_1 can be transferred to another method as an input parameter of type t_2. In this paper, we apply data mappings to the relations between methods, called *binding*.

Before addressing the binding relations between methods, we define several notations. For a given mapping, M, and type, t, $mappable_M(t) = \{t' \mid (t', t) \in M\}$. Let Δ be the output result tree of a method, m_1, i.e., Δ is an instance of $output(m_1)$. Then, we can find a node from Δ that can be mapped to a parameter of type t, which is defined as $bindings(\Delta, t) = \{\pi \mid$ The node at $\pi(\Delta)$ has a type in $mappable(t)\}$. Let *input(m₂)* be a parameter type list denoted as $[p_1, p_2, ..., p_k]$. Then, we can find a set of bindings for the parameter list such as

$bindings(\Delta, [p_1, p_2, ..., p_k]) = \{[\pi_1, \pi_2, ..., \pi_k] \mid \pi_i \in bindings(\Delta, p_i)$ for $1 \leq i \leq k\}$.

For two methods, m_1 and m_2, let Δ be an instance of *output(m₁)* and $[p_1, p_2, ..., p_k] =$ *input(m₂)*. If there is more than one binding in $bindings(\Delta, [p_1, p_2, ..., p_k])$, then we say m_1 binds m_2, and denotes $m_1 \rightarrow m_2$.

For our running example, an output tree instance of the "ReadEvent" method, Δ_1, is shown in Figure 3(b). If *input*(CreateReserve3) = {eventId, role}, then output tree Δ_1 covers CreateReserve3 because it contains eventId and rname, where (rname, role) ∈ M and M is a given set of data mappings. A tree with no role element would not cover CreateReserve3. Furthermore, trees often have multiple candidates to bind for a given type t. In this example, there are more than one rname elements that can map to input parameter role. Consider the CreateReserve2 method, where *input*(CreateReserve2) = {eventId, location, time}. There are many location and time elements in Δ_1. Therefore, a user has to select elements to bind for input parameters.

If there is a unique binding from an output tree of m_1 to the input parameters of m_2, we can identify the binding data without user interactions. For example, Δ_1 in Figure 3(b) binds method m_2 deterministically if m_2 = "Search Exhibits Related to the Event" and *input(m₂)* = {eventId }. In this paper, our goal is to present the conditions for deterministic binding and generate navigation menu codes automatically.

Definition 1. Let Σ be a tree type and input(m₂) = $[p_1, p_2, ..., p_k]$. Then, Σ is said to *d_bind* method m_2 if the following condition is satisfied:

for each input parameter p_i of m_2, $1 \leq i \leq k$,

there is a unique path π_i s.t. $|\pi_i(\Sigma)| = 1$ and $\pi_i(\Sigma) \in$ *mappable(p_i)*.

3.3   Repeat Binding for Tree Type Definitions

When the tree has a repeat structure, deterministic binding is often possible by the selection of one of the repeat parts in the current repeat context. However, it is not easy to determine which method is bound by the current repeat context. Moreover, if the repeat structure is nested, this becomes more complicated, and it would be quite a burden to check every output tree instance. Therefore, we introduce the concept of repeat binding, where a given repeat context allows deterministic bindings, and present a method for statically finding the bindings from the tree type definition.

A repeat node is defined from the tree structure definition, where the max-occurs attribute of the node is larger than 1. In Figure 2(a), there are three repeat nodes: part, when, and role. Non-repeated descendents (terminal nodes) are gathered as closure for a repeat node. For example, *closure*(event) = {eventId, title, description,...}.

Let Σ = *output(m₁)*, where m_1 is a method and R is a repeat node of Σ. The closure subtree of Σ for R, denoted by *closure*(Σ, R), is a subtree type that includes all of the ascendant repeat nodes of R and their closure nodes, as well as the subtree of R. For example, *closure*(Σ, part) is the tree that includes *closure*(event) ∪ *closure*(part).

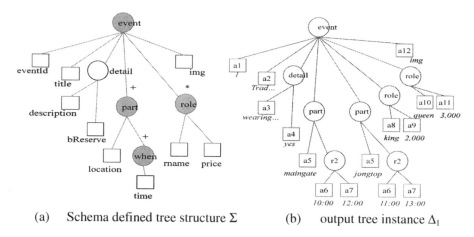

(a)   Schema defined tree structure Σ   (b)   output tree instance Δ₁

Fig. 2. The output tree definition and an instance of `event` resource

If closure(Σ, R) d_binds m_2, this means that there is a unique binding in the closure tree for every input parameter in input(m_2). In the above example, *closure*(Σ, part) *d_binds* [eventId, location] and *closure*(Σ, a10) d_binds [eventide, location, time]. For a given node, *n*, we are interested in finding the corresponding methods that become d_binded by *n*.

Definition 2. For two given methods, m_1 and m_2, let Σ = *output*(m_1), *input*(m_2) = [p_1, p_2, ..., p_k] and R be a repeat node of Σ. Then,
bindingContext(m_1, R) = {(m_2, [π_1, π_2, ..., π_k]) |
where *closure*(Σ, R) d_binds *input*(m_2), and
there is no ascendent R' of R s.t. *closure*(Σ, R') d_binds *input*(m_2)}.

4   Implementation

4.1   System Architecture and Generated Result Pages

The proposed approach was implemented in the Javascript code generation system developed by the authors[7]. Figure 3 shows the system architecture, including the code generator and type analyzer. The system reads WADL files and the schema type definitions. In addition, the data mapping relations are given in front. The generated code results consist of an html page and several JS files. The system generates request and handler functions for each service method. Then, input and output view placeholders are created in the html code if necessary.

Then, the bindingContext is serialized as a Javascript table, as shown in Figure 3. Response handlers generated by the system uses the binding context information for dynamically generating context popup menus. Because of the paper length restrictions, we omit the details of computing the repeat cover and bindingContexts.

Figure 4 shows two types of menus, one for the view menus in (a) and one for the context popup menus in (b) and (c). The response handler functions generated by

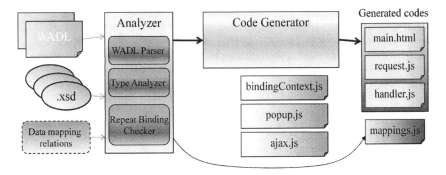

Fig. 3. System architecture of code generation system

the code generator module are responsible for creating the output presentation view dynamically, as well as generating context menus depending on the binding contexts. Because the corresponding mashup connections appear on the context, the result page allows a reasonable complexity for the often-complicated mashup relations between methods. Moreover, using the context popup menus, a user can request that the method transfer the current context data without further interactions

(a) View menu   (b) context menu on location   (c) context menu on time

Fig. 4. Types of context menus for navigating services

5   Conclusion

In this paper, we presented a code generation approach to developing client systems that support a dynamic service environment and client side service composition. Moreover, we proposed the concept of deterministic data binding from repeated output data to the input parameters of another method. For a given set of data mappings between services, we investigated the d_bind condition from the current context and discussed the generation of user interface-context popup menus.

Compared to other proposals for client-side service integration frameworks, our approach enables an efficient and lightweight code generation system, and the result page code allows users to control the data and service composition using a simple and convenient interface. We presented a historical tourism service in order to validate our method.

We are currently working on extending various schema constructs and tree structures in terms of the proposed concept, repeat binding. Moreover, we plan to extend our research to a consideration of parameter properties such as the default and required fields.

References

1. Jhingran, A.: Enterprise information mashups:integrating information, simply. In: VLDB 2006, pp. 3–4 (2006)
2. Yu, J., et al.: Understanding mashup development. IEEE Internet Computing 12(5), 44–52 (2008)
3. Lecue, L.F., Salibi, S., Bron, P., Moreau, A.: Semantic and Syntactic Data Flow in Web Service Composition. In: IEEE International Conference on Web Services, ICWS 2008, pp. 211–218 (2008)
4. Moreau, A., Malenfant, J.: Data Flow Repair in Web Service Orchestration at Runtime. In: ICIW 2009, pp. 43–48 (2009)
5. Liu, X., Hui, Y., Sun, W., Liang, H.: Towards Service Composition Based on Mashup. In: IEEE Congress on Services, pp. 332–339 (2007)
6. Nestler, T.: Towards a Mashup-driven End-User Programming of SOA-based Applications. In: iiWAS 2008, pp. 551–554 (2008)
7. Lee, L.E., Seo, K.-J.: Designing Client View Navigations Using Rest Style Service Patterns. In: WEBIST 2010 (2010)
8. Daniel, F., Casati, F., Benatallah, B., Shan, M.-C.: Hosted Universal Composition: Models, Languages and Infrastructure in mashArt. In: Laender, A.H.F., Castano, S., Dayal, U., Casati, F., de Oliveira, J.P.M. (eds.) ER 2009. LNCS, vol. 5829, pp. 428–443. Springer, Heidelberg (2009)
9. Pietschmann, S., Waltsgott, J., Meißner, K.: A Thin-Server Runtime Platform for Composite Web Applications. In: ICIW 2010, pp. 390–395 (2010)
10. Web application description language (WADL),
   http://www.w3.org/Submission/wadl

Integration Retrieval of History Data and Sensing Information Using SGLN Code in Extended RFID Application

Seungwoo Jeon[1], Gihong Kim[1], Bonghee Hong[1], and Joonho Kwon[2]

[1] Dept. of Computer Engineering, Pusan National University,
Busan, Republic of Korea
[2] Institute of Logistics Information Technology, Pusan National University
Busan, Republic of Korea
{i2825t,buglist,bhhong,jhkwon}@pusan.ac.kr

Abstract. The current logistics system is constructed considering only one environment. For example, if the tag is attached to the item, the user can manage only historical data of the item. However, the user demands various kinds of data such as location data or condition data of item, it is impossible for the existing system to process this kind of data. Due to the various requirements of the user, the logistic environment becoming complicated and various devices will be needed from processing complicated logistics environment. For example, GPS device is used for getting outdoor location information of item and Passive Tag is used for getting indoor location information. Also, sensor node or sensor tag is used for sensing condition of item or surroundings. However, when the user queries the system, the tables of the data created from various devices must be joined. In this time, because of join, the problem of performance can occur. For solving this problem, this paper proposes method that agrees with the representations of join field using SGLN code.

Keywords: RFID; Join; sensor.

1 Introduction

The Existed Logistics System was established by considering only one environment that manages the history data of the goods attaching RFID tag. For example, ammunition management system of Ministry of National Defense, port and logistics system of Ministry of Maritime Affairs and Fisheries, and so on can be called only one information management system.[1][2] These systems are providing simple history information such as kind of goods, expiration date, location.

However, the next logistics environment will be multifarious and complicated because the users are demanding not only history data but also sensing information and so on.[3][4][5] Especially, if the user want to know the condition of the medicine that can be sensitive to temperature and humidity, the system will have to provide state information in real time.[5]

In this situation, it is impossible for the existed logistics system such as EPCIS to process the requirements of the users. In other words, we will have to extend EPCIS

C. Lee et al. (Eds.): STA 2011 Workshops, CCIS 187, pp. 71–76, 2011.
© Springer-Verlag Berlin Heidelberg 2011

for being satisfied with various requirements. To extend EPCIS, firstly, the system have to add the devices such as sensor node, sensor tag to process state information. Also, the system will store the information created from the devices, and when the users query the system to know state of the goods, the system will have to indicate the results that join history data and state information. However, the problems of performance are occurred due to joining in this time. In this paper, we propose method for solving the problem of performance due to joining in EPCIS.

Next section introduces related works. And section 3 introduces a target environment of this paper. Section 4 delineate data analysis and the problem in the target environment. In section 5, we suggest approach for solving the problem and show the result of test. Finally, section 6 describes conclusion of this research and further works.

2 Related Work

2.1 EPCIS(EPC Information Services)

The EPCglobal suggests the standard network architecture.[6] The EPCglobal network architecture includes ALE(Application Level Event), EPCIS Capturing Application, EPCIS Repository, EPCIS Accessing Application, etc. The role of ALE is filtering and collection about RFID data. And the role of EPCIS Capturing Application is creating business event. The role of EPCIS is storing and searching about EPC level event. The EPCIS is a standard of EPC Information service. The event of EPC information has four types. First, the object event represents observations of EPCs. Second, the aggregation event represents aggregations, items in cases or cases in pallets. Third, the quantity event represents the quantity of the products. Fourth, the transaction event represents the business transactions.

2.2 SGLN (Serialized Global Location Number) Code

SGLN code uses to express the physical location such as building or warehouse. And, the code is used by readpoint field, bizLocation field of EPCIS event.[6]

Table 1. General syntax of SGLN code

General Syntax	urn:epc:id:sgln:CompanyPrefix.LocationReference.ExtensionComponent
Example	urn:epc:id:sgln:0614141.12345.400

This table shows general syntax of SGLN code. CompanyPrefix part represents code of specific company and the GS1 grants this part to each company. LocationReference part uniquely represents a specific physical location. Finally, ExtensionComponent part is assigned by the managing entity to an individual unique location. CompanyPrefix and LocationReference are assigned by total 12 digits, the rule that decide digits of these parts is different each country.

3 Target Environment

The target environment of this paper is the RFID application considering with sensing information created from sensor node and history data of the item attached RFID tag.

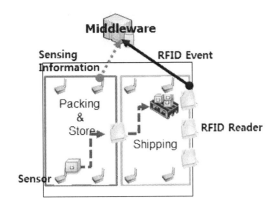

Fig. 1. Target Environment

There are RFID readers in the warehouse, some of which are installed at entrance, or between room and room. When the tags come in the warehouse or room, firstly, RFID readers will scan the tag and they transmit tag data to RFID middleware. Also, there are sensor nodes in the warehouse, all of which are installed at wall in the room. They transmit state information of room to RFID middleware. The item attached RFID tag moves to another place such as room, truck, warehouse.

4 Data Analysis and Problem Definition

4.1 History Data Analysis and Sensing Information Analysis

History data means object event among RFID events. As discussed in related work, object event represents physical object data distinguished by EPC. And when the tag passes reader, the event is acquired, the fields of the event are composed of EPC code, location, event time and so on.

Table 2. Object event of RFID events

	1	2	3
EPC	sgtin:1.1.8	sgtin:1.1.8	sgtin:1.1.8
Location	sgln:1.1.1	sgln:1.1.1	sgln:1.1.1
Event Time	2010-08-02T-09:00:50.764	2010-08-02T-09:01:10.221	2010-08-02T-09:01:91.101

Sensing information store temperature, humidity created from sensor nodes, the fields of which are composed of sensor node id, location, event time, sensing type, sensing value. And because sensor node periodically generates the sensing information in real time, the information is more volume than RFID events.

Table 3. Sensing information

	1	2	3
Sensor	A.0.1	A.0.2	A.0.3
Location	A.0.1	A.0.2	A.0.3
Event Time	2010-08-02T-09:0050.764	2010-08-02T-09:01:10.221	2010-08-02T-09:01:91.101
Sensing Type	Temperature	Temperature	Temperature
Sensing Value	10	11	10.4

4.2 Problem Definition

When the user queries to the RFID application, this application will have to return results joined between history data and sensing information. Firstly, we were able to know that common fields of each data table are event time and location through data analysis. However, because viewpoint acquired from each event is different, the event time isn't suitable join field. Therefore, the location field should be connected.

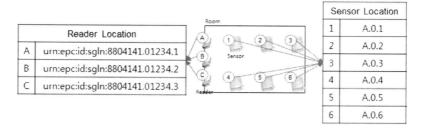

Fig. 2. Representations of each location field

But, because representations of each location field are different, we are in need of one table such as reference table in other to join between these tables. And because of the reference table, counts of total search are three times, the problem grown by response time of the counts occurs.

5 Approach

5.1 Basic Idea

Using SGLN code, the representations of each location field can make the same. It is possible for the code to reduce search time or response time. It is the basic idea of this paper. Left of fig. 3 shows query plan with reference table. Firstly, join between the location field of RFID event table and the location field of reference table, then join again between the location field of reference table and sensing information table. Right of fig. 3 shows query plan using SGLN code. Of course, the plan using the code is fewer join counts than the plan with reference table.

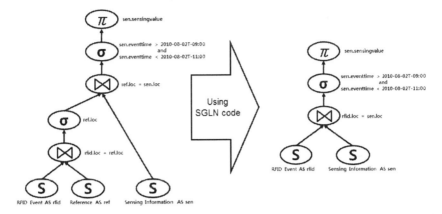

Fig. 3. Cut Back the counts of the joining tables by using SGLN code

5.2 Test

Before test regarding performance, firstly make a test case according to each condition for test analysis. Test Q1 finds sensing value with EPC, time and location. On the other hand, Test Q2 finds EPC with sensing value, time and location. Test Q3 finds location using EPC, sensing value and time. For measuring the performance, each test data such as history data, sensing information has stored 10 million counts.

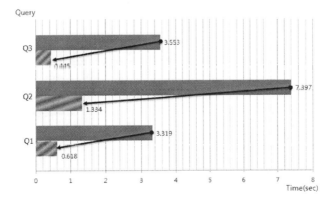

Fig. 4. Test result

Fig. 4 shows test result according to test case. Deviant crease line graphs show test result using SGLN code, another graphs show test result using reference table. We're able to know that the response time of the former graph is shorter than the latter graph.

6 Conclusion

We have considered only one logistics environment until now and the system has been made for one environment, too. However, because logistics industry is going to be grew and logistics environment is also complicated, the existing system no longer process complicated environment. In order to process complicated environment, we need various devices, and need to extend the existing system such as EPCIS middleware for processing data created from various devices. But, because the representations of join field are different, need the reference table, it will occur the performance problem.

For solving this problem, this paper proposes method that agrees with the representations of join field using SGLN code. And in other to prove this method about performance, test one case with reference table and another case using SGLN code. As a result, the latter is better performance than former.

Acknowledgements

This work was supported by the Grant of the Korean Ministry of Education, Science and Technology (The Regional Core Research Program/Institute of Logistics Information Technology).

References

1. Park, J.-W., Choi, S.-C.: A study on the application of RFID for ammunition management system. Jounal of Military Operations Research Society of Korea 31(2), 13–27 (2005)
2. Choi, J.-H., Kim, S.-Y., Lee, H.-C.: The plan of the introduction of RFID technology for developing port logistics (December 2007)
3. Lee, J.-D., Kim, H.-S., Kim, T.-H., Seo, H.-J.: RFID-based Automatic Entity Information Management System for Smart Refrigerator. Journal of Korean Society for Internet Information 9(1), 43–54 (2008)
4. Han, M.-J.: A development of Agro-Foods Warehouse Management System based on RFID/USN (December 2007)
5. Lee, B.-G.: Design & Implementation of Drug Management System based on RFID. Journal of Korea Information Processing Society 13-D(7), 977–984 (2006)
6. EPCglobal, EPC Information Services (EPCIS) Version 1.0.1 Specification (September 21, 2007)

Real-Time Quantity Inspection Method for Moving Tags in RFID Middleware

Goo Kim[1], Wooseok Ryu[1], Bonghee Hong[1], and Joonho Kwon[2]

[1] Dept. of Computer Engineering
[2] Institute of Logistics Information Technology
Pusan National University
Busan, Republic of Korea
{daekeun7,wsryu,bhhong,jhkwon}@pusan.ac.kr

Abstract. Huge amount of goods passes to the customers, which are produced in factories or packaged by the box in wholesalers. At this time, if does not inspect the exactly number of products in the box while packaging, high cost is occurred by the incident. That is scarce number of products in the box. This means that cost and time waste increases in the logistics. In order to efficiently inspect the exact number of products in the box, in this paper, a technique is suggested to inspect number of products using RFID system which includes RFID Tags, Reader and Middleware. Furthermore, this paper contains a study on the method to inspect the number of products. It overcomes the weak points of the existing methods.

Keywords: quantity inspection technique; RFID Tags; Real-time; RFID Middleware.

1   Introduction

With the Internet population growing, huge amount of goods passes to the customers, which are produced in factories or packaged by the box in wholesalers. At this time, if does not inspect the exactly number of products in the box, it is packaged by several number of the products; cost and wasteful time are caused by the incident. Therefore, the requirement is raised in order to inspect the number of products in one box efficiently.

The existing inspection methods includes artificial checking or checking the weight of box[1] which is filled by several numbers of products. However, those approaches have restrictions. Artificial checking is done using the eyes of people. And, the case of box weight checking also has some problem, since products' weight are different.

Therefore, in this paper, a technique is suggested to inspect the number of products with an RFID Tag, Reader, Middleware[3,4,5] in the real-time.

This paper contains 6 Chapters: in Chapter 2, problem definition is mentioned; in Chapter 3, approach and solution are introduced; in Chapter 4, the experiment for real-time inspection technique; in Chapter 5, the conclusion and the future study are described.

C. Lee et al. (Eds.): STA 2011 Workshops, CCIS 187, pp. 77–83, 2011.
© Springer-Verlag Berlin Heidelberg 2011

2   Problem Definition

Fig 1 shows tag reading patterns in real-time environment. Tags reading patterns show some problems about quantity inspection in real-time. As Fig 1 shown, all tags are detected in 3 read cycles. However, it use the repeatPeriod and duration mechanism in RFID middleware which specified by EPCglobal[5], it needs 18 seconds for all tags detection. That means, about 11sec additional time are spent. Consequently, a technique is suggested to reduce the wasted time. It is important factor to inspect the number of products. Because, the goal of quantity inspection technique is to reduce all logistics processing time and cost.

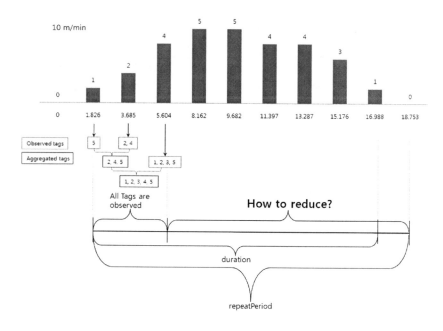

Fig. 1. Problem definition

3   Approach and Solution

In order to reduce the inspection time, we suggest an Accessing App.[4] which can process user query. It inspects number of products and gives the reports to users.

Query analyzer, in Accessing App., should receive query from the user. And then analyzed query is sent to RFID Middleware by Query sender. After then, Reports receiver receive the reports, which are received read cycle interval, from RFID Middleware. Then, Result sender can get the results, it is analyzed by Reports parser. Finally, Result sender should give the results to the user. The results were compared with registered query.

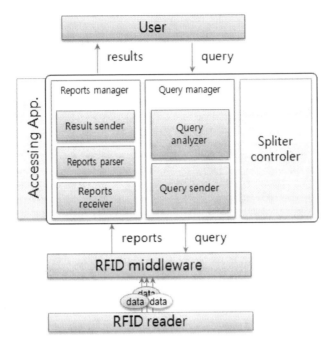

Fig. 2. Accessing App.

4 Experiment

4.1 Environment Composition

In this paper, the environment targeted in real-time boxes movement, containing multiple products used in the conveyor belt.

RFID tags are attached to the each product in the box passes through the RFID Reader's antenna range At this time, the RFID Middleware, which is specified by

Fig. 3. RFID Reader and 900MHz RFID Tags

EPCglobal can received tag data from the RFID Reader, and then RFID Middleware send the tag data to Accessing App. In order to inspect the exactly number of tags, the user can register to the query for quantity inspection of products, after that the user also can receive the results of the quantity inspection.

Finally, in Figure 4, Accessing App. can control conveyor belt with the spliter; blue dotted line in Figure 4. If the box has exactly number of tags, it can pass "OK" line, else it should go "REJECT" line.

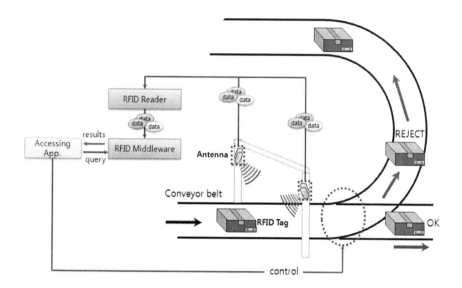

Fig. 4. Target Environment

4.2   Experiment Setting

When setting up the environment by using RF, the settings depend on the variety environment configurations. So, several problems are detected. The antenna was connected to the RFID Reader which can control the frequency of the strength by tread the RFID tag. If the frequency of the strength is strong, unnecessary tags can be read.

In other case, when using multiple antennas for one RFID Reader, the RFID Reader will process the duplication of RFID tag data. Which was caused by tag data processing loading. Accordingly, in this paper, the target environment was set up similarly to the real environment[2].

In this paper, through the analysis of target environment, as shown in Fig 5, only one RFID antenna should be used to reduce the load due to the duplication of RFID tag data. And also, the strength of RF(for tags reading) was set up 200(10=1dB, max=300). In order to avoid unnecessary tags reading.

Fig. 5. RFID Reader Antenna for Tags reading

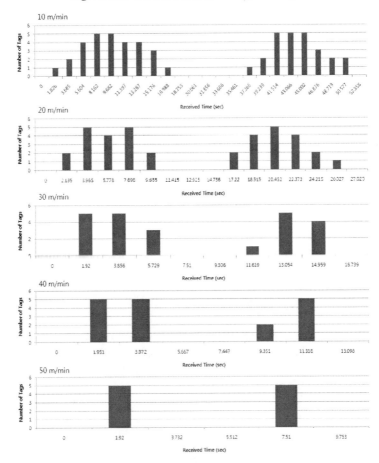

Fig. 6. Tags reading pattern by velocity changing

4.3   Case Study

Using the analyzed target environment executed a variety of case studies. The goal of these cast study is to know RFID Reader reading performance and patterns.

1st case; 5 RFID Tags are used. Running tags reading, increasing the velocity of conveyor belt. The purpose of this test case is to check the observed tag patterns when the velocity of tags is changing.

2nd case; 5 RFID Tags are used. Running tags reading, increasing the velocity of conveyor belt. The purpose of this test case is to check reader's performance for tags complete reading.

The time of read cycle used in the two test cases is 2000ms.

Fig 6 shows the experiment results of velocity changing for 10m/min~50m/min using 5 tags. As the figure shows, all tags can read by minimizing the distance (vertical angle tags and antenna) between tags and antenna. But, when the velocity is equal to 10m/min(Fig7), all the tags were unable to be read within one read cycle. All tags can be detected within 3 times of read cycle. Fig 7 shows the IDs of detected tag.

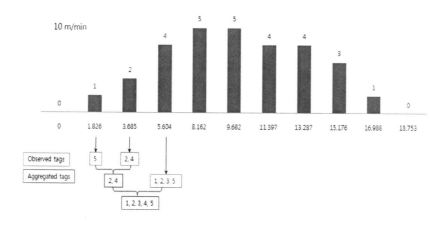

Fig. 7. Tags reading pattern by 10m/min

From the experiment results of the second test case, we can know the reader's performance when the velocity is changing. In order to know the complete reading rate, we increased the velocity of conveyor by 10m/min each time and checked the detected tags within the reader's antenna range.

Fig 8 shows when the velocity of conveyor is less than 60m/min, all tags can be detected. But, when the velocity is more than 60m/min, missed reading is occurred. As this figure shows, with an increase of the velocity of the conveyor, complete reading rate of all tags is reduced.

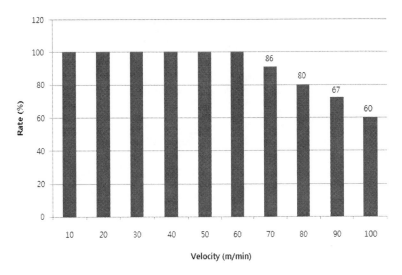

Fig. 8. Tags complete reading rate by velocity changing

5   Conclusion and Future Study

The cost reduction issue becomes increasingly important, as the distribution industry is developing and the cost of distribution is increasing. So, in this paper, a quantity inspection technique is proposed to reduce the cost and the time.

Based on the technique suggested in this paper, we will focus our future studies on the following areas; firstly, a middleware system study for efficient management on real time tag data; secondly, a study on hardware setups for improving the performance of recognition.

Acknowledgements

This work was supported by the Grant of the Korean Ministry of Education, Science and Technology (The Regional Core Research Program/Institute of Logistics Information Technology).

References

1. Wan-Seon, S.: Multi-product Lot Quantity Verification: A Weighting Inspection Approach. Journal of Korean Institute of Industrial Engineers 19(4)
2. Alien Technology, "Reader Interface Guide, All Fixed Readers" (September 2008)
3. EPCglobal, "Reader Protocol Standard, Version 1.1", Ratified Standard (June 21, 2006)
4. EPCglobal, "The EPCglobal Architecture Framework", EPCglobal Final Version 1.2 Approved (September 10, 2007)
5. EPCglobal, "The Application Level Events (ALE) Specification, Version 1.1 Part I: Core Specification", EPCglobal Rarified Specification as of February 27 (2008)

An Improved Active Learning in Unbalanced Data Classification

Woon Jeung Park

Strategic Planning Team
Korea Institute of Patent Information
146-8 Donggyo-dong, Mapo-gu, Seoul, Korea
tomato0720@kipi.or.kr

Abstract. This paper is concerned with the unbalanced classification problem which occurs when there are significantly less number of observations of the target concept. The standard machine learning algorithms yield better prediction performance with balanced datasets. However, in real application, it is quite common to have unbalanced dataset with a certain class of interest having very small size. It will be problematic since the algorithm might predict all the cases into majority classes without loss of overall accuracy. In this paper, we propose an efficient way of selecting informative for active learning which does not necessitate a search through the entire dataset and allows active learning to be applied to very large datasets. Experimental results show that the proposed method decreases the prediction error of minority class significantly with increasing the prediction error or majority class a little bit.

Keywords: active learning, unbalanced data, selective sampling, beta distribution, classification, Class Probability Output Network (CPON).

1 Introduction

Classification is a supervised learning method which acquires a training dataset to form its model for classifying unseen examples. A training dataset is called unbalanced if at least one of the classes is represented by significantly less of instance than the others. Real world applications often face this problem because naturally normal examples which constitute the majority class in classification problems are generally abundant; on the other hand the examples of interest are generally rare and form the minority class. Another reason for class unbalance problem is limitations on collecting instances of some classes. In unbalanced data classification, the class boundary learned by standard machine learning algorithms can be severely skewed toward the majority class. As a result, the prediction error of minority class can be excessively high.

In Classification tasks, it is generally more important to correctly classify the minority class instances. In real-world applications mispredicting a rare event can

C. Lee et al. (Eds.): STA 2011 Workshops, CCIS 187, pp. 84–93, 2011.

result in more serious consequences than mispredicting a common event. For example in the case of cancerous cell detection, misclassifying non-cancerous cells leads to additional clinical testing but misclassifying cancerous cells leads to very serious health risk. Due to their design principles, most of the machine learning algorithms optimize the overall classification accuracy hence sacrifice the prediction efficient active learning framework which has high prediction performance to overcome this serious data mining problem.

In addition to the naturally occurring class unbalance problem, the unbalanced data situation may also occur in one-against-rest schema in multiclass classification. Assuming there are N different classes, one of the simplest multiclass classification schemes built on top of binary classifiers is to train N different binary classifiers. Each classifier is trained to distinguish the examples in a single class from the examples in all remaining classes. When it is desired to classify a new example, the N classifiers are run, and the classifier which has the highest classification confidence is chosen. Therefore, even though the training data is balanced, issues related to the class unbalance problem can frequently surface.

Active learning has been pronounced by some researchers [7, 8] as a sampling method has been done to show that it works well with unbalanced data. The main idea of active learning is that the most informative patterns would be near the decision boundaries. Thus, exactly decision boundary is desired to select exactly informative patterns. However, in unbalanced data classification, the boundary learned by standard machine learning is not proper because this boundary can be skewed toward the majority class.

Class Probability Output Network (CPON) is a method of postprocessing for the probabilistic scaling of classifier's output. The output of a classifier is analyzed and the distribution of the output is described by the beta distribution parameters. For more accurate approximation of class output distribution, the beta distribution parameters as well as the kernel parameters describing the discriminant function are adjusted in such a way to improve the uniformity of beta cumulative distribution (CDF) values for the given class output samples. Thus, CPON make a decision boundary which reflects the skewed standard classifier's output. So, we apply the approximation of class output distribution instead of the distance between decision boundary and samples to select informative instances for training; active learning can indeed be a useful technique to address the class unbalance problem and we can apply active learning to very large datasets by using the approximated CDF of class output samples. Thus, proposed active learning strategy can apply to unbalanced data without high computational costs. In section 1, the classifications using discriminant functions and active learning are presented. Section 3 brings a description of the CPON method and the proposed active learning method, in section 4, the simulation for pattern classification problems is performed. Finally, in Section 5, the conclusion is presented.

2   Pattern Classifiers

2.1   Pattern Classifiers

Pattern classifiers provide an output $\hat{y}$ as a discriminant value for the given input pattern $\mathbf{x}$. First, let us consider a binary classification problem. Then, the discriminant function h can be formulated as

$$\hat{y} = h(\mathbf{x}) \tag{1}$$

where $\mathbf{x} \in X$ (an input space, an arbitrary subset of $\mathbf{R}^d$) represents the d dimensional input pattern and $\hat{y} \in Y$ (an output space, a set of $\{-1, +1\}$).

Suppose we have K classes. Then, one of methods of implementing multiclass discriminant function is to construct K discriminant functions for each class; that is

$$\hat{y}_k = h_k(\mathbf{x}), \quad \text{for } k = 1, ..., K \tag{2}$$

From these class outputs, the decision is made by the maximum discriminant value such as

$$\text{class} = \arg \max_k \hat{y}_k \tag{3}$$

In general, the discriminant function h_k can be constructed by a linear combination of kernel functions; that is

$$h_k(\mathbf{x}) = \sum_{j=1}^{m_k} w_{kj} \phi_{kj}(\mathbf{x}) \tag{4}$$

where m_k, w_{kj}. and ϕ_{kj} represent the number of kernel functions, the jth weight value, and the kernel function for the kth discriminant function, respectively.

2.2   Active Learning

In some neural network applications it is very time consuming and/or expensive to acquire training data. Therefore it is desirable to only use patterns with maximal information about the function. Informally, we would expect that the most valuable patterns would be near the decision boundaries. These patterns are presented as a query. A method where the learner points out good patterns is often called active learning and is a special case of a resampling technique. The basic assumption is that those patterns in the input space yielding the largest error are those points we would benefit the most from including in the training set.

More generally we begin with a preliminary, weak classifier that has been developed with a small set of labeled samples. There are two related methods for then selecting an informative pattern – that is, a pattern for which the current classifier is least certain. In confidence-based query selection the classifier computes discriminant function $h_k(\mathbf{x})$ for the k categories, k = 1... K. An informative pattern x is one for which the two largest discriminant functions have nearly the same value; such patterns lie near the current decision boundaries. The second method, voting-based or committee-based query selection, is similar to the previous method but is applicable to multi-classifier systems. Each unlabeled pattern is presented to each of the k component classifiers; the pattern that yields the greatest disagreement among the k resulting category labels is considered the most informative pattern, and is thus presented as a query to the oracle. Voting-based query selection can be used even if the component classifiers do not provide analog discriminant functions. In both confidence-based methods, the pattern labeled by the oracle is then used for training the classifier in the traditional way.

3   Proposed Method

The standard machine learning algorithms yield better prediction performance with balanced datasets. However, in real world applications, we often face class unbalanced problem. Some researchers suggest using active learning strategy to deal with the class unbalanced problem. The main idea of active learning is that not all the instances are equally important in the training sets. This idea led a question how to select the most informative examples in the datasets. Various methods of selecting informative samples are introduced [5-8]. And the main idea of these methods is that the closest instances to the hyperplane are considered to be the most informative instances. However, it needs too much time to calculate the distances between the hyperplane and classifier's outputs. Furthermore, the class boundary learned by standard machine learning algorithms can be skewed toward the majority target class. Therefore, we proposed a new method that select informative samples depend on the decision boundary of CPON.

3.1   Class Probability Output Network

The distribution of the classifier's output can be approximated by the beta distribution under the assumption that the classifier's output has unimodal distribution. The probability density function (PDF) f_Y and cumulative distribution function (CDF) of beta random variable Y whose values lie between 0 and 1 are

$$f_Y(y \mid \alpha, \beta) = \frac{1}{B(\alpha, \beta)} y^{\alpha-1}(1-y)^{\beta-1} \tag{5}$$

and

$$F_Y(y \mid \alpha, \beta) = \frac{1}{B(\alpha, \beta)} \int^y x^{\alpha-1}(1-x)^{\beta-1} dx \tag{6}$$

where α and β represent positive constants for the beta density function, and $B(\alpha, \beta) = \int_0^1 x^{\alpha-1}(1-x)^{\beta-1} dx$ is the beta function.

Form the data, the parameters α and β can be estimated directly

$$\alpha = \bar{Y}\left(\frac{\bar{Y}(1-\bar{Y})}{S_Y^2} - 1\right), \quad \beta = (1-\bar{Y})\left(\frac{\bar{Y}(1-\bar{Y})}{S_Y^2} - 1\right) \tag{7}$$

where $\bar{Y} = \frac{1}{n}\sum_{i=1}^n Y_i$ and $S_Y^2 = \frac{1}{n-1}\sum_{i=1}^n (Y_i - \bar{Y})^2$ are the sample mean and sample variance.

However, in general, these estimates do not always provide the optimal values of beta distribution parameters due to not enough samples. If these estimates are accurate, the distribution of the CDF of data, that is $F_Y(Y_i)$, $i = 1,...,n$, becomes uniformly distributed. From this point of view, we need to check the uniformity of $F_Y(Y_i)$, $i = 1,...,n$, using the hypothesis test such as the K-S test. If the data $F_n^*(Y_i)$, $i = 1,...,n$, pass the hypothesis test of uniform distribution, it implies that the estimates of α and β are good enough to represent the distribution of the classifier's output. However, in some cases, this hypothesis of uniform distribution may be rejected due to the inaccurate estimation of beta distribution parameters. In this case, α and β are adjusted to improve the uniformity of $F_n^*(Y_i)$, $i = 1,...,n$.

First, the CDF F_n^* of beta distribution can be approximated by using the following trapezoidal rule

-   Let the normalized classifier's output Y_i, $i = 1,...,n$, be sorted in ascending order where $Y_0 = 0$ and $Y_n = 1$;

-   Then the area under the curve of f_Y between $Y_0 = 0$ and $Y_n = 1$ can be divided into n strips each with a width of $\Delta Y_i = Y_i - Y_{i-1}$ and the shape of each strip is approximated as a trapezium. And the area a_i of ith strip is approximated as

$$a_i = \frac{\Delta Y_i}{2}\left(f_Y(Y_i) + f_Y(Y_{i-1})\right). \tag{8}$$

Adding up these areas gives us an approximated value for the CDF

$$F_n^*\left(y = Y_j \mid \alpha, \beta\right)$$
$$\approx \sum_{i=1}^{j} \frac{\Delta Y_i}{2}\left(f_Y(Y_i) + f_Y(y_{i-1})\right). \tag{9}$$

Using this trapezoidal rule, the beta distribution's parameters α and β can be adjusted to improve the uniformity of F_n^* as

$$\Delta_i = F_n^*(Y_i) - F_n^*(Y_{i-1})$$
$$\approx \frac{Ci}{2}\left(Y_i^{\alpha-1}(1-Y_i)^{\beta-1} + Y_{i-1}^{\alpha-1}(1-Y_{i-1})^{\beta-1}\right) \tag{10}$$

where C_i represents a constant defined by

$$C_i = \Delta Y_i / B(\alpha, \beta) . \tag{11}$$

Then, the sample mean and variance of Δ_i, $i = 1, ..., n$, are determined by

$$\overline{\Delta} = \frac{1}{n}\sum_{i=1}^{n}\Delta_i \text{ and } S_\Delta^2 = \frac{1}{n-1}\sum_{i=1}^{n}(\Delta_i - \overline{\Delta})^2 . \tag{12}$$

Here, to improve the uniformity of $F_n^*(Y_i)$, the beta distribution's parameters α and β are adjusted:

$$\alpha^{new} = \alpha^{old} + \eta\Delta\alpha \tag{13}$$

and

$$\beta^{new} = \beta^{old} + \eta\Delta\beta \tag{14}$$

where η represents a positive constant referred to as the learning rate. Here, $\Delta\alpha$ and $\Delta\beta$ can be determined in such a way to minimize the sample variance S_Δ^2, that is

$$\Delta\alpha = -\frac{\partial S_\Delta^2}{\partial\alpha}$$
$$= -\frac{2}{n-1}\sum_{i=1}^{n}(\Delta_i - \overline{\Delta})\left(\frac{\partial\Delta_i}{\partial\alpha} - \frac{1}{n}\sum_{j=1}^{n}\frac{\partial\Delta_i}{\partial\alpha}\right) \tag{15}$$
$$= -\frac{1}{n-1}\sum_{i=1}^{n}C_i(\Delta_i - \overline{\Delta})(\alpha-1)\left(A_i - \frac{1}{n}\sum_{j=1}^{n}A_j\right)$$

where

$$A_i = Y_i^{\alpha-1}(1-Y_i)^{\beta-1} + Y_{i-1}^{\alpha-1}(1-Y_{i-1})^{\beta-1}$$

In the similar way,

$$\Delta\beta = -\frac{1}{n-1}\sum_{i=1}^{n}C_i(\Delta_i - \overline{\Delta})(\beta-1)\left(B_i - \frac{1}{n}\sum_{j=1}^{n}B_j\right) \tag{16}$$

where

$$B_i = Y_i^{\alpha-1}(1-Y_i)^{\beta-2} + Y_{i-1}^{\alpha-1}(1-Y_{i-1})^{\beta-2} .$$

This update rule of beta distribution parameters provides more accurate estimation of the distribution of classifier's output samples by assuring the higher confidence of the uniformity of $F_n^*(Y_i)$. The uniformity of empirical CDF of Y_i is also dependent upon the kernel parameters describing the discriminant function. From this point of view, the kernel parameter is selected to maximize the uniformity of empirical CDF of Y_i in CPON.

After training the CPON, the classification for an unknown sample can be determined by the beta distribution for each class. For the multi-class classification problem, we consider two groups of samples in each class, that is, the "+" group of samples that belong to the class, and the "−" group of samples that belong to the rest of classes. Each conditional probability represents a class probability that the given instance belongs to the "+" group among two groups, that is, the "+" and "−" groups. If the probabilities of the "+" and "−" groups are the same, that is, $\Pr\{C_k^+\} = \Pr\{C_k^-\}$, the posterior probability of class membership for the given normalized output $\overline{y}_K$, becomes

$$\Pr\left\{C_k^+ \mid Y_k^+ \le \overline{y}_K \text{ or } Y_k^- \ge \overline{y}_K\right\} = \frac{F_{Y_k^+}(\overline{y}_K)}{F_{Y_k^+}(\overline{y}_K) + 1 - F_{Y_k^-}(\overline{y}_K)} \tag{17}$$

The final decision of the class is determined by investigating the class which has the maximum posterior probability of class membership, that is,

$$\text{class} = \arg \max_k \Pr\left\{C_k^+ \mid Y_k^+ \le \overline{y}_K \text{ or } Y_k^- \ge \overline{y}_K\right\} \tag{18}$$

3.2   Proposed Method

The strategy of selecting instances within some range such as a margin addresses the unbalanced dataset classification very well. Thus, an accurate decision boundary is desired because informative instances defined by depending on the distance from the decision boundary. We want to utilize CPON to find the decision boundary and to improve the accuracy over the minority class without much sacrificing the accuracy over the majority class. If we apply the CPON to classifiers, we can get an accurate decision boundary and the estimated distribution of the output using the beta distribution parameters. We utilize the estimated distribution to select informative instance instead of the distance from the decision boundary. Then, we can reduce the version space as fast as possible to reach the solution faster in order to avoid certain costs associated with the problem. For the possibility of a non-symmetric version space, there are more complex selection methods suggested, but it has been observed that the advantage of those are not significant when compared to their high computational cost. We constrain our discussion to a standard two-class classification problem.

< Proposed algorithm >

Given: Set $S = \{(x_i, y_i), i = 1, ..., n\}$ with labels $y_i \in \{-1, +1\}$.

Step1. For the given sample set S, divide into the training sample set S_{train} and test sample set S_{test}.

Step2. Train the classifier using the training sample set S_{train}.

Step3. Estimate the CDF of the classifier's output using (6), (13), and (14).
  a. Classifier's outputs are divided into minority class and majority class.
  b. For each class, normalize the outputs of classifiers such that the range of values is between 0 and 1 and calculate the mean and variance.
  c. Estimate the parameters α and β for each class using (7).
  d. Hypothesis test of uniform distribution.
          If hypothesis of uniform distribution is rejected
  d-1. adjust the parameters α and β using (13)-(16).
  e. Calculate the posterior probability of class membership using (17)

Step4. Select the instances within some range of the CPON's decision boundary as informative instances
$$S_{\text{new}} = \{(x_i, y_i), i = 1, ..., s\}.$$

Step5. Retrain the classifier using the informative instances
$$S_{\text{new}} = \{(x_i, y_i), i = 1, ..., s\}.$$

Step6. Calculate a new decision boundary of the new classifier by Step3.

Step7. Make the final decision of the class using (17) and (18).

4   Simulation and Results

For the simulation for classification problems, we selected the data set from the UCI database [9] and the Korea patent data. To see the effect of CPON to select the balanced informative instances, two strategies of selecting informative instances methods are compared. One method select the informative instances based on the decision boundary of standard machine learning (S.M.L) and the other method select the informative instances based on the decision boundary of CPON. The unbalanced data situation may also occur in one-against-rest schema. Table 1 presents the ratio of each class of train data and two compared informative instance sets. The balanced dataset of UCI database is used.

Table 1. Comparison of the informative instances' ratio

	Train data	S.M.L	CPON
Class1	0.4608	0.0952	**0.2857**
Class2	0.0784	0.0476	**0.0952**
Class3	0.4608	0.0476	**0.3333**

From Table 1, we can see that the set of informative instances based on CPON is more balanced than S.M.L.

Table 2. The ratio of the IPC in the Korea patent dataset

Section	Ratio (%)	Section	Ratio (%)
A	7.62	E	2.26
B	18.78	F	10.76
C	12.32	G	18.05
D	2.71	H	27.50

The Korea patent dataset consists of publicly available 167634 patents and contains much quantitative information about the patent. There are eight sections which represent the International Patent Classification (IPC) and each patent belongs to one of the IPC. Table 2 presents the ratio of the IPC in the Korea patent dataset.

Automatic IPC sorting problem also faces an unbalanced classification problem. To solve this problem, Perceptron, Active learning with Perceptron (A.L with S.M.L), and Active learning with CPON (A.L with CPON) are applied and test error and the error of minority class are compared. One-against-rest schema is used to solve this problem, so there are eight different binary classifiers. We constrain our discussion to these binary classification problems. After training of classifiers, each classifier was evaluated using the tenfold cross-validation method.

Table 3. Comparison of test error and false-negative rate

	Perceptron		A.L with S.M.L		A.L with CPON	
	test error	Minority error	test error	Minority error	test error	Minority error
A	**0.0778**	0.9899	0.8924	**0.0187**	0.3253	0.3542
B	0.6957	**0.0779**	0.2893	0.9981	**0.2394**	0.6933
C	0.1260	0.9314	0.1223	0.9995	**0.1049**	0.5303
D	**0.0273**	1.0	0.0299	0.9964	0.1550	**0.4886**
E	**0.0223**	0.9964	0.0225	0.9955	0.1431	**0.5653**
F	0.1267	1.0	0.6396	**0.1907**	**0.1072**	0.6313
G	**0.1831**	0.9903	0.2093	0.9179	0.2814	**0.2588**
H	0.2804	0.9554	0.3701	0.5180	**0.2687**	**0.0938**

The results in Table 3 depict the proposed method (A.L with CPON) decreases the prediction error of minority class (minority error) significantly with increasing the prediction error or majority class a little bit.

5   Conclusion

Classification is a supervised learning method which acquires a training dataset to form its model for classifying unseen examples. The unbalanced data classification problem has been known to impact the prediction performance of classification algorithms. We propose an efficient active learning method which selects informative instances using CPON. Experimental results show that the proposed method decreases the prediction error of minority class significantly.

References

1. Park, W.J., Kil, R.M.: Pattern Classification With Class Probability Output Network. IEEE Trans. Neural Netw. 20(20), 1659–1673 (2009)
2. Rosas, H., Kil, R.M., Han, S.W.: Automatic media data rating based on class probability output networks. IEEE Trns. Consumer Elect. 56(4), 2296–2302 (2010)
3. Park, W.J.: Prediction of a Patent Property Using the Class Probability Output Network. In: 2nd International Conference on ITCS (August 2010)
4. Qiao, X., Liu, Y.: Active weighted learning for unbalanced multicategory classification. Biometrics, 1–10 (2008)
5. Ertekin, S., Huang, J., Bottou, L., Lee Giles, C.: Learning on the Border: Active Learning in Imbalanced Data Classification. In: Proc. of ACM 16th CIKM (November 2007)
6. Jie, S., Xiaoling, L., Xizhi, W.: An Improved AdaBoost Algorithm for Unbalanced classification Data. In: 2009 Sixth International Conference on Fuzzy Systems and Knowledge Discovery (2009)
7. Abe, N.: Invited talk: Sampling approaches to learning form imbalaned datasets: Active learning, cost sensitive learning and beyond. In: Proc. of ICML Workshop: Learning from Imbalanced Data sets (2003)
8. Provost, F.: Machine learning from imbalanced datasets 101. In: Proc. Of AAAI Workshop on Imbalanced Data Sets (2000)
9. Murphy, M., Aha, D.W.: UCI Repository of Machine Learning Databases. Univ. California at Irvine, Irvine (1994), http://www.archieve.ics.uci.edu/ml/

A Study on Aircraft Position Calculation Algorithm in Compliance with the Wind Parameter

Dong-Hwa Park and Hyo-Dal Park

Dept. of Electronic Engineering
Inha University, Incheon, Korea
parkdh96@hotmail.com, hdpark@inha.ac.kr

Abstract. Aircraft's position calculation is basic work for Trajectory modeling, conflict detection and air traffic flow management. This paper proposes a novel algorithm based vincenty's formulas for aircraft position calculation calculation, which is combined with the vincenty's formulas. We demonstrated through simulations with wind parameter and experimental results show that our aircraft position calculation exhibits much better performance in accuracy.

Keywords: ATC, ATM, ATFM, wind parameter.

1   Introduction

The air traffic control (ATC) system improves safety and efficiency of air traffic by preventing collisions against other aircraft and obstacles and managing aircraft's navigation status[1].

To achieve these purposes, the air traffic control system identifies aircraft and displays its location, displays and distributes flight plan data, provides flight safety alerts, and processes controllers' requests[2].

Despite technological advances in navigation, communication, computation and control, the Air Traffic management (ATM) system is still, to a large extent, built around a rigidly structured airspace and centralized, mostly human-operated system architecture. The Increasing demand for air traffic is stressing current ATM practices to their limit[3]. According to the recent increase in air traffic a more efficient air traffic control is required. The continuous traffic increase is now pushing the current system to its limits, and the need for alternatives of higher capacity arises[3].

The accuracy of trajectory predictions in En-route airspace impacts ATM conflict predictions and Estimated Times of Arrival (ETA) to control fixes. For the airspace user, inaccurate trajectory predictions may result in less-than-optimal maneuver advisories in response to a given traffic management problem[3][4].

A limiting factor in the accurate prediction of aircraft trajectories is the difficulty in obtaining precise trajectory calibration and intent data for individual flights. Trajectory calibration data refers to aircraft state, aircraft performance, and atmospheric characteristics that influence the external forces acting on the aircraft.

C. Lee et al. (Eds.): STA 2011 Workshops, CCIS 187, pp. 94–102, 2011.

Many aircraft position calculation algorithm account for this uncertainty[3]. On the other hand, only limited research has been done on stochastic position detection.

In this paper we propose aircraft position calculation algorithm. The remainder of this paper is structured as follows. In the next section, wind parameter and aircraft position detection techniques and theoretical background about aircraft position control algorithm is presented. We present some experimental results of our proposed scheme in Section 3, and finally conclude with the conclusion in Section 4.

2   Aircraft Position Detection

2.1   Aircraft Position in Compliance with the Wind Parameter

Consider a fairly simplified model for aircraft position in compliance with the wind parameter problem. A flow is defined as a set of flights between a departure aerodrome, an arrival aerodrome and en-route navigation. The following simplifications are made.

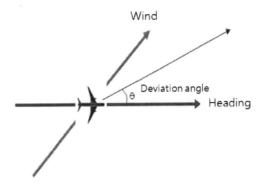

Fig. 1. Typical model of a aircraft position in compliance with the wind parameter

2.2   Parameter for Position Calculation

For position calculation, we must consider about concept of speed and conversion between other speeds, speed variation by altitude changing and wind parameter.

Fir, airspeed is the speed of an position calculation relative to the air. Among the common conventions for qualifying are : Indicated Airspeed (IAS), Calibrated Airspeed (CAS), True Airspeed (TAS) and Ground speed (GS).

IAS is the airspeed indicator reading uncorrected for instrument, position, and other errors. From current European Aviation Safety Agency (EASA) definitions : Indicated airspeed means the speed of an aircraft as shown on its pitot static airspeed indicator calibrated to reflect standard atmosphere adiabatic compressible flow at sea level uncorrected for airspeed system errors.

Most airspeed indicators show the speed in knots (i.e. nautical miles per hour). Some light aircraft have airspeed indicators showing speed in miles per hour.

CAS is indicated airspeed corrected for instrument errors, position error and installation errors.

CAS is CAS values less than the speed of sound at standard sea level (661.4788 knots) are calculated as follows :

$$V_c = A_0 \sqrt{5 \left[\left(\frac{Q_c}{P_0} + 1 \right)^{\frac{2}{7}} - 1 \right]} \qquad (1)$$

Where

V_c is the CAS.

Q_c is the impact pressure sensed by the pitot tube.

p_0 is 29.92126 inches Hg at standard sea level.

A_0 is 661.4788 knots; speed of sound   speed at standard sea level.

This expression is based on the form of Bernoulli's equation applicable to a perfect, compressible gas. The values P0 and A0 are consistent with the International Standard Atmosphere (ISA).

TAS is the physical speed of the aircraft relative to the air surrounding the aircraft. The true airspeed is a vector quantity. The relationship between the true airspeed(V_t) and the speed with respect to the ground(V_g) is

$$V_t = V_g - V_w \qquad (2)$$

Where

V_w is wind speed vector.

Aircraft flight instruments, however, don't compute true airspeed as a function of groundspeed and wind speed. They use impact and static pressures as well as a temperature input. Basically, true airspeed is calibrated airspeed that is corrected for pressure altitude and temperature. The result is the true physical speed of the aircraft plus or minus the wind component. True Airspeed is equal to calibrated airspeed at standard sea level conditions.

The simplest way to compute true airspeed is using a function of Mach number

$$V_t = A_0 \bullet M \sqrt{\frac{\tau}{\tau_0}} \qquad (3)$$

Where M is Mach number, τ is Temperature (kelvins) and τ_0 is Standard sea level temperature (288.15 kelvins)

Second, speed variation by altitude changing means that when aircraft are climb or descent.

The rate of climb (RoC) is the speed at which an aircraft increases its altitude. this is most often expressed in feet per minute and can be abbreviated as ft/min. Else where, it is commonly expressed in meters per second, abbreviated as m/s. The rate of climb in an aircraft is measured with a vertical speed indicator (VSI) or instantaneous vertical speed indicator (IVSI). The rate of decrease in altitude is referred to as the rate of descent or sink rate. A decrease in altitude corresponds with a negative rate of climb.

There are two airspeeds relating to optimum rates of ascent, referred to as Vx and Vy.

Vx is the indicated airspeed for best angle of climb. Vy is the indicated airspeed for best rate of climb. Vx is slower than Vy.

Climbing at Vx allows pilots to maximize the altitude gain per unit ground distance. That is, Vx allows pilots to maximize their climb while sacrificing the least amount of ground distance. This occurs at the speed for which the difference between thrust and drag is the greatest (maximum excess thrust). In a jet airplane, this is approximately minimum drag speed, or the bottom of the drag vs. speed curve. Climb angle is proportional to excess thrust.

Climbing at Vy allows pilots to maximize the altitude gain per unit time. That is, Vy, allows pilots to maximize their climb while sacrificing the least amount of time. This occurs at the speed for which the difference between engine power and the power required to overcome the aircraft's drag is the greatest (maximum excess power). Climb rate is proportional to excess power.

Vx increases with altitude and Vy decreases with altitude. Vx = Vy at the airplane's absolute ceiling, the altitude above which it cannot climb using just its own lift.

Last, we consider about wind parameters. Wind parameter can divide two components(weather fonts and thermal wind) on a large scale.

Weather fronts are boundaries between two masses of air of different densities, or different temperature and moisture properties, which normally are convergence zones in the wind field and are the principal cause of significant weather. Within surface weather analyses, they are depicted using various colored lines and symbols

The air masses usually differ in temperature and may also differ in humidity. Wind shear in the horizontal occurs near these boundaries. Cold fronts feature narrow bands of thunderstorms and severe weather, and may be preceded by squall lines and dry lines.

Cold fronts are sharper surface boundaries with more significant horizontal wind shear than warm fronts. When a front becomes stationary, it can degenerate into a line which separates regions of differing wind speed, known as a shear line, though the wind direction across the feature normally remains constant. Directional and speed shear can occur across the axis of stronger tropical waves, as northerly winds precede the wave axis and southeast winds are seen behind the wave axis.

Horizontal wind shear can also occur along local land breeze and sea breeze boundaries.[

Thermal wind is a meteorological term not referring to an actual wind, but a difference in the geostrophic wind between two pressure levels p_1 and p_0, with $p_1 < p_0$; in essence, wind shear. It is only present in an atmosphere with horizontal changes in temperature.

In a barotropic atmosphere, where temperature is uniform, the geostrophic wind is independent of height. The name stems from the fact that this wind flows around areas of low (and high) temperature in the same manner as the geostrophic wind flows around areas of low (and high) pressure.

$$f_{VT} = K \times \nabla(\phi_1 - \phi_0) \tag{4}$$

where the ϕ_x are geopotential height fields with $(\phi_1 > \phi_0)$, f is the Coriolis parameter, and K is the upward-pointing unit vector in the vertical direction. The thermal wind equation does not determine the wind in the tropics. Since f is small or zero, such as near the equator, the equation reduces to stating that $\nabla(\phi_1 - \phi_0)$ is small. This equation basically describes the existence of the jet stream, a westerly current of air with maximum wind speeds close to the tropopause which is (even though other factors are also important) the result of the temperature contrast between equator and pole.

3   Proposed Aircraft Position Calculation Algorithm

Aircraft's position consists of latitude and longitude. In accordance, for measuring the distance between waypoints over a flight information region, the curvature of the Earth must be taken into consideration.

As a rough estimate, we could assume the Earth is a sphere.

$$dN = R \vartheta \emptyset \tag{5}$$

$$dE = R cos \vartheta \emptyset \lambda \tag{6}$$

where R is the radius of the Earth (average of 6378.1 km) and the differences in latitude and longitude are in radians, the distance is 447.47 km. This method is valid assumption over very small distances, however, over large distances we need to account for the non-uniformity of the Earth. The Earth is not actually a sphere, it is an ellipsoid of revolution, 21 km shorter on the North - South direction than the East - West direction.

The flattening at the poles is caused by the centifugal force of the spinning Earth. Because of this flattening, the radius if the Earth is not a constant value as we assume for Spherical Earth coordinates.

A more accurate method of measuring the distance between two points on the surface of the Earth is Vincenty's Formula. It is accurate to 0.5 mm over a distance of a few centimeters to nearly 20,000 km.

Given the coordinates of the two points (φ_1, λ_1) and (φ_2, λ_2) the vincenty's inverse method finds the azimuths α_1, α_2 and ellipsoidal distance s.

Calculate reduced latitude U_1 ($\arctan[(1-f)\tan\varphi_1]$, U_2($\arctan[(1-f)\tan\varphi_2]$, and L, and set initial value of $\lambda = L$ .Then iteratively evaluate the following equations until λ converges.

$$sin\sigma = \sqrt{(cosU_2 sin\lambda)^2 + (cosU_1 sinU_2 - sinU_1 cosU_2 cos\lambda)^2} \tag{7}$$

$$cos\sigma = sinU_1 sinU_2 + cosU_1 cosU_2 cos\lambda \tag{8}$$

$$\sigma = arctan\frac{sin\sigma}{cos\sigma} \tag{9}$$

$$cos(2\sigma_m) = cos\sigma - \frac{2sinU_1 sinU_2}{cos^2\alpha} \tag{10}$$

$$sin\alpha = \frac{cosU_1 cosU_2 sin\lambda}{sin\sigma} \tag{11}$$

$$cos^2\alpha = 1 - sin^2\alpha \tag{12}$$

$$C = \frac{f}{16} cos^2\alpha[4 + f(4 - 3cos^2\alpha)] \tag{13}$$

$$\lambda = L + (1 - C)f sin\alpha\{\sigma + Csin\sigma[cos(2_{\sigma m}) + Ccos\sigma(-1 + 2cos^2(2_{\sigma m})]\} \tag{14}$$

When λ has converged to the desired of accuracy, evaluate the following:

$$u^2 = cos^2\alpha\frac{a^2 - b^2}{b^2} \tag{15}$$

$$A = 1 + \frac{u^2}{16384}\{4096 + u^2[-768 + u^2(320 - 175u^2)]\} \tag{16}$$

$$B = \frac{u^2}{1024}\{256 + u^2[-128 + u^2(74 - 47u^2)]\} \tag{17}$$

$$\Delta\sigma = Bsin\sigma\{cos(2_{\sigma m}) + \frac{1}{4}B[cos\sigma(-1 + 2cos^2(2_{\sigma m}) \tag{18}$$

$$(-3 + 4sin^2\sigma)(-3 + 4cos^2(2_{\sigma m}))]\}$$

$$s = bA(\sigma - \Delta\sigma) \tag{19}$$

$$\alpha_1 = arctan(\frac{cosU_2 sin\lambda}{cosU_1 sinU_2 - sinU_1 cosU_2 cos\lambda}) \tag{20}$$

$$\alpha_2 = arctan (\frac{cosU_1 sin\lambda}{-sinU_1 cosU_2 + cosU_1 sinU_2 cos\lambda}) \tag{21}$$

We can compute azimuths(α_1, α_2) and distance s.

4   Experimental Results of Proposed Scheme

This section describes the method for computing the wind parameter used to compute the accurate position and our position calculation algorithm.

First of all, we need aircraft's position and its speed. Aircraft's position consists of latitude and longitude. For calculating aircraft's position at specified time, we need airspeed (TAS or GS), wind speed and wind direction. Aircraft's position can calculate using vincenty's formula at specified time. For using position prediction algorithm, predict aircraft's position and other parameters are shown in the table 1.

Table 1. Simulation parameters

Item	Simulation parameters	
	Simulation 1	*Simulation 2*
Start point	North 352834	West 1203434
Through point	North 213459	West 802343
Direction	271 Degree	87 Degree
TAS(Knot)	600	400
Wind direction	70	170
Wind speed	8	4

For using position prediction algorithm, Simulation 1 is shown in the figure 2.

```
Input Lat, Long 1 (ex.0530902N,0015040W):0352834N,1203434W
Input Lat, Long 2 (ex.0521219N,0000833W):0213459N,0802343W
Lat1 : 35.476111  Lon1 : -120.576111   Lat2 : 21.583056   Lon2 : -80.395278
True Course : 271.566998
Input Heading(Degree):271
Input True Air Speed(Knot):600
Input Wind Direction(Degree):70
Input Wind Velocity(Knot):8
Climb(or Descent) rate(ft/min) (+:Climb, -:Descent) (ex : +010) : +000
Rate : 0.000000
 TAS : 600.000000       Wind Velocity : 8.000000
 True Heading : 271.000000     Wind Direction  : 70.000000
Drift Angle : 0.004901
***********************************************************************
distance : 4179.454558[km]
Ground Speed : 607.410528[Knot]
Ground Speed : 1124.924298[Km/h]
Time        : 3.715321
***********************************************************************
```

Fig. 2. Result of Simulation 1

The direction about the real point should be 271.566998 degrees and then the attitude control angle should be   +0.004901 degrees in accordance with the current aircraft direction and wind direction. Actual speed of the aircraft is 607.410528 knot when considering the pace and wind speed, in other words, 1124.92km/h. We could be obtained the conclusion that it takes 3.715321(3 hours 42 minutes 55 seconds) to pass the point at this speed.

For using position prediction algorithm, Simulation 2 is shown in the figure 3.

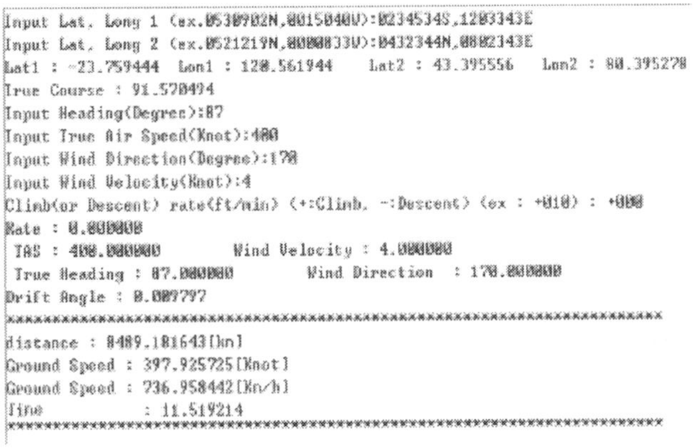

```
Input Lat, Long 1 (ex.0530702N,0015040W):0234534S,1203343E
Input Lat, Long 2 (ex.0521219N,0080033W):0432344N,0802343E
Lat1 : -23.759444  Lon1 : 120.561944    Lat2 : 43.395556   Lon2 : 80.395278
True Course : 91.570494
Input Heading(Degree):87
Input True Air Speed(Knot):400
Input Wind Direction(Degree):170
Input Wind Velocity(Knot):4
Climb(or Descent) rate(ft/min) (+:Climb, -:Descent) (ex : +010) : +000
Rate : 0.000000
 IAS : 400.000000       Wind Velocity : 4.000000
 True Heading : 87.000000      Wind Direction  : 170.000000
Drift Angle : 0.009797
xxxxxxxxxxxxxxxxxxxxxxxxxxxxxxxxxxxxxxxxxxxxxxxxxxxxxxxxxxxxxxxxxxxxxx
distance : 8489.181643[km]
Ground Speed : 397.925725[Knot]
Ground Speed : 736.958442[Km/h]
Time      : 11.519214
xxxxxxxxxxxxxxxxxxxxxxxxxxxxxxxxxxxxxxxxxxxxxxxxxxxxxxxxxxxxxxxxxxxxxx
```

Fig. 3. Result of Simulation 2

The direction about the real point should be 91.578494 degrees and then the attitude control angle should be   +0.800808 degrees in accordance with the current aircraft direction and wind direction. Actual speed of the aircraft is 397.925725 knot when considering the pace and wind speed, in other words, 736.958442km/h. We could be obtained the conclusion that it takes 11.519214 hours(11 hours 31 minutes 9 seconds) to pass the point at this speed.

By computing aircraft position and wind parameter, we can calculate aircraft's position

In this paper we propose aircraft position calculation in compliance with wind parameter.

Experimental results show that our algorithm exhibits much better performance in accuracy. The applicability of the proposed algorithm is manifold during the trajectory prediction and modeling such as, rocket positioning control, aeronautical traffic flow management system(ATFM).

From now on, it is further suggested that the proposed algorithm may be extended to the trajectory modeling, which may further improve the 4D trajectory prediction.

Acknowledgments. This research was supported by a grant(code#) from Air Transportation Advancement Program funded by Ministry of Land, Transport and Maritime affairs of Korean government.

References

1. Sridhar, B., Grabbe, S.R., Mukherjee, A.: Modeling, Optimization in Traffic Flow Management. Proceedings of the IEEE 96(12), 2060–2080 (2008)
2. Kuchar, J.K., Yang, L.C.: A Review of Conflict Detection and Resolution Modeling Methods. IEEE Transactions On Intelligent Transportation Systems 1(4), 179–189 (2000)

3. Vela, A.E., Salaun, E., Solak, S.: A Two-Staqge Stochastic Optimization model For Air Traffic Conflict Resolution under Wind Certainty. In: 28th Digital Avionics Systems Conference 2009, pp. 2.E.5-1–2.E.5-13.
4. Xi, L., Jun, Z., Yanbo, Z., Wei, L.: Simulation Study of Algorithm for Aircraft Trajectory Prediction Based on ADS-B Technology. In: 2008 Asia Simulation Conference – 7th Intl. Conf. on Sys. Simulation and Scientific Computing, pp. 322–327 (2008)
5. Smith, T.F., Waterman, M.S.: Identification of Common Molecular Subsequences. J. Mol. Biol. 147, 195–197 (1981)

For Aviation Security Using Surveillance System[*]

Deok Gyu Lee and Jong Wook Han

Electronic and Telecommunications Research Institute
161 Gajeong-dong, Yuseong-gu, Daejeon, Rep. Of Korea
{deokgyulee,hanjw}@etri.re.kr

Abstract. As the national airspace system grows increasingly interconnected to partners and customers both within and outside the Rep. of Korea government, the danger of cyber-attacks on the system is increasing. Because of low-cost computer technology and easier access to malware, or malicious software code, it is conceivable for individuals, organized crime groups, terrorists, and nation-states to attack the Rep. of Korea air transportation system infrastructure.[4] An apparatus and a method for processing image information are provided. The apparatus for processing image information includes an image capturing device and an image information server for receiving and storing an image captured by the image capturing device and adds information on the image capturing device and signature information to image data obtained by the image capturing device. Accordingly, the device information and the signature information can be added to the image data obtained by the image capturing device to maintain security of the image data and use the image data as digital proof when a specific event is generated.

Keywords: Aviation Security, Surveillance System, Authentication, Authorization.

1 Introduction

As the national airspace system grows increasingly interconnected to partners and customers both within and outside the Rep. of Korea government, the danger of cyber-attacks on the system is increasing. Because of low-cost computer technology and easier access to malware, or malicious software code, it is conceivable for individuals, organized crime groups, terrorists, and nation-states to attack the Rep. of Korea air transportation system infrastructure.

Consider an airport in which passengers and employees can enter common areas, like transportation facilities, and waiting areas. However, secured areas, like luggage transport and service stations, are available for authorized employees only. The highest security areas, such as the air traffic control room, are accessible to specialized personnel who are appropriately authorized. The keyword here is "authorization", meaning that people who are not authorized to access a physical location should not be

[*] This research was supported by a grant (code# 07aviation-navigation-03) from Aviation Improvement Program funded by Ministry of Construction & Transportation of Korean government.

allowed physical or electronic access to that location. In the surveillance world, the exact same rules apply and the potential recipient of the surveillance data must have the same authorization that an ordinary person of any trade would have to be physically or electronically present at that location. However, during emergency operations, controlled dissemination of sensitive data may become necessary in order to obtain support services or to prevent panic. It has been shown that during crisis people require clear instructions so that their maximum cooperation is obtained. However, these instructions should not release unauthorized information or reveal the existence of such information.

This paper relates to an apparatus and a method for processing image information, and more particularly, to an image information processing apparatus and method capable of adding information on an image capturing device and signature information to image data and storing the image data to maintain security of the image data and use the image data as digital proof.

2   Related Work

With the development of image photographing technology, techniques for maintaining security of image data captured by an image capturing device and protecting copyright are proposed. For example, captured images are transmitted to a limited image information output device and reproduced or identification information such as watermarking is embedded in image data to protect copyright of image information[8].

In the case of embedding watermarking in image information, it is possible to confirm the copyright holder of the image information even though the image information is displayed at or transmitted to an undesired place and prevent the image information from being illegally copied. Furthermore, users can watch the image information without having any difficulty and track the source of the image information and image information copy routes when watermarking is embedded in the image information.

However, watermarking does not have legal force capable of preventing the image information from being illegally copied or transmitted although it can show the copyright holder or the source of the image information and allow users to confirm image information copy routes and the source of the image information. Accordingly, security of image information cannot be efficiently maintained only with watermarking when the image information includes personal information related to privacy or data requiring the maintenance of security[9.12].

A distributed architecture for multi-participant and interactive multimedia that enables multiple users to share media streams within a networked environment is presented in "An architecture for distributed, interactive, multi-stream, multi-participant audio and video". In this architecture, multimedia streams originating from multiple sources can be combined to provide media clips that accommodate look-around capabilities. SMIL has been the focus of active research "The use of smil: Multimedia research currently applied on a global scale" and "About the semantic verification of SMIL documents", and many models for adaption to real world scenarios have been provided. A release control for SMIL formatted multimedia objects for pay-per-view movies on the Internet that enforces DAC is described in "Regulating access to smil formatted pay-per-view movies". The cinematic structure consisting of acts, scenes, frames of an actual movies are written as a SMIL document without losing the sense of a story. Here access is restricted to the granularity of an act in a movie. A secure and progressively updatable SMIL document "Sputers: A secure traffic surveillance and emergency response architecture" is used to enforce RBAC and respond to traffic emergencies. In an emergency response situation, different recipients of the live feeds have to be discriminated to people playing different roles[8-14].

Multilevel security (MLS) has been widely studied to ensure data confidentiality, integrity, and availability . MLS systems provide controlled information flow(from higher level to the lower level) based on the security classification of the protection objects (e.g., data items) and subjects of the MLS system (e.g., applications running in behalf of a user). Damiani et al "Securing xml based multimedia content" also discuss feature protection of XML format images. Its primary focus is controlled dissemination of sensitive data within an image. They propose an access control model with complex filtering conditions. This model uses SVG to render the map of a physical facility. While this model could be used to represent our model, it has limitations when compared to flexibility and adaptability to certain issues particular to physical security in the multilevel hierarchy. Bertino at al" An access control model for video database systems" provide a security framework to model access control in video databases. They provide security granularity, where objects are sequences of frames or particular objects within frames. The access control model is based on he concepts of security objects, subjects, and the permitted access modes, like viewing and editing. The proposed model is provides a general framework of the problem domain, however it is not explained how access control objects to be released are formalized and enforced.

While most models addresses the need of multimedia, their approach does not incorporate semantics of multimedia. None of the approaches are completely satisfactory for surveillance multimedia. They primarily address textual documents and exploit the granular structure of XML documents. Multimedia for various reasons as discussed above has to be treated differently because there is a sense of temporal synchrony and continuity involved. Synchronization and integration of different and diverse events to produce sensible information is nontrivial when compared to textual data. The process of retrieval without losing the sense of continuity and synchronization needs sophisticated techniques and algorithms which all of the above models do not completely address. Although our approach to provide controlled information flow in real-time multimedia systemsis based in concepts similar to MLS, the developed methods and techniques are also applicable in other security models, like Role-Based or Discretionary Access Control models.

3   ACRS(Aviation Control Room Surveillance)

It is an object of the paper to provide an image information processing apparatus and method for adding information on an image capturing device and predetermined signature information to image data obtained using the image capturing device to protect the image data from infringement of security such as illegal copy and transmission and adding information on the place and time at which the image data is obtained to the image data to use the image data as digital proof.

An apparatus for processing image information according to the paper comprises: an image capturing unit for generating image data and collecting information on the image capturing unit; an image processing unit for adding at least one of the information on the image capturing unit and signature information to the image data using the image data and the information on the image capturing unit transmitted from the image capturing unit; and an image storage unit for storing the image data output from the image processing unit.

A method for processing image information according to the paper comprises: an image capturing step of generating image data and collecting information on the image capturing step; an image processing step of adding at least one of the information on the image capturing step and signature information to the image data; and an image storing step of storing the image data.

An apparatus for processing image information using image data according to the paper comprises: a device information unit for embedding information on the device that generates the image data in the image data; a signature information unit for embedding signature information in the image data; and a storage unit for storing the image data having at least one of the information on the device and the signature information added thereto.

A method for processing image information using image data according to the paper comprises: a device information step of embedding information on the device that generates the image data in the image data; a signature information step of embedding signature information in the image data; and a storing step of storing the image data having at least one of the information on the device and the signature information added thereto.

The papper can acquire image data included in a captured image and add information on the device that captures the image and signature information to the image data to efficiently maintain security of the image data and use a captured image with respect to a specific event as digital proof.

3.1   Security Framework for Physical Environment

The Security framework for physical environment contains a few essential components, such as an authentication, an authorization, and a security policy. They work at each smart door and often cooperate with a smart surveillance established by a smart image-unit in the physical environment. Since the smart door is installed at the border of each physical domain and every physical environment must pass through it, it is supposed to be a core component and suitable in providing security functions described in security framework for physical environment. Whenever a new access to physical environment is found, it should be able to authenticate and authorize it and enforce security policy based on security rules set by the corresponding smart security administrator [3].

Figure 1 depicts the overall architecture of secure physical environment.

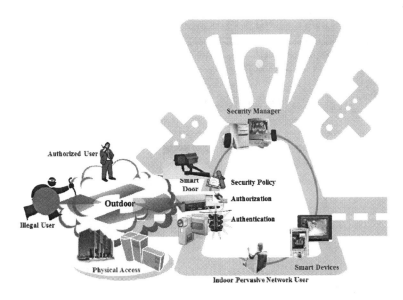

Fig. 1. Architecture of secure physical environment

FIG. 1 is a view illustrating a configuration of an image photographing system to which an image information processing apparatus according to the paper is applied. Referring to FIG. 2, the image photographing system includes an image capturing device for capturing an image and converting the captured image into image data, an image information server for receiving and storing the image data, and an application server for providing various application services using the image data stored in the image information server.

The image capturing device includes an imaging capturing unit for converting an optical image formed through a lens into image data and an image processor for receiving the image data and adding signature information or device information of the image capturing unit to the image data.

The image capturing unit that is a device capable of capturing an image can be a closed-circuit television (CCTV), a digital camera or a video camera, for example. The image capturing unit includes a lens for condensing light and a charge-coupled device (CCD) for converting the light condensed by the lens into image data, recognizes an object through the lens and images the recognized object to generate an optical image. This optical image can be converted into image data through a CCD sensor. The image data generated by the image capturing unit is transmitted to the image processor.

The image processor receives the image data from the image capturing unit, processes the image data and embeds signature information in the image data. The image processor can be constructed as additional hardware or included in the image capturing unit. In the current embodiment, it is assumed that the image processor exists as an additional module separated from the image capturing unit.

The image processor adds at least one of information on the image capturing unit and signature information to the image data transmitted from the image capturing unit. By doing so, the image data can be protected from arbitrary access and control. The signature information can be added to the image data at regular intervals.

The image information server stores the image data to which the information on the image capturing unit or the signature information has been added by the image processor. The image information server includes a storage unit capable of storing the image data having the information on the image capturing unit or the signature information added thereto and can be connected to a communication network such as the Internet or a mobile communication network to transmit the image data processed by the image processor to a communication terminal. That is, the image data processed by the image processor can be stored in the image information server and applied to the application server through the communication network such as the Internet.

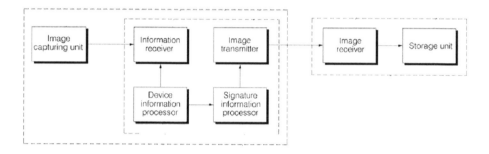

Fig. 2. Block diagram of an image capturing device

The application server provides a variety of application services to a mobile terminal of a communication service subscriber using the communication network at the request of the communication service subscriber. For example, the application server extracts the stored image data and transmits the image data to a mobile terminal at the request of the user of the mobile terminal. The application server can store the image data to which information such as signature information has been added by the image processor or the image information server and transmit the stored image data to the terminal of the communication service substrate to prevent the image data from being illegally copied and edited.

In another embodiment, the image information server can add the signature information or the information on the image capturing unit to the image data captured by the image capturing unit. In this case, the image processor transmits the image data and the information on the image capturing unit received from the image capturing unit to the image information server, and the image information server adds the information on the image capturing unit or the signature information to the image data transmitted from the image processor. The image data processed by the image information server can be applied to the application server through the communication network such as the Internet. This will be explained in more detail later with reference to FIG. 3.

FIG. 2 is a block diagram of the image capturing device and the image information server illustrated in FIG. 1 according to an embodiment of the paper, which shows a case in which the image processor adds the information on the image capturing unit or the signature information to the image data.

Referring to FIG. 2, the image photographing device includes the image capturing unit and the image processor. The image processor includes an information receiver, a device information processor, a signature information processor, and an image transmitter. The image information server includes an image receiver and a storage unit.

The image capturing unit is a device capable of capturing an image, obtaining image data from the captured image and collecting information on the image capturing unit. For example, a CCTV, a digital camera, a video camera or a communication terminal including a camera module can be used as the image capturing unit. The image data obtained by the image capturing unit is transmitted to the image processor and undergoes a data processing operation of adding signature information or the information on the image capturing unit thereto.

The image processor adds the information on the image capturing unit or the signature information to the image data generated by the image capturing unit. The information receiver included in the image processor receives the image data generated by the image capturing unit and the information on the image capturing unit and the device information processor adds the information on the image capturing unit to the image data transmitted from the information receiver. The signature information processor adds the signature information to the image data transmitted from the device information processor and the image transmitter transmits the image data having the information on the image capturing unit or the signature information added thereto to the image information server.

Here, positions of the device information processor and the signature information processor can be changed each other. That is, the signature information can be added first, and then the information on the image capturing unit can be added.

The information receiver receives the image data generated by the image capturing unit and transmits the information to the device information processor. The information on the image capturing unit can include an identifier given to the image capturing unit or information on the place and time at which the image capturing unit obtains the image data. When the image capturing unit is a CCTV, for example, the information on the image capturing unit can include the place where the CCTV is installed and the time when the CCTV records the image. When the image capturing unit is a communication terminal, the information on the image capturing unit can include an identification number given to the communication terminal.

The device information processor adds the information on the image capturing unit to the image data transmitted from the information receiver. That is, the place and time at which the image data is obtained or the identification number of the image capturing unit that captures the image data can be added to the image data as the information on the image capturing unit. The image data can be used as digital proof of a specific event when the place and time at which the image data is captured is added thereto and the source of the image data can be easily detected when the identification number of the image capturing unit is added thereto. The device information processor transmits the image data having the information on the image capturing unit added thereto to the signature information processor.

The signature information processor can embed signature information including a predetermined encryption key in the image data transmitted from the device information processor. According to an embodiment, the signature information processor can add public key based signature information, symmetric key based signature information or public key and symmetric key based signature information to the image data.

The public key based signature information can be generated according to Rivest Shamir Adleman (RSA) algorithm and the symmetric key based signature information can be generated according to Vernam or data encryption standard (DES) algorithm. The symmetric key based signature information requires transmission of an additional secret key and is difficult to authenticate with safety although it is encrypted at a high speed. On the other hand, the public key based signature information does not require transmission of the additional secrete key and is easily authenticated with safety while it is encrypted at a low speed. Accordingly, an algorithm of generating the signature information can be selected according to a degree to which maintenance of security of the image data is required.

When the signature information is added to the image data, the image data can be accessed only using a predetermined decryption key. Accordingly, the possibility that the image data is exposed to hacking or illegal copy according to arbitrary access can be reduced when the signature information is added to the image data. The application server that provides the image data to communication subscribers can provide the decryption key to only an authenticated communication subscriber through a text message to maintain security of the image data.

The signature information can be added to the image data at regular intervals.

The image data having the information on the image capturing unit and the signature information added thereto is transmitted to the image transmitter. That is, at least one of the information on the image capturing unit and the signature information is added to the image data transmitted from the image capturing unit and transmitted to the image transmitter.

The image transmitter transmits the image data received from the signature information processor to the image information server.

The image receiver receives the image data from the image transmitter. The storage unit stores the image data transmitted from the image receiver. The image data transmitted from the image receiver has at least one of the information on the image capturing unit and the signature information added thereto.

The image information server can determine whether the decryption key transmitted from the application server corresponds to the encryption key embedded in the image data, extract the image data stored in the storage unit and transmit the image data to the application server when the application server requests the image information server to transmit the image data through the communication network.

FIG. 3 is a block diagram of the image capturing device and the image information server illustrated in FIG. 1 according to another embodiment of the paper, which shows a case in which the image information server adds the information on the image capturing unit or the signature information to the image data.

Referring to FIG. 3, the image capturing device includes the image capturing unit and the image processor and the image information server includes a receiver, a device information processor, a signal information processor and a storage unit.

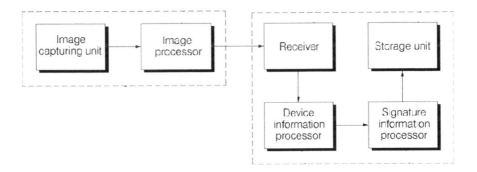

Fig. 3. Block diagram of an image capturing device

The image capturing unit is a device capable of recognizing an object through a lens and a sensor, obtaining image data from the recognized object and collecting information on the image capturing unit. The image processor transmits the image data and the information on the image capturing unit received from the image capturing unit to the image information server.

The receiver included in the image information server receives the image data and the information on the image capturing unit transmitted from the image processor and the device information processor receives the image data and the information on the image capturing unit from the receiver and embeds the information on the image capturing unit in the image data. The signature information processor adds predetermined signature information to the image data having the information on the image capturing unit added thereto and the storage unit stores the image data including the signature information.

The receiver receives the image data and the information on the image capturing unit from the image processor.

The device information processor embeds the information on the image capturing unit in the image data and transmits the image data to the signature information processor. The information on the image capturing unit depends on the type of the image capturing unit. For example, when the image capturing unit is a CCTV, the information on the image capturing unit can include the place where the CCTV is installed and the time when the CCTV obtains the image data. When the image capturing unit is a communication terminal including a camera module, the information on the image capturing unit can include the identification number of the communication terminal.

The source of the image data can be easily searched when the identification number of the image capturing unit is embedded in the image data and the image data can be used as digital proof when the place and time at which the image capturing unit captures the image data is added thereto. The information on the image capturing unit can be recorded in a meta data region of the image data.

The signature information processor can embed signature information including a predetermined encryption key in the image data transmitted from the device information processor.

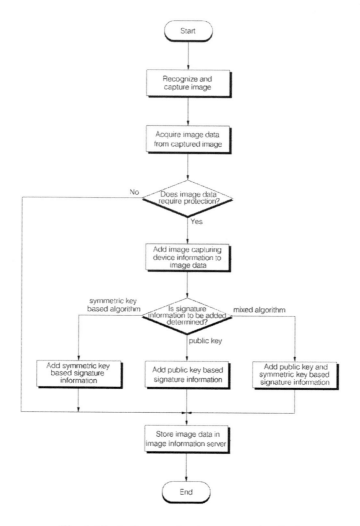

Fig. 4. Block diagram of an image capturing device

The signature information processor can generate the signature information according to a predetermined algorithm and embed the signature information in the image data. The signature information can be generated according to a public key based algorithm or a symmetric key based algorithm. In general, the case that the image information server embeds the information on the image capturing unit and the signature information in the image data requires a data processing speed and available capacity greater than the data processing speed and available capacity required for the case that the image photographing device embeds the information on the image capturing unit and the signature information in the image data. Accordingly, it is desirable to generate the signature information using the public key based algorithm that easily performs safe authentication and does not require an addition secret key to be transmitted while having a low encryption speed. The image data to which the signature information has been added is stored in the storage unit of the image information server.

The signature information can be added to the image data at regular intervals.

The storage unit stores the image data transmitted from the signature information processor. The image data transmitted from the signature information processor has at least one of the information on the image capturing unit and the signature information added thereto.

The image information server can receive a predetermined decryption key from the application server and compare the decryption key with the encryption key included in the image data to determine whether the image data is transmitted when the application server requests the image information server to transmit the image data through the communication network.

FIG. 4 is a flow chart of an image information processing method using the image photographing system illustrated in FIG. 1.

Referring to FIG. 4, the image capturing unit included in the image capturing device recognizes an image and captures the image in operation.

Then, the image capturing unit acquires image data from the image captured in operation. For example, the image capturing unit included in the image capturing device can condense light through a lens and convert the light that has passed through the lens into image data using a CCD sensor.

The image data can include meta data and main data. The main data can include information on the captured image and the meta data can include information that explains the main data.

When the image data is obtained, the image capturing device determines whether it is required to protect the image data in operation. It can be determined whether the image data requires protection according to the type of the image capturing device or setting up by a user who captures the image.

When it is determined that the image data does not require protection in operation, the image data is transmitted to the image information server without undergoing additional image data processing in operation.

When it is determined that the image data requires protection in operation, information on the image capturing device is added to the image data in operation. For example, the information on the image capturing device can correspond to information on the image capturing unit that captures the image data and be added to the image data by the image processor of the image capturing device or the image information server. That is, when the image processor is configured in the form of a module independent from the image capturing unit or has sufficient data processing speed and capacity, the image processor can add the information on the image capturing device to the image data. However, when the image processor do no have sufficient data processing speed and capacity or is configured in the form of software installed in the image capturing unit, the image information server can add the information on the image capturing device to the image data.

When the information on the image capturing device is embedded in the image data in operation, the type of signature information to be added to the image data is determined in operation. The signature information can be generated according to symmetric key based algorithm, public key based algorithm or public key and symmetric key based algorithm and embedded in the image data.

When the signature information according to the symmetric key based algorithm is embedded in the image data in operation, safe authentication is difficult to perform and an additional secret key is required although encryption speed is high due to low algorithm complexity. Accordingly, it is desirable to use the symmetric key based algorithm in consideration of data processing load applied to the image processor in the case where the image processor embeds the signature information in the image data.

When the signature information according to the public key based algorithm is embedded in the image data in operation, safe authentication can be achieved and transmission of an additional secret key is not needed in spite of high algorithm complexity. Accordingly, it is desirable to use the public key based algorithm using the data processing speed and capacity of the image information server, which are greater than those of the image processor when the image information server embeds the signature information in the image data.

When the signature information according to the public key and symmetric key mixed algorithm is embedded in operation, a public key is generated using the public key based algorithm first, and then a data encryption key with respect to the public key based algorithm is generated using the symmetric key based algorithm. Although the public key and symmetric key mixed algorithm can secure safe authentication as compared to the cases where the public key based algorithm and symmetric key based algorithm are used in operations, it is desirable to use the mixed algorithm when the image information server can embed the signature information in the image data because algorithm complexity is high.

The signature information can be added to the image data at regular intervals.

When the signature information has been embedded in the image data in operations, the image data having the signature information added thereto is stored in the image information server in operation. When the application server requests the image information server to transmit the image data through the communication network, the image information server can compare the decryption key transmitted from the application server with the encryption key included in the image data stored in the image information server to determine whether the requested image data is transmitted.

While the paper has been particularly shown and described with reference to exemplary embodiments thereof, it will be understood by those of ordinary skill in the art that various changes in form and details may be made therein without departing from the spirit and scope of the paper as defined by the following claims.

According to the paper, image data can be protected from security infringement such as illegal copy and arbitrary transmission. Furthermore, information on the place and time at which an image is captured is added to the image data such that the image data can be used as digital proof.

4   Conclusion

We have presented a surveillance framework for audio-video surveillance of multi-level secured facilities during normal and pre-envisioned emergencies. This paper relates to an apparatus and a method for processing image information, and more particularly, to an image information processing apparatus and method capable of adding information on an image capturing device and signature information to image data and storing the image data to maintain security of the image data and use the image data as digital proof. However, it is also important to address data integrity and source authentication issues. These issues, along with the development of a complete and comprehensive prototype system are part of our future work.

References

1. Damiani, E., De Capitani di Vimercati, S.: Securing xml based multimedia content. In: 18th IFIP International Information Security Conference (2003)
2. Damiani, E., De Capitani di Vimercati, S., Paraboschi, S., Samarati, P.: Securing XML documents. In: Zaniolo, C., Grust, T., Scholl, M.H., Lockemann, P.C. (eds.) EDBT 2000. LNCS, vol. 1777, pp. 121–122. Springer, Heidelberg (2000)
3. Kodali, N., Wijesekera, D., Farkas, C.: Secrets: A Secure Real-Time Multimedia Surveillance System. In: Proc. of the 2nd Symposium on Intelligence and Security Informatics (2004)
4. Faa'S Nextgen Air Traffic Control System. A CIO's Perspective on Technology and Security Georgetown University Institute for Law, Science, and Global Security & Billington CyberSecurity (February 28, 2011)
5. Damiani, E., De Capitani di Vimercati, S., Paraboschi, S., Samarati., P.: A fine grained access control system for xml documents. ACM Transactions on Information and System Security 5 (2002)
6. Gu, X., Nahrstedt, K., Yuan, W., Wichadakul, D., Xu., D.: An xml-based quality of service enabling language for the web (2001)
7. Kodali, N., Farkas, C., Wijesekera, D.: Enforcing integrity in multimedia surveillance. In: IFIP 11.5 Working Conference on Integrity and Internal Control in Information Systems (2003)
8. Kodali, N., Farkas, C., Wijesekera, D.: Multimedia access contol using rdf metadata. In: Workshop on Metadata for Security, WMS 2003 (2003)
9. Kodali, N., Wijesekera, D.: Regulating access to smil formatted pay-per-view movies. In: 2002 ACM Workshop on XML Security (2002)
10. Kodali, N., Wijesekera, D., Michael, J.B.: Sputers: A secure traffic surveillance and emergency response architecture. Submission to the Journal of Intelligent Transportaion Systems (2003)
11. Pihkala, K., Cesar, P., Vuorimaa, P.: Cross platform smil player. In: International Conference on Communications, Internet and Information Technology (2002)
12. Rutledge, L., Hardman, L., Ossenbruggen, J.: The use of smil: Multimedia research currently applied on a global scale (1999)
13. Rutledge, L., van Ossenbruggen, J., Hardman, L., Bulterman, D.C.A.: Anticipating SMIL 2.0: the developing cooperative infrastructure for multimedia on the Web. Computer Networks 31(11-16), 1421–1430 (1999)
14. Schmidt, B.K.: An architecture for distributed, interactive, multi-stream, multi-participant audio and video. In: Technical Report No CSL-TR-99-781. Stanford Computer Science Department (1999)

An Efficient Intrusion Detection Scheme for Wireless Sensor Networks

Chunming Rong[1], Skjalg Eggen[2], and Hongbing Cheng[1,3]

[1] Department of Electronic Engineering & Computer Science,
University of Stavanger, 4036, Stavanger, Norway
[2] Department of Informatics, Oslo University, Boks 1072 Blindern 0316 Oslo, Norway
[3] College of Computer, Nanjing University of Posts&Telecommunications,
Nanjing, 210003, China

Abstract. As a hot issue, wireless sensor network have gained widely attention. WSNs in general and in nature are unattended and physically reachable from the outside world, they could be vulnerable to physical attacks in the form of node capture or node destruction. These forms of attacks are hard to protect against and require intelligent prevention methods. It is necessary for WSNs to have security measures in place as to prevent an intruder from inserting compromised nodes in order to decimate or disturb the network performance. In this paper we present an intrusion detection algorithm for wireless sensor networks which does not require prior knowledge of network behavior or a learning period in order to establish this knowledge. We have taken a more practical approach and constructed this algorithm with small to middle-size networks in mind, like home or office networks. The proposed algorithm is also dynamic in nature as to cope with new and unknown attack types. This algorithm is intended to protect the network and ensure reliable and accurate aggregated sensor readings. Theoretical simulation results in three different scenarios indicate that compromised nodes can be detected with high accuracy and low false alarm probability.

Keywords: Wireless Sensor Network; Intrusion Detection; Security.

1   Introduction

A wireless sensor network[1] is a network consisting of multiple wireless sensors, also called nodes, which cooperate in sensing some sort of physical or environmental conditions, such as temperature, sound, vibrations, light, movement etc. These networks can consist of everything from 10's of nodes for sparsely populated networks, up to 100's of thousands of nodes in densely populated networks. The individual sensor nodes are small and have limited energy, computational power and memory. This puts some restraints on the applications and protocols which are designed for use in such networks. Wireless sensor network (WSN) is an emerging important research area. The variety in and number of applications is growing in wireless sensor networks. They range from general engineering, environment science, health service, military, etc. Wireless sensor network range from sparse networks with 10's of nodes to populated networks with 1000's, possibly 10000's or 100000's of sensor collecting data from the environments. These wireless sensor nodes are tiny devices with limited energy,

C. Lee et al. (Eds.): STA 2011 Workshops, CCIS 187, pp. 116–129, 2011.

memory, transmission range, and computational power. A base station is usually present in the network, which receives the sensor data from the sensors. Such a base station is usually a powerful computer with more computational power, energy and memory. Currently most research in wireless sensor networks have focused on routing protocols, data aggregation and clustering protocols. However, in most circumstances, wireless sensor networks require some amount of security in order to maintain high survivability and integrity of the network. Many emerging and future applications could require strong security in place, in order to function acceptably.

For military applications, WSNs could be placed behind enemy lines in order to detect and track enemy soldiers and vehicles. In indoor environment, sensor networks could be deployed in order to detect intruders and security violations via a wireless home security system. In office buildings, sensor networks could be deployed as a temperature monitoring/regulating or fire alarm system, etc.

Because WSNs in general and in nature are unattended and physically reachable[2] from the outside world, they could be vulnerable to physical attacks in the form of node capture or node destruction. These forms of attacks are hard to protect against and require intelligent prevention methods. It is necessary for WSNs to have security measures in place as to prevent an intruder from inserting compromised nodes in order to decimate or disturb the network performance.

The rest of the paper is organized as follows, in Section 2, security concern on data access is described and in Section 3, identity based encryption and biometric authentication for secure data access in cloud computing is proposed. In Section 4, we give a detail analysis and experiment results of the proposed approach. Conclusions are drawn in Section 5.

2   Security in Wireless Sensor Network

Security[3] in wireless sensor networks will and should become a hot topic in future WSN research. Security protocols should be developed and deployed in the same time as the routing and aggregation protocols, instead of adding them later on as patches to existing holes in order to create a robust platform to deploy security critical applications. Sensors are often deployed in accessible areas, which add the risk of physical attack. This is why wireless sensor networks pose unique challenges. Security protocols and techniques used in traditional wired networks cannot be applied directly. Due to the scarce resources of wireless sensor networks, sensor nodes are limited in their energy, computation, and communication capabilities. New light weight, multi layered security schemes need to be developed in order to detect and prevent the new forms of attacks these networks are subject to, while using as little as possible of the scarce resources that exist in the networks.

2.1   Threat Models

Attacks come in different sizes and shapes and can be conducted from the inside and the outside of the network. External attackers are attackers that are not legally part of the network. They could be part of another network which is linked to the target network using the same infrastructure or same communication technology. These nodes can carry out attacks without being authorized on the target network. These attackers could also be an outside node, not part of the network, but with jamming or eavesdropping capabilities. Internal attackers are compromised nodes which are authorized on the target network. These nodes are capable of more sophisticated attacks because they are seen as authorized by the network and fellow nodes. As an example they can produce false routing information to the network, and in this manner decimate the network or simply route attractive traffic through itself in order to collect data or maybe choose not to forward the packets consequently disrupting the connection. They could also be placed in strategic positions to report false sensor readings in order to "pollute" picture the sensor data presents.

The attacker can be either active or passive Passive attackers do not disrupt service. Eavesdropping is a good example of a passive attack, in this attack the attacker only listens to traffic that it can intercept. The attacker does not do anything active in the sense of attracting traffic to itself through the network. Active attackers alter data, obscure the operation or cut off nodes from neighbors. An active attacker must be able to inject packets to the network. A good example of an active attack is injecting false routing information to the network in order to decimate the network or route interesting traffic through itself. Active attackers can target the physical layer by jamming the transmissions of wireless signals or by destroying the hardware at certain nodes. Attackers can also target the network layer protocols such as routing by injecting false routing information, and they can target the application layer by injecting false information onto the network. In essence wireless sensor networks need protection on multiple layers in order to make attacks more difficult to carry out.

2.2 Security Requirements

As we have discussed previously, wireless sensor networks are subject to passive eavesdropping as well as active interfering over several layers. This can lead to leaking of sensitive information which is observed by a passive eavesdropper, message contamination or node impersonation by an active attacker. In this section we will examine the security requirements[4] which are essential for a secure, high survivability wireless sensor network.

Confidentiality: Unlike wired networks, an attacker does not need to gain physical access to cables/switches for wiretapping or compromise routers and other nodes in order to conduct eavesdropping. Due to the fact that all signals are transmitted over the air, an attacker can eavesdrop on any node it chooses, as long as it is within radio coverage. In order to prevent information traveling through the network from being compromised, confidentiality is a necessary requirement. Compromised nodes present a serious threat to confidentiality, because by compromising a node, an attacker can gain access to the cryptographic keys used to protect the communication.

Authentication: Authentication is necessary to distinguish legitimate sensor nodes from intruders. Authentication is also necessary in order to determine that the received data came from a authorized sensor node, and not injected by an attacker trying to falsify information.Authentication is also crucial in cluster formations, where sensor nodes form clusters according to location, sensing data etc. Authentication is needed in order to ensure that   nodes inside the cluster only accepts data from authorized nodes in the same cluster.

Integrity: Integrity is an important criterion, as information moving through the network could be altered. Without integrity we would not be able to trust the information received from the sensor network.

Freshness: Freshness is important, because attackers could replay packets to confuse the network. Freshness requirement ensures that only fresh unused data are accepted.

Secure management: Secure management is needed from the base station in order to securely manage distribution of cryptographic keying material, securely form clusters and adding or removing member of clusters.

Availability: Availability is a crucial requirement because it ensures that the services of the network are available at the time it is needed. DoS attacks could disrupt the availability of wireless sensor networks, so it is necessary to ensure that such attacks have as little impact as possible.

3   The Proposed Intrusion Detection Algorithm

In this section, we review some knowledge and then we show the proposed intrusion detection algorithm for wireless sensor networks.

3.1   Preliminary

Our algorithm is based on the proposal of F.Liu, X.Cheng and D.Chen [5], but with some small modifications. While their approach operates with two neighborhoods, our algorithm operates with three. The third neighborhood is a result of the data aggregation scheme, as it introduces the cluster as a separate neighborhood N_1^*,this is needed because of the assumption we make that the subject of the sensor measurements is locked to the region of the cluster, and may differ from the subject of the sensor measurements of the other nodes N_1 and N_2 .Hence the sensor measurements will only be evaluated by the intrusion detection algorithm inside the cluster. The next modification we introduce is a different calculation of the threshold for decision making regarding whether a node is to be regarded as an outlier node or not. We propose a dynamically computed threshold which depends on the actual distribution of the Mahalanobis squared distances [6] We introduce this modification because we assume that it will reduce the number of falsely accused nodes in the network, when no outliers are present.   The third modification we propose is the use of two different values for α in the calculation   when the use of $X_q^2(\alpha)$. We propose to increase the value of α when the thresholds for the cluster neighborhood is to be calculated. We find this necessary as a result of the assumption that the clusters will be very sparse networks with few nodes and, as we will   observe in the simulation results, the false detection probability tends to increase as the neighborhood becomes increasingly sparse. This is a result of the algorithm having less information to calculate the robust statistics of the Mahalanobis squared distances The fourth and final modification I introduce, is the use of MAD as the sample standard deviation in the "False information filtering" protocol [7]. The reason I introduce this modification is that the MAD calculations is less effected by the presence of outliers, as it relies on the median instead of the mean. Hence, it should be more effective in detecting realoutliers.

3.2   The Proposed Intrusion Detection Algorithm

This proposed algorithm uses the anomaly detection technique in detection of intrusion and collects attribute vectors for each node in its neighborhood and comprises a data set consisting of all attribute vectors.

3.2.1   Assumptions

We consider a cluster based sensor network with N sensors uniformly distributed in clusters within the network area. We assume that the data aggregation is only done by the clusterhead of each cluster, and there is only one level of clusters (i.e flat aggregation topology).

All sensors have the same capabilities, and communicate through bidirectional links. We assume sensors in the clusters are burdened with similar workloads and sensor readings. We assume sensors in the close proximity of each other, also in different clusters, behave similarly under normal conditions.

An *insider attacker*[8] is a sensor under the control of an adversary. It has the same network resource as a normal sensor, but its behavior is different compared to others. For example, an insider attacker may drop or broadcast excessive packets, report false readings that deviate significantly from other readings of neighboring sensors, etc. We assume each sensor works in promiscuous mode intermittently and listens for activities of direct neighbors. Which means, sensor x can overhear the message to and from the immediate neighbor x_i no matter whether or not x_i is involved in the communication. The monitoring is conducted intermittently, and x_i's networking behavior is modeled by a q-component attribute vector $f(x_i) = (f_1(x_i), f_2(x_i), ..., f_q(x_i))^T$ with each component describing x_i's activity in one aspect. For each fixed $j(1 \leq j \leq q)$, the component $f_j(x_i)$ represents the actual monitoring result, such as the number of packets being dropped or broadcasted during one monitoring period. Therefore, $f_j(x_i)$ can be continuous or discrete. We assume that the base station has a complete overview of the entire network and controls the initial clustering and cluster head elections. We also assume that the base station controls the adding of new sensor nodes to the network. We assume that there exists a clustering protocol that can handle the reelection of cluster heads based on remaining energy levels, and that this protocol can handle cluster head removal in case of faulty or compromised cluster heads detected by the intrusion detection system. We assume that in any local area of the sensor field, all $f(x_i)$, where x_i's neighbors are normal sensors, follow the same multivariate normal distribution. After an internal adversary is detected, the cluster head of that node should remove it from the cluster and send a report to the base station. In addition, we assume there exists a MAC layer protocol to coordinate neighboring broadcastings such that no collision occurs.

3.2.2   Algorithm Description

In this section we describe the operations of the proposed intrusion detection system.

- **Clustering method**

  Due to the assumption that the base station has a complete overview over the network, prior to deployment, we propose that the base station coordinates the clustering operation, and elects the cluster head of each cluster after the sensor nodes are deployed in the working environment. For the remaining network lifetime the election of new cluster heads are performed within the individual cluster based on remaining reported energy level of nodes. New cluster heads are elected at a timely manner, when the current cluster head fails or if the current cluster head is found to be an insider attacker by the IDS. New nodes are not allowed into the clusters unless the base station explicitly organizes the introduction of the new node.

- **Intrusion detection**

  Our algorithm consists of four main phases with some sub-phases to each main phase. The phases are:

1. Information collection phase

Information collection for N_1 and N_2

Information collection phase for cluster (sensor data)

2. Information filtering phase

Information filtering phase for N_2

3. Outlier detection phase

Outlier detection phase for N_1 and N_2

Outlier detection phase for cluster

4. Voting phase

Voting phase for N_1 and N_2

Voting phase for cluster

The four phases are described as follows:

Information collection phase

a. Information collection in N_1 and N_2

Let $N_1(x)$ denote a bounded closed set of R^2 that can be directly monitored by sensor x. Specifically, $N_1(x)$ is x's one-hop neighborhood.

Let $N(x) \supseteq N_1(x)$ denote another closed set of R^2 that contains the sensor x and additional $n-1$ nearest sensors. The set $N_2(x)$ represents another neighborhood of x, whose selection is determined by the node density in the network. For a dense network, we can simply choose $N_2(x) = N_1(x)$, while for a sparse network, $N_2(x)$ may include x's two-hop neighbors, sensor x monitor the activities of sensors in $N_1(x)$ and express the results using q-component attribute vectors. Then, the observed results are broadcasted within the neighborhood $N_2(x)$, so that sensor x obtains a set $F_1(x)$ of attribute vectors, where $F_1(x) = \{f(x_i) = (f_1(x_1), f_1(x_2), ..., f_1(x_i))^T \,|\, x_i \in N_2(x)\}$, during this phase sensor x will have acquired a dataset which should represent the true activities of the neighborhood $N_2(x)$.

b. Information collection within the cluster

Let $N_1^*(x)$ denote a bounded closed set of R^2 that can be directly monitored by sensor x. Specifically, $N_1^*(x)$ is x's cluster. Sensor x monitors the activities of sensors in $N_1^*(x)$ and express the results using $q-1$- component attribute vectors. Then, the observed results are broadcasted within the neighborhood $N_1^*(x)$ *together with x's sensor reading*, so that sensor x obtains a set $F_2(x)$ of attribute vectors, where $F_2(x) = \{f(x_i) = f_1(x_i), f_2(x_i), ..., f_{q-1}(x_i), f_q(x_i))^T \,|\, x_i \in N_1^*(x)\}$, where $f_q(x_i)$ is the sensor readings of x_i, during this phase sensor x will have acquired a dataset which should represent the true activities of the neighborhood $N_1^*(x)$.

Information filtering phase

After the information collection phase for $N_1(x)$ and $N_2(x)$, sensor x will have acquired a dataset $F_1(x)$ which should represent the true activities of the neighborhood $N_2(x)$. However there may exist insider attackers within the neighborhood $N_1(x)$ which could have modified and forwarded a monitoring result of one or more nodes in the neighborhood $N_2(x) - N_1(x)$. Hence, node x should filter the results as much as possible in order to produce accurate detections of outliers according to the modified *"trust-based information filtering protocol"* proposed by [8]. Based on the direct neighborhood monitoring, sensor x assigns a trust value to each 1-hop neighbor $x_i \in N_1(x)$. The trust value $T(x_i)$ is in the range $\{0, 1\}$, where values closer to 1 indicates a higher trust in that the neighbor x_i is a normal sensor. The consideration is that the sensors in close proximity should behave similarly. This indicates that $T(x_i)$ can be computed according to the degree of x_i's deviation from the neighborhood activities.

a. Insider attacker detection phase for $\tilde{N}_2(x)$

Sensor x detects if any insider attackers exist by studying the data set $\tilde{F}_1(x)$. The detection is conducted by computing the Mahalanobis squared distance of each nodes attribute vector and comparing it to the threshold θ_0 calculated with the chi-squared value $X_q^2(\alpha)$. Sensor x_i is determined to be an insider attacker if the distance is larger than the threshold θ_0. The detection phase is conducted in the following manner:

1. Compute the Orthogonalized Gnanadesikan- Kettenring (OGK) robust estimates of the sample set $\tilde{F}_1(x)$ means μ and covariance matrix Σ as described in Ref[9].

2. Compute the Mahalanobis squared distances of each $f(x_i)|x_i \in \tilde{N}_2(x)$

3. Compute the threshold θ_0 as described in Ref[10].

4. Compare the calculated Mahalanobis squared distances to the threshold θ_0.

5. Mark the nodes with Mahalanobis squared distances larger than the threshold θ_0 as insider attackers. Mark the nodes with Mahalanobis squared distances lesser than the threshold θ_0 as normal nodes.

6. Broadcast the result from previous the step within the neighborhood $N'(x)$, where $\tilde{N}_2(x) \subseteq N'(x)$. Choosing a larger neighborhood $N'(x)$ ensures that more nodes participate in the voting. At the same time node x will receive the results from others and registers the votes about its neighbors in $N_1^*(x)$.

7. After x receives the broadcasted results, it count the number of positive detections for each node in $N_1^*(x)$. If the proportion of positive detections for a node $x_i \in N_1^*(x)$, Then that node is decided to be an insider attacker.

a. If x Is the cluster head; it removes the confirmed insider attacker from the cluster and notifies the base station.

b. If x is a regular cluster node; it waits to see if the cluster head removes the confirmed attacker from the cluster.

c. If the cluster head does nothing, x broadcasts an alarm message within the cluster specifying the confirmed insider attacker. If x receives alarm messages from other nodes in the cluster, it counts the number of received alarm messages.

i. If the majority of the cluster has confirmed the specified node as an insider attacker, the cluster head is deemed as an insider attacker and removed by the cluster nodes. A new node is elected as cluster head and removes the confirmed insider attacker.

ii. If the majority of the cluster has not confirmed the specified node as an insider attacker, x regards the detection as an error.

d. If the cluster head tries to remove a node which is not detected by the other nodes in the cluster as an insider attacker, the other nodes will collude in removing the cluster head in the same manner as c.

b. Insider attacker detection phase for the cluster $N_1^*(x)$

Sensor x detects if any outliers exist by studying the data set $F_1^*(x)$. The detection is conducted by computing the Mahalanobis squared distance of each nodes attribute vector and comparing it to the threshold θ_0 calculated with the chi-squared value $X_q^2(\alpha)$. Sensor x_i is determined to be an insider attacker if the distance is larger than the threshold θ_0. The detection phase is conducted in the following manner:

1. Compute the Orthogonalized Gnanadesikan- Kettenring (OGK) robust estimates of the sample set $F_1^*(x)$ means μ and covariance matrix Σ as described in Ref[9]

2. Compute the Mahalanobis squared distances of each $f(x_i)|x_i \in N_1^*(x)$.

3. Compute the threshold θ_0 as described in Ref[10].

4. Compare the calculated Mahalanobis squared distances to the threshold θ_0.

5. Mark the nodes with Mahalanobis squared distances larger than the threshold θ_0 as insider attackers. Mark the nodes with Mahalanobis squared distances lesser than the threshold θ_0 as normal nodes.

6. broadcast the result from previous the step within the neighborhood $N_1^*(x)$. At the same time node x will receive the results from the other nodes in $N_1^*(x)$

7. After x receives the broadcasted results, it count the number of positive detections for each node in $N_1^*(x)$ .If the proportion of positive detections for a node $x_i \in N_1^*(x)$, Then that node is decided to be an insider attacker.

a. If x Is the cluster head; it removes the confirmed insider attacker from the cluster and notifies the base station.

b. If x is a regular cluster node; it waits to see if the cluster head removes the confirmed attacker from the cluster.

c. If the cluster head does nothing, x broadcasts an alarm message within the cluster specifying the cluster head as an insider attacker.

i. If the majority of the nodes in the cluster broadcast an alarm, the cluster head is deemed as an insider attacker and removed by the cluster nodes.
A new node is elected as cluster head and removes the confirmed insider attacker.

ii. If the majority of the nodes in the cluster broadcast an alarm, x regards the detection as an error.

d. If the cluster head tries to remove a node which is not detected by the other nodes in the cluster as an insider attacker, the other nodes will collude in removing the cluster head in the same manner as c.

4   Simulation

Simulations are preformed in Wolfram Mathematica version 6.0.0 in three different scenarios. Needed package loaded: "MultivariateStatistics`". System: Windows Vista Ultimate SP1Graphs and tables are constructed in Microsoft Excel, Microsoft office 2007.

During this section we denote insider attackers as outliers or outlying nodes. In order to observe how our modifications perform, we compare the results with the results of the original algorithm proposed by Ref[11]. In our simulation results we denote our proposal for the dynamic threshold by θ', and the original proposal for the fixed chi-squared threshold by θ. We will simulate various scenarios in which insider attackers are present, and evaluated the theoretical performance of the algorithm. We have limited the simulations to evaluate the performance of the algorithm on one node $x_i \in N(x)$, with a neighborhood $N_1^*(x)$, consisting of the 1-hop neighbors in the cluster, a neighborhood $N_1(x)$ consisting of all 1-hop neighbors (including the neighbors in the cluster), and a neighborhood $N_2(x)$ consisting of all 1 and 2-hop neighbors, where $N_1^*(x) \in N_1(x) \in N_2(x) \in N(x)$ We will evaluate the algorithm in sparse networks with a cluster neighborhood $N_1^*(x)$ consisting of 5 nodes, and the 1-hop neighborhood $N_1(x)$, consisting of 10 nodes, while the neighborhood $N_2(x)$ consists of 20 nodes. The behavior of each node is modeled by a vector containing q=3 attributes. As stated in Ref[12]., the IDS only examine the sensor readings as an attribute within the cluster. Hence we only evaluate the sensor readings in the simulation scenario for $N_1^*(x)$ we evaluate how our algorithm performs in the neighborhood $N_2(x)$, containing 20 nodes, while the percentage of outliers varies from 0 to 50%. We also evaluate how our proposal for the dynamic threshold θ' performs as opposed to the fixed chi-squared threshold θ proposed by Ref[12], by comparing false alarm probability as well as the detection accuracy for both thresholds θ' and θ in $N_2(x)$ The thresholds θ and θ' are calculated with $X_3^2(0,975)$ for $N_1(x)$ and $N_2(x)$ and $X_3^2(0,9999)$ for $N_1^*(x)$. The reason for increasing the detection threshold in $N_1^*(x)$ is the tendency of the outlier detection algorithm to increase in false alarm probability in sparse networks and no outlying nodes are present. This is a result of the data set $F_2(x_i)$ becoming small, and less information is used in calculating the robust statistics. Figures 1 and 2 below illustrate this tendency. However we can observe that the detection accuracy does not suffers so much from this increase in the threshold, because the robust statistics employed in the calculation of the Mahalanobis distances will still punish outliers by assigning them with significantly larger distances in comparison to the normal nodes.

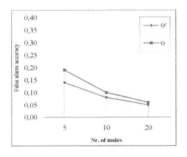
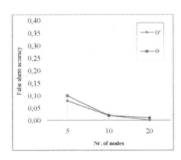

Fig. 1. False alarm accuracy ($x_{3\,(0,975)}^2$)   **Fig. 2.** False alarm accuracy($x_{3\,(0,9999)}^2$)

Figure 1 illustrates the false alarm probability when the number of nodes varies from 5 to 20 with 0 % outliers, and the threshold is calculated with $X_3^2(0,975)$. Figure 2 illustrates the false alarm probability when the number of nodes varies from 5 to 20 with 0 % outliers, and the threshold is calculated with $X_3^2(0,9999)$. Observe that the false alarm accuracy is brought back to an acceptable level with a larger chisquared chisquared percentile, and that the proposed dynamic threshold θ' has a lower false alarm probability than the fixed threshold θ.

In the first scenario there are 20 nodes in the neighborhood $N_2(x)$ of which the percentage of outliers varies from 0 to 50%. We evaluate how our proposal for the dynamic threshold θ' performs as opposed to the fixed chi-squared threshold θ by comparing false alarm probability as well as the detection accuracy for both thresholds.

1.   For normal nodes, the attributes are generated with $\mu_i = (10,50,100)$ and $\sigma_i = (1,5,10)$,

2.   For outliers in one attribute, the attribute values are generated with $\mu_i = (20,100,200)$ and $\sigma_i = (1,5,20)$,

3.   For outliers with three outlying attributes, the attribute values are generated with $\mu_i = (20,100,200)$ and $\sigma_i = (1,5,20)$.

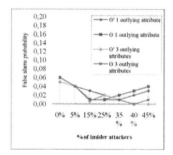   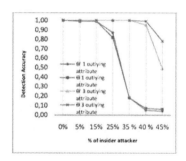

Fig. 3. False alarm probability n = 20   **Fig. 4.** Detection accuracy n = 20

In Figure 3, θ' denotes our proposal for the dynamic threshold, while θ denotes the original proposal for the static threshold. Figure 3 illustrates the false alarm probability when the percentage of outliers varies from 0 to 40% with 20 nodes. Figure 4 illustrates the detection accuracy when the percentage of outliers varies from 0 to 40% with 20 nodes.

In the second scenario there are 10 nodes in the neighborhood $N_1(x)$ of which the percentage ofoutliers varies from 0 to 40%. As in the first scenario we observe how our proposal for thedynamic threshold θ' performs as opposed to the fixed chi-squared threshold θ by comparing the false alarm probability as well as the detection accuracy for both thresholds.

1. For normal nodes, the attributes are generated with $\mu_i = (10,50,100)$ and $\sigma_i = (1,5,10)$,

2. For outliers in one attribute, the attribute values are generated with $\mu_i = (10,50,200)$ and $\sigma_i = (1,5,20)$,

3. For outliers with three outlying attributes, the attribute values are generated with $\mu_i = (20,100,200)$ and $\sigma_i = (1,5,20)$.

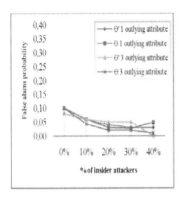

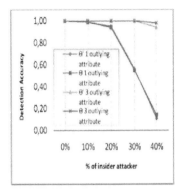

Fig. 5. False alarm probability n = 10   **Fig. 6.** Detection accuracy n =10

Figure 5 illustrates the false alarm probability when the percentage of outliers varies from 0 to 40% with 10 nodes.

Figure 6 illustrates the detection accuracy when the percentage of outliers varies from 0 to 40% with 10 nodes.

In the third scenario there are 5 nodes in the neighborhood $N_1^*(x)$, and the percentage of outliers vary from 0 to 40% (0 to 2 nodes). As in the two previous scenarios, we also here evaluate how our proposal for the dynamic threshold θ' performs as opposed to the fixed chi-squared threshold θ by comparing the number of false positives with the use of both values as thresholds.

However we have chosen to increase the chi-squared threshold to the 0,9999 percentile as a result of the increase of false alarm probability we observed earlier, when the number of nodes in the neighborhood decreases.

1. For normal nodes, the attributes are generated with $\mu_i = (10,50,100)$ and $\sigma_i = (1,5,10)$,

2. For outliers in one attribute, the attribute values are generated with $\mu_i = (10,50,200)$ and $\sigma_i = (1,5,10)$,

3. For outliers with three outlying attributes, the attribute values are generated with $\mu_i = (20,100,200)$ and $\sigma_i = (1,5,10)$.

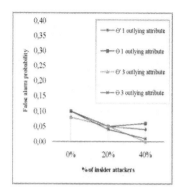 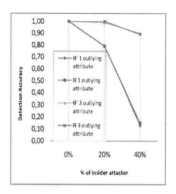

Fig. 7. False alarm probability n = 10   **Fig. 8.** Detection accuracy n =10

Figure 7 illustrates the false alarm probability when the percentage of outliers varies from 0 to 40% with 5 nodes.

Figure 8 illustrates the detection accuracy when the percentage of outliers varies from 0 to 40% with 5 nodes.

All of the simulation results in the three different scenarios indicate that compromised nodes can be detected with high accuracy and low false alarm probability using our proposed intrusion detection algorithm.

5   Conclusions

In this paper we have presented a novel intrusion detection algorithm for wireless sensor networks to act as second line of defense in conjunction with the preventive measures, such as encryption and authentication. We have taken a more practical approach in our assumptions and tried to develop an algorithm for small home or office sensor networks with few nodes.

Our IDS algorithm does not require prior knowledge of network behavior or a learning period in order to establish this knowledge. The proposed algorithm is also dynamic in nature as to cope with new and unknown attack types. By exploiting the similarity in behavior of nodes in proximity of each other, our IDS algorithm can achieve a high detection accuracy and low false alarm probability as indicated by the theoretical simulation study, and by using the OGK robust estimate of the mean for the sensor readings distribution within the clusters, our algorithm can achieve high accuracy of aggregation results, even with smart attackers trying to influence the aggregation result by seeding the aggregator node with slightly outlying sensor readings.

A nice property of the algorithm is that it can be "tailored" to fit various scenarios as a result of the possibility of monitoring different aspects of networking behavior simultaneously. Another nice property of our IDS algorithm is that it has low memory usage, as it doesn't require a specification file for normal behavior or a pattern recognition file for known attacks.

Acknowledgement

This work was supported in part the Natural Science Foundation of Jiangsu normal higher university under Grant No. 09KJB510021.

References

[1] Maronna, R.A., Martin, R.D., Yohai, V.J.: Robust Statistics: Theory and Methods, vol. ch. 6.9.1, pp. 205–208. Wiley Publisher, Chichester (2006)

[2] Hussain, S., Mohamed, M.A., Holder, R., Almasri, A., Shukur, G.: Performance evaluation based on the robust mahluationbis distance and multilevel modelling using two new strategies (February 2008)

[3] Filzmoser, P.: A multiivariate outlier detection method

[4] Alberts, P., Kuhn, M.: Security in ad hoc networks: A general intrusion detection architecture enhancing trust based approaches. In: First International Workshop on Wireless Information Systems, 4th International Conference on Enterprise Information Systems (2002)

[5] Liu, F., Cheng, X., Chen, D.: Insider Attacker Detection in Wirelss Sensor Networks. In: IEEE Proceedings INFOCOM 2007 (2007)

[6] Alqallaf, F.A., Konis, K.P., Douglas Martin, R., Zamar, R.H.: Scalable robust covariance and correlation estimates for data mining. In: ACM SIGKDD 2002, Edmonton, Alberta, Canada, pp. 14–23 (2002)

[7] Ngai E.C.H.: Intrusion Detection for Wireless Sensor Networks. Ph.D. – Term 2 Paper (2005)

[8] Sarma, H.K.D., Manipal, S., Kar, A.: Security Threats in Wireless Sensor Networks (2006)

[9] Newsome, J., Shi, E., Song, D., Perrig, A.: The Sybil Attack in Sensor Networks: Analysis & Defenses (2004)

[10] Staniford-Chen, S., Cheng, S., Crawford, R., Dilger, M.: GRIDS – A Graph Based Intrusion Detection System for Large Networks. In: The 19th National Information Systems Security Conference (1996)

[11] Brutch, P., Ko, C.: Challenges in intrusion detection for wireless sensor networks. In: Proceedings 2003 Symposium on Applications and the Internet Workshops, pp. 368–373 (2003)

[12] Lancaster, H.O.: The chi-squared distribution. Wiley, Chichester (1969)

Policy Based Management for Security in Cloud Computing

Adrian Waller[1], Ian Sandy[1], Eamonn Power[2], Efthimia Aivaloglou[3],
Charalampos Skianis[3], Antonio Muñoz[4], and Antonio Maña[4]

[1] Thales UK, Research and Technology, Reading, UK
[2] TSSG, Waterford Institute of Technology, Waterford, Ireland
[3] Department of Information and Communication Systems Engineering,
University of the Aegean, Samos, Greece
[4] University of Málaga
{adrian.waller,ian.sandy}@thalesgroup.com, epower@tssg.org,
{eaiv,cskianis}@aegean.gr, {amunoz,amg}@lcc.uma.es

Abstract. Cloud computing is one of the biggest trends in information technology, with individuals, companies and even governments moving towards their use to save costs and increase flexibility. Cloud infrastructures are typically based on virtualised environments, to allow physical infrastructure to be shared by multiple end users. These infrastructures can be very large and complex, with many end users, making their configuration difficult, error-prone and time-consuming. At the same time, the fact that diverse end users share the same physical infrastructure raises security concerns, and can lead to a significant impact from misconfiguration or being slow to react to attacks. In this paper, we focus on the use of Policy Based Management techniques to manage cloud infrastructure, identifying the requirements, surveying the state-of-the-art, identifying the challenges and proposing potential solutions.

Keywords: Policy Based Management; Virtualisation; Cloud Computing.

1 Introduction

Cloud computing is one of the biggest trends in Information Technology (IT) today. By enabling data and services to reside on outsourced and shared computing platforms, significant cost savings and more flexibility can be achieved compared to deploying and maintaining one's own infrastructure. For this reason, companies and even governments are moving towards their use, but the potential sensitivity of their data means that cloud providers must manage their large and complex infrastructures in a robust way. Current trends in IT suggest that software systems will become very different from their counterparts today, due to a greater adoption of Service-Oriented Architectures (SOAs), the wider deployment of Software as a Service (SaaS), and the increased use of wireless and mobile technologies [1][2]. In line with these trends, cloud computing platforms are built on top of large-scale, heterogeneous infrastructures that are made available to a large number of end users with very disparate needs. In this setting, the management of non-functional properties such as security and

C. Lee et al. (Eds.): STA 2011 Workshops, CCIS 187, pp. 130–137, 2011.

privacy will be of an increased and critical importance. In this paper we look at the use of Policy Based Management (PBM) techniques to securely manage cloud infrastructure. In section 2, we describe the background to cloud management, the use of PBM in this context, and the requirements for a solution based on PBM. In section 3, we survey the state-of-the-art and identify the key challenges for such a solution. Finally, in section 4 we outline some potential solution approaches and future work that we are pursuing in the PASSIVE project [3].

2 Background and Requirements

The NIST definition of cloud computing [4] refers to a model of resource management that enables convenient access to a shared pool of configurable computing resources that can be easily provisioned and released with minimal effort from the service provider. It goes on to categorise the service models as Infrastructure as a Service (IaaS), Platform as a Service (PaaS) and Software as a Service (SaaS). IaaS allows the provisioning of servers (using virtual machines (VM)), storage and network resources rapidly using either a console interface or an API. The goal of this paper is to outline a component that resides beneath the console/API and spans the underlying resources to enable fine-grained resource control and provide assurance regarding the integrity of the resources being managed. We propose an approach using PBM of the virtualisation resources for cloud providers. In essence, PBM is a technique for specifying the behaviour of a system under different circumstances. The use of policies allows the response of the system to a given situation to be changed quite simply, by changing the policy, without the need to modify the underlying software. In a dynamic system such as presented by cloud computing, the system must handle changing policies as the system runs, which gives rise to a number of issues that have to be solved in order to create an effective system:

- The PBM system has to take in policies covering a variety of topics in addition to security (e.g. resource allocation), and from a variety of sources. These policies may be expressed in multiple languages at different levels of abstraction, and must be translated into a common language for use at the point decisions are made.
- The decision making process using the defined policies must be correct, and the implementation of the policy actually has to happen (i.e. be enforced, and be consistent throughout the cloud). This implies the need for assurance in both the PBM decision making, as well as the selection, reconfiguration and composition of the components that are used to implement the decision.
- Having multiple policies from multiple sources will almost certainly result in a conflict at some stage, which will need to be resolved.
- Last but not least, a PBM system's activities will, of course, need to be performed in such a way so as not to impact on the performance and cost of the cloud.

In the following section, we consider the relevant state-of-the-art and major challenges in developing a PBM solution to meet these requirements.

3 State-of-the-Art and Challenges

3.1 Policy Based Management

A common theme in the state-of-the-art is the use of formal or logic-based methods. Systems with a rigorous formal foundation both for the specifications and for the semantics of authorisation allow rigorous guarantees of the security policies [5]. A problem is that the policy to be applied may actually be a composite of different requirements from different sources. One proposed solution in access control is an algebra with formal semantics which allows a number of simple policies to be combined into the required complex policy [6]. A significant challenge remains to develop a formal policy language which is suitable for expressing policies for a range of areas such as security, access control, monitoring and resource management. Part of the challenge would be to make the language as easy to use as possible without compromising its formal properties, which may require the development of a natural-language front-end with associated translation, such as proposed for the PERMIS editor [7]. Another potential benefit of a formal language would be in making the detection and resolution of conflicts between policies easier, which is in itself a challenge that needs addressing [8]. A recent survey of conflict resolution techniques found them to be mostly unsuitable for live management systems [9]. Algorithms and techniques for conflict detection and resolution are needed both when the policies are being created or edited and when they are being evaluated. The best approach to conflicts may be to avoid them altogether by paying close attention to writing policies to ensure that they cannot conflict (e.g. [9]) but this is unlikely to be a successful strategy in an environment as complex and dynamic as a cloud. Within a cloud, Virtualised Environments (VEs) are typically used, and PBM has been proposed for managing them. Performance for such an approach is a key challenge within VEs, and an example of work in this area is to transfer the security enforcement and program analysis roles to a policy-directed FPGA [10].

3.2 Cloud PBM Architectures

Policies can be enforced at various layers of the systems architecture of cloud computing environments. Policies controlling resource access or inter-VM communication can be enforced at the hypervisor layer, while more fine-grained policies can be enforced at the VM operating system layer. Policies controlling the formation of coalitions of VMs or setting restrictions on their collocation may be defined on a central management VM instead of on each host of the infrastructure. The sHype security architecture [11] enables the enforcement of policy based access control for the shared virtual resources and the information flows between operating systems hosted on common hardware platforms. Following the FLASK access control architecture [12], sHype keeps the access control policy separate from access control enforcement. The policy management function offers the means to create and maintain policy instantiations that are efficient to use at the hypervisor level. The OpenTC architecture [13] enables the definition and enforcement of a wide range of security policies. It includes a trusted virtualisation layer, a Trusted Platform Module (TPM) with strong isolation properties between virtual machines, and a security services layer. Similar to the sHype architecture, the definition and management of the security policies is performed at the application layer, in a dedicated management virtual machine. A layered architecture for access control in virtualised systems running sHype for mandatory access control (MAC) was proposed in [14]. The operating system kernel (SELinux) layer implements MAC to confine data received from the other VMs. The Shamon shared reference monitor [15] that has been proposed for enforcing MAC policies across a distributed set of VMs also implements a layered approach. It enforces MAC reference monitoring from the hypervisor (Xen) and the operating system (SELinux) and IPsec network controls. Shamon offers support for coalitions of VMs on multiple physical hypervisors. In more recent proposed solutions enabling trusted multi-tenant virtual datacentres [16], the notion of coalitions of VMs has evolved to the concept of Trusted Virtual Domains (TVDs) [17] that allow the grouping of VMs that collaborate. The Trusted Virtual Datacentre (TVDc) security solution [16] groups VMs into TVDs and relies on the enforcement of MAC policies by sHype for isolating them. While the architectures that enable the formation of coalitions [15] or TVDs [16] allow the enforcement of fine-grained policies for controlling cooperation among the coalitions, one challenge that remains is the flexible organisation and management of the coalition members which could be useful for scenarios with frequent VM membership changes, such as for cloud infrastructures hosting virtual desktops. An additional challenge for controlling VM placement and collocation is to enable the definition of placement rules based on both static and dynamic attributes of the hosts and the VMs, and the security characteristics supported by the platform.

3.3 Assurance in Decision Making

To achieve high assurance, policies need to be precisely and unambiguously specified, and accurately implemented. Policies may also conflict, and therefore these conflicts need to be detected and resolved if correct behaviour is to be observed. The ideal approach to achieve this would be the use of a logic-based formal language, allowing the correctness of the policies to be mathematically proven. Unfortunately, there appear to be no readily available formal policy languages suitable for an environment such as cloud computing, where policies cover a range of activities from access control to resource management. DHARMA [18] is a formal language, but since it is principally a reference monitor it is not really suitable or easily adaptable to meet these needs. More general purpose policy languages such as APPEL [19] and PONDER [20] do exist, as do more specialised ones such as XACML [21] for access control or UCON [22] for usage control. However, none of these are formal. Another difficulty with formal languages, or indeed any language that can be implemented in an automated policy system, is that they require a lot of skill to be used effectively, which is unlikely to be found in a user who is not a programming or technical expert (or, indeed, a formal methods expert). A potential solution would be a natural language front-end as the interface to the user. This would, by necessity, have a restricted vocabulary and grammar and would need to be translated into the underlying machine-readable language. Ideally, there would only be one translation step, built on formal methods, that would generate machine instructions from user input and be provably correct. This is unlikely to be realised in the short-term and intermediate stages will be needed, with a consequent greater difficulty in showing that the policy has been correctly interpreted and enforced. Verification and validation of the low-level policies is also needed, and should include detecting and resolving conflicts between policies. In the absence of a formal language with its inherent property of proof of correctness, testing will have to be more rigorous and more extensive to provide this. Even so, it is not possible to provide the same level of confidence with any realistic testing regime, although this approach can be less expensive as it does not require specialist staff to be available.

3.4 Software Security Certification

In addition to assurance in policy decision making, assurance in the security and privacy properties of the modified system resulting from a policy decision is also needed. In principle, certification appears a plausible, practical and well-established solution for increasing users' trust and confidence, where a certificate attests security properties of entities (software and hardware products, systems and services). However, looking more closely at the specific characteristics of cloud computing scenarios, we see that current software system certification schemes are not appropriate. Software certification is currently based on evaluation processes carried out by experts following pre–defined and publicly accepted criteria that analyse the software using different techniques, ranging from testing to formal modelling. These processes are mostly manual and require considerable amounts of effort, and thus time and investment. The relying party of a certificate needs not only to trust the authenticity of the certificate, but also the experts, and the certification scheme. This trust is established by the scheme being run by accredited authorities, the accreditation of the experts themselves, and the certificate being officially approved. In current schemes certificates are awarded to traditional, monolithic software systems and become invalid when a system performs run time selection and composition of components [23]. However, in a cloud computing scenario, several independently produced applications may coexist on a virtualised environment, which in turn is supported by a distributed computing architecture. Clearly, this approach of providing certificate–based assurance of security does not scale well to scenarios that are characterised by dynamism, high degrees of distribution, and ever–changing environments. The main reasons for this are that existing schemes produce certificates and explanations intended for human users and aim to help them decide whether or not to use/buy the system. Also, certificates refer to a particular version of the product or system. In general, changes in the system structure require a process of re–certification. Certification schemes like the Common Criteria (CC)[24] contain an assurance class on flaw remediation, but it is rarely used and does not provide methodological support for analysing the security impact of system changes. An additional challenge is the need to cover both individual software services and the environment in which they operate at execution time. Some support exists in CC to deal with composite systems (i.e. derive a system certification from certificates of its components), but a perfect match between assumptions and component guarantees is required, which is still too restrictive to be practical in our scenarios. An important aspect of cloud scenarios is dynamism. Unfortunately, current software certification schemes do not support dynamic replacement of components or runtime binding of systems. Even in CC v3.1 [24], changing components requires new evaluator/expert interaction and repetition of (or parts of) the evaluation and certification. Moreover, current certificates lack a machine-readable, semantics-aware format for expressing security properties. Thus, they cannot be used to support and automate run time security assessment, although this issue of providing machine-readable versions of security certifications is being addressed in the ASSERT4SOA project [25]. As a result, today's certification schemes simply do not provide, from an end user perspective, a reliable way to assess the trustworthiness of a composite application in the context where (and at the moment when) it will be actually executed.

4 Future Work and Acknowledgements

The work in this paper arises from the PASSIVE project [3]. PASSIVE is developing a policy-based security architecture for cloud computing which will address many of the challenges raised in this paper. PASSIVE is a Specific Targeted Research Project (STREP) supported by the European 7th Framework Programme, Contract number ICT-2.1.4-257644, Project starting date 1st June 2010 (duration 24 months).

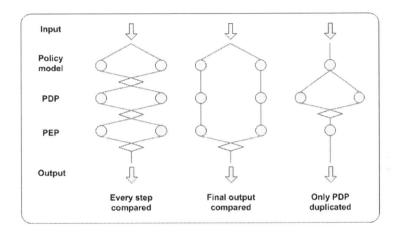

Fig. 1. Options for multiple redundant implementations in PBM

One approach we are pursing to providing high-assurance is the provision of multiple independent implementations of important components, whose outputs are compared and must agree. Unanimity will ensure that only the correct output is obtained or an error condition will be raised. Majority voting can allow continued operation, albeit with a perhaps less than ideal output with the discrepancy flagged for urgent investigation. The implementations need to be as independent as possible (e.g. carried out by different teams possibly using different programming languages), giving much greater confidence that the outcome is correct. Potentially, the whole section between the user natural language-based interface and the resulting machine instructions (i.e. the whole policy system) could be done this way. This would suggest a need for multiple policy languages in addition to the code that makes decisions based on the policies, and that which enforces those decisions. There are different ways of exploiting the duplication, the two extremes being that the different implementations run separately and only the final outcomes are compared or that the outcomes of each step are compared as the process runs. The diagram illustrates this as well as the situation with only one part duplicated (the Policy Decision Point, (PDP)).

Another approach we will take is the so-called 'policy continuum' [26]. This approach provides a means to represent the various constituency languages needed to support security policy definition at various levels. It also supports the mapping of high-level goals to low-level tasks and actions. This mapping is supported by the use of a common information model, which seeks to represent, in an abstract way, the behaviour and characteristics of a system without regard to details such as platform, language etc. Such information models have been used and demonstrated in projects such as AutoI [27] where virtual infrastructure and associated management policies were modelled and used to manage, monitor and orchestrate Internet services. The information model allows data to be harmonised between constituencies. This permits access to information gathered from outside of the constituency to be associated with current constituency entities. This, in turn, allows more useful information to be inferred and used. An example here would be the use of intrusion detection system data on a given node to decide how resources are allocated in surrounding nodes by provisioning systems. This ability for common information sharing between diverse components such as those described above in the duplicated decision point approach would support such a solution. Both components could have their output represented in common terms and thus compared or prioritised. PASSIVE is currently designing a solution and a demonstrator will be available at the end of the project (Summer 2012).

References

1. Software as a Service Market Will Expand Rather than Contract Despite the Economic Crisis, IDC Finds (January 2009),
   http://www.idc.com/getdoc.jsp?containerId=prUS21641409
   (accessed March 2010)
2. Robinson, J.J.: Demand for software-as-a-service still growing (May 2009),
   http://www.information-age.com/channels/
   commsand-networking/perspectives-and-trends/1046687/
   demand-forsoftwareasaservice-still-growing.thtml
   (accessed March 2010)
3. PASSIVE project, http://ict-passive.eu/
4. http://csrc.nist.gov/groups/SNS/cloud-computing/ (July 10, 2009)
5. Chapin, P.C., Shalka, C., Wang, X.S.: Authorization in Trust Management: Features and Foundations. ACM Comput. Surv. 40(3), Article 9 (August 2008)
6. Bonatti, P., De Capitani Di Vimercati, S., Samarati, P.: An Algebra for Composing Access Control Policies. ACM Trans. Inf. Syst. Secur. 5(1), 1–35 (2002)
7. Inglesant, P., Sasse, M.A., Chadwick, D., Shi, L.L.: Expressions of Expertness: The Virtuous Circle of Natural Language for Access Control Policy Specification. In: Symposium On Usable Privacy and Security (SOUPS) 2008, Pittsburgh, PA, USA, July 23-25 (2008)
8. Dunlop, N., Indulska, J., Raymond, K.: Methods for Conflict Resolution in Policy-Based Management Systems. In: Proceedings of the 7th International Conference on Enterprise Distributed Object Computing (EDOC 2003), pp. 1–12 (2003)

9. Chadha, R.: A Cautionary Note about Policy Conflict Resolution. In: Proc. IEEE Military Comms Conference 2006, MILCOM 2006, Washington, DC, October 23-25 (2006)
10. Bratus, S., Locasto, M.E., Ramaswamy, A., Smith, S.W.: Traps, Events, Emulation, and Enforcement: Managing the Yin and Yang of Virtualization-based Security. In: VMSEC 2008, Fairfax, Virginia, USA, pp. 49–58 (October 31, 2008)
11. Sailer, R., Valdez, E., Jaeger, T., Perez, R., van Doorn, L., Griffin, J.L., Berger, S.: sHype: Secure Hypervisor Approach to Trusted Virtualized Systems. IBM Research Report RC23511, 2005 (2005)
12. Spencer, R., Smalley, S., Loscocco, P., Hibler, M., Andersen, D., Lepreau, J.: The flask security architecture: system support for diverse security policies. In: Proceedings of the 8th Conference on USENIX Security Symposium, vol. 8 (1999)
13. Kuhlmann, D., Landfermann, R., Ramasamy, H. V., Schunter, M., Ramunno, G., Vernizzi, D.: An Open Trusted Computing Architecture - Secure Virtual Machines Enabling User-Defined Policy Enforcement. OpenTC report, 2006 (2006)
14. Payne, A.D., Sailer, R., Cáceres, R., Perez, R., Lee, W.: A layered approach to simplified access control in virtualized systems. ACM SIGOPS Operating Systems Review 41(7), 12–19 (2007)
15. McCune, J.M., Jaeger, T., Berger, S., Caceres, R., Sailer, R.: Shamon: A System for Distributed Mandatory Access Control. In: Computer Security Applications Conference, pp. 23–32 (2006)
16. Berger, S., Cáceres, R., Pendarakis, D., Sailer, R., Valdez, E., Perez, R., Schildhauer, W., Srinivasan, D.: TVDc: Managing Security in the Trusted Virtual Datacenter. ACM SIGOPS Operating Systems Review 42(1), 40–47 (2008)
17. Bussani, A., Griffin, J.L., Jansen, B., Julisch, K., Karjoth, G., Maruyama, H., Nakamura, M., Perez, R., Schunter, M., Tanner, A., van Doorn, L., Herreweghen, E.V., Waidner, M., Yoshihama, S.: Trusted Virtual Domains: Secure foundation for business and IT services, Research Report RC 23792, IBM Research (November 2005)
18. Chander, A., Dean, D., Mitchell, J.C.: A distributed high assurance reference monitor. In: Zhang, K., Zheng, Y. (eds.) ISC 2004. LNCS, vol. 3225, pp. 231–244. Springer, Heidelberg (2004)
19. Montangero, C., Reiff-Marganiec, S., Semini, L.: Logic–Based Detection of Conflicts in APPEL Policies. In: Arbab, F., Sirjani, M. (eds.) FSEN 2007. LNCS, vol. 4767, pp. 257–271. Springer, Heidelberg (2007)
20. Damianou, N., Dulay, N., Lupu, E., Sloman, M.: Ponder: A Language for Specifying Security and Management Policies for Distributed Systems. The Language Specification Version 2.3. Imperial College Research Report DoC 2000/1 (October 20, 2000)
21. OASIS website (February 2011), http://www.oasis-open.org
22. Zhang, X., Parisi-Presicce, F., Sandhu, R., Park, J.: Formal Model and Policy Specification of Usage Control. ACM Trans. Inf. Syst. Secur. 8(4), 351–387 (2005)
23. Alvaro, A., de Almeida, E.S., de Lemos Meira, S.R.: Software component certification: A survey. In: Proc. of 31st EUROMICRO Conference on Software Engineering and Advanced Applications, Porto, Portugal (August–September 2005)
24. Common Criteria for Information Technology Security Evaluation, ISO/IEC Standard 15408, version 3.1(2008)
25. ASSERT4SOA Project (March 2011), http://www.assert4soa.eu/
26. Davy, S., Jennings, B., Strassner, J.: The Policy Continuum - A Formal Model. In: Proc. Modelling Autonomic Communications Environments, Multlicon, Multicon, Berlin. Lecture Notes, vol. 6, pp. 65–78 (2007)
27. AUTOI ICT-216404, Deliverable D4.1 - Initial Management Plane (December 2008)

Management of Integrity-Enforced Virtual Applications

Michael Gissing, Ronald Toegl, and Martin Pirker

Institute for Applied Information Processing and Communications (IAIK),
Graz University of Technology, Inffeldgasse 16a, A-8010 Graz, Austria
m.gissing@tugraz.at,
{ronald.toegl,martin.pirker}@iaik.tugraz.at

Abstract. The security of virtualization platforms can be improved by applying
trusted computing mechanisms such as enforcing the integrity of the hypervisor.
In this paper we build on a recently proposed platform that extends this trust on
to applications and services. We describe a process that covers the fully
integrity-enforcing life-cycle of a trusted virtual application. Our architecture
allows applications the safe transition between trusted states, even in case of
updates of the hypervisor. We also detail the technical realization in our
prototype implementation.

Keywords: Trusted Computing, Virtualization, Integrity Enforcement.

1 Introduction

Commodity PC platforms [1] now provide *hardware virtualization*; under the control
of a singleton *hypervisor* this enables the creation, execution and hibernation of
partitions (i.e. virtual machines), each hosting a guest operating system and the virtual
applications building on it.

Another extension of the PC architecture, the concept of *Trusted Computing*, offers
trust anchors such as the *Trusted Platform Module (TPM)* [19] and chipset extensions
for safer computing [8]. These hardware primitives can be used to determine the
software configuration of a system. A platform service may then collect and report
expressive information on its configuration - which is an important precondition to
leverage integrity enforcement in distributed systems.

The combination of virtualization and Trusted Computing offers complementary
benefits. The TPM can be used to ensure the hypervisor code is free from
manipulations at startup, or to detect sophisticated attacks like Blue Pill[1] that take over
control of a platform in a way that software detection mechanisms alone cannot
identify. Virtualization on the other hand offers a natural separation of different *virtual
applications*, thus providing a smaller attack surface, allowing the isolation of security
critical tasks or simplified handling of complex software stacks. Accordingly, a
number of security-oriented virtualization platforms have been proposed or (partially)
prototyped using specialized hypervisors to enable software configuration reporting

---

[1] http://blackhat.com/presentations/bh-usa-06/
BH-US-06-Rutkowska.pdf

C. Lee et al. (Eds.): STA 2011 Workshops, CCIS 187, pp. 138–145, 2011.

[12,4], to protect code integrity [13,7,16] or to isolate critical code at runtime [7,17,5,11]. This protection can also be extended to federated virtual machines in trusted virtual data centers [2,3].

Such *trusted virtualization platforms* therefore offer powerful security features to virtual applications that go beyond what general purpose virtualization solutions require. However, to leverage these advantages, novel processes and mechanisms for the management of virtual applications throughout their life-cycle are needed.

In this paper, we describe how virtual application images are imported, stored, initialized, run, shut-down and removed from the integrity-enforcing and fully isolating acTvSM trusted virtualization platform [14,15,18]. We report on a practical platform-operator oriented process and also outline our implementation details.

The remainder of this paper is organized as follows. In Section 2 we give a short overview on the acTvSM platform, its Trusted Computing integration and its capabilities. Section 3 describes the life-cycle management of a trusted virtual application on the acTvSM platform, while Section 4 concentrates on the update process of the base system layer. Section 5 summarizes the components and integration of our implementation. We conclude in Section 6.

2   acTvSM: A Trusted Virtualization Platform

2.1 Overview

The acTvSM platform [14,15,18] is a prototype implementation of a Trusted Computing enriched platform management architecture, which enforces integrity guarantees to itself as a software platform and the applications and the services it hosts. The platform takes advantage of the Linux Kernel-based Virtual Machine (KVM) hypervisor, which is operated in a complex security configuration, which we call *Base System*.

A secure boot process using Intel's *Trusted Execution Technology (TXT)* [8] ensures execution of a known-good hypervisor configuration via the GETSEC[SENTER] CPU instruction that guarantees a defined, secure[2] system state. During boot a *chain-of-trust* is built by measuring the relevant components, such as boot-loader and OS kernel, into the TPM's *Platform Configuration Registers (PCRs)*. A *measurement m* in this context is a 160 bit SHA-1 hash which is stored in PCR i using the one-way *extend* operation: $extend_i(m) = PCR_i^{t+1} = SHA-1(PCR_i^t//m)$.

For a PCR's initial power-on state ($t = 0$) we write *initial$_i$* and for *several m$_j$* $j = 1..n$ we write $extend_i\{m_j, .., m_n\}$. Note that this operation is the only way to alter the content of a PCR and depends on the previous value. To achieve a certain value in a PCR the same measurements have to be extended in the same order, otherwise the result would be different. The TPM also serves as access-controlled, autonomous storage for two policies which are enforced. First, *a Launch Control Policy (LCP)*, which is evaluated by an *Authenticated Code Module (ACM)* provided by Intel, defines which secure boot loader is allowed to run as a so *called Measured Launch Environment (MLE)* [9]. Second, a *Verified Launch Policy (VLP)*, which is evaluated

---

[2] Note that the TXT implementation in the current generation of hardware is still susceptible to certain attacks, e.g. [20] or [21]. We assume this will improve as the technology matures.

by the secure boot loader, defines which subsequent Kernel and initial ram disk are allowed to be loaded and executed. Furthermore, mechanisms in the Intel TXT chipset offer isolated partitions of main memory and restrict *Direct Memory Accesses (DMA)* I/O to defined areas.

Based on these PCR measurements access to data can be restricted to a known-good platform state. This can be achieved using the TPM's ability to seal data. Sealing and unsealing means to encrypt – respectively decrypt – data inside the TPM with a key which is only available inside the TPM and where usage of the key is restricted to a defined PCR configuration. Under the assumption that the TPM is a tamper-resistant device this is a robust way to guarantee that sealed data can only be accessed under a predefined platform state. An important novel aspect of the acTvSM architecture is that the measurements are predictable so the PCR values can be calculated *a priori* and data can be sealed to *future* trusted states after a planned configuration update.

One of the platform's peculiarities is a structured set of file systems. For instance, measurements of the base system are taken over its whole file system. To achieve the same measurement on every boot we use a read-only file system. Comparable to a Linux Live-CD, an in-memory file system is merged to form the runtime file system. Services and applications are stored on encrypted logical volumes. For each volume, a set of key slots allows to assign different access keys, which are sealed to trusted platform states. Additional fall-back keys allow back-up and migration by authorized administrators, even if a TPM should fail. Images can be read-only (therefore measurable) or mutable.

2.2 Platform Trust State Transitions

After finishing the boot process the acTvSM platform runs in *Update Mode*, in which a remote maintenance shell can be started. In this mode the platform is in a well-defined known-good configuration. This allows access to all data which were sealed to this configuration. When a *virtualized application*, i.e. a partition with an autonomous software configuration (OS, libraries etc. up to networked services), gets started from its encrypted volume(s), the platform enters *Application Mode*. In this mode further access to data sealed to the Update Mode is blocked.

Beginning from platform power on, the system transits between four system states S_{BIOS}, S_{boot}, S_{update} and $S_{application}$. The BIOS state covers whatever happens before the boot loader calls GETSEC[SENTER]. As this instruction always returns in a trusted state, we need not consider S_{BIOS} any further. Later in the boot process the S_{boot} state is reached where ACM and MLE have been measured and the secure boot loader has already launched the kernel and the code contained in the initial ramdisk is in charge.

More formally,

$$S_{boot} := \{ \; initial_{14}, initial_{15},$$
$$extend_{18}\{\textbf{secure boot loader, linux kernel}\},$$
$$extend_{19}\{\textbf{initrd}\}\}.$$

Before control is handed over to the base system it is measured, so the *update* state is produced by extending this measurement:

$$S_{update} := \{S_{boot}, extend_{14}\{\texttt{base system}\}\}.$$

So S_{update} represents the PCR values when the platform has reached Update Mode and is fully functional. Finally, $S_{application}$ is defined to be different from S_{update} by extending with a random token and reflects the configuration of Application Mode:

$$S_{application} := \{S_{update}, extend_{15}\{\texttt{random}\}\}.$$

3 Management of Applications

To make a virtualization platform a trusted one, the management of applications has to consider additional requirements. The implications of measuring for integrity and sealing to states can be explained by looking at the detailed lifecycle of a virtualized application.

Installation. An application image may be generated without restrictions using conventional tools, either locally or on some remote host. Therefore, we only need to describe the mechanisms that perform the installation of it into the trusted platform. To ensure security-at-rest, on installing an application all data on the target platform has to be stored in an encrypted way, including temporary files. Since the Base System has no persistent R/W storage, we allocate extra encrypted temporary disk space to transfer the application from the network. When all necessary data is present on the target, the actually needed disk space is allocated. More specifically, two volumes, the *Application Specific Logical Volume (ASLV)* and the *Application Specific Configuration Logical Volume (ASCLV)* are allocated and encryption is set up for these volumes. The image of the application is written to the ASLV while the configuration file of the application is copied to ASCLV. If needed, an application can also use a second virtual hard disk. This allows for example to split an application into a read-only (measureable binaries) and a writable (data) part. The encryption keys to the freshly created volumes are sealed to the current platform state and stored in a key store. For example the key k_{ASLV} which encrypts ASLV is sealed to state S_{update}. The sealing process during installation guarantees that the application can only be started if the platform is in the correct state. Obviously, all temporary data has to be removed safely after the installation process to prevent unintended access to the application.

Execution. Launching an application is the next step. We outline this process in Figure 1. First, in S_{update}, the sealed keys of all ASCLVs are unsealed and the volumes are decrypted and mounted into the system's file system hierarchy. The associated configuration files are evaluated and based on *Application Group Configurations (AGCs)* files, the applications which shall be started are determined. Afterwards, the ASCLVs are un-mounted and the cryptographic keys belonging to them are removed from memory. Then the ASLVs of individual applications are mounted using the proper sealed keys. Only within S_{update}, a `ssh` daemon is active in the hypervisor to allow maintenance operations. This restriction is ensured by sealing the ssh private key to this state. Before the first application is actually launched, a randomly chosen value gets extended to a PCR. This marks the transition from S_{update} to $S_{application}$ and prevents access to data which was sealed to S_{update}.

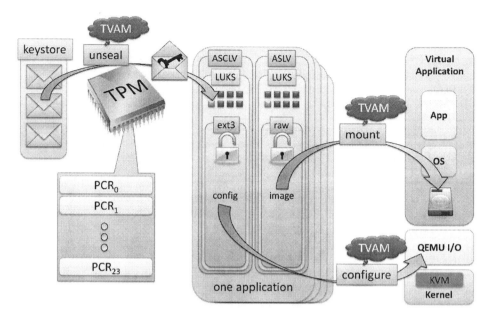

Fig. 1. To launch an application at first the encryption keys for the logical volumes ASCLV and ASLV have to be unsealed using the TPM, which holds the proper platform configuration in its PCRs. Afterwards the keys can be used to decrypt the volumes. The configuration contained by ASCLV's file system is evaluated and the virtual application is set up properly. The content of ASLV is provided to the application as its hard disk.

Consequently, even if an attacker manages to break the security perimeter of one virtual application, she will not be able to read or manipulate other applications' disk storage. Upon the mode transition, the `ssh` daemon is stopped and the in-memory `ssh` server keys are deleted as well. In an optional step, the chain-of-trust to the virtual application can be extended by a measurement of the ASLV before it is mounted.

$$S_{service} := \{ S_{application}, \; extend_{13}\{\texttt{application image}\} \}.$$

Together with the ability to use the physical TPM, a virtualized application can perform services relying on this chain-of-trust. According to the configuration, the network interfaces for the virtual application are set up and the application is finally launched.

Update. A virtual application update is possible in two ways. The first is to update the application while it runs with the tools provided by the application itself. For example, a virtual Linux system can be easily updated using its package management system. When no administrative connection is possible to the application or it uses a read only image, then the platform provides a facility to exchange the whole content of the ASLV. Changing the configuration which is stored in the ASCLV can be done by either editing the existing file or replacing it with a new one. The platform will mount the file system ASCLV on request. Besides the application self-update these operations are only possible in S_{update} because access to the sealed keys is needed. Note that the state of the platform does not change when an application gets updated.

Removal. When an application should be removed from the platform, primarily the corresponding cryptographic keys must be removed. Additionally the allocated disk spaces ASLV and ASCLV have to be freed.

4 Base System Update

An update to the hypervisor layer is more complex as all application keys directly depend on its state. Hypervisor updates are therefore a major functionality in the management of virtual applications. Due to the in-memory file system structure, the administrator can change the system at will in Update Mode, but all changes will be void after the next power cycle. As after every reboot the acTvSM platform should reach a known-good-state, the administrator needs a functionality to freeze a current, ephemeral and (by her responsibility) trustworthy system state. We denote this future states S'_{update} and S'_{boot} respectively. However, the TPM still holds the measurements for S_{update} that cannot be replaced without a platform reset.

Instead, we need to define a new chain-of-trust that will end in trusted platform state S'_{update} after reboot. To this end, at first a new base-system image gets created and hashed. With this data, the future values of the PCRs are precalculated. This state prediction allows sealing keys to the future state S'_{update} before the new base-system version was ever booted. Now the new image is copied to a newly allocated *Base System Logical Volume (BSLV)*, encryption is enabled and the corresponding key is sealed to S'_{boot}. The next step is to update the VLP in the TPM so that the secure boot loader will accept the new configuration during secure boot. Next, a new entry in the boot loader configuration is created. At this point the new system would be able to boot into the new system state, but access to the installed applications would not be possible. So all the cryptographic keys, including those for application images, have to be unsealed from S_{update} and sealed to the new platform state S'_{update}. At last all temporary data is safely discarded. This ensures a trustworthy transition between trusted states.

5 Implementation

The acTvSM platform extends a conventional Linux system with security and management features. The boot loader GRUB loads the secure boot loader tboot[3], which is Intel's prototype implementation of an MLE. The base system consists of a *Debian GNU/Linux* lenny with a version 2.6.32 Linux kernel. Virtualization is done using the *Kernel-based Virtual Machine (KVM)* [10] hypervisor and *QEMU* I/O Emulation. For hard disk space management Logical Volume Manager (LVM)[4] is used. Encryption of logical volumes is done by the dm-crypt subsystem of Linux, while the keys are handled with *Linux Unified Key Setup (LUKS)* [6]. LUKS authorization data is stored as data blobs sealed to the TPM which can be stored on an unencrypted file system. TPM operations are implemented with *jTpmTools* and *jTSS* from IAIK's "Trusted Computing for Java" project.

---

[3] http://tboot.sourceforge.net/
[4] http://sourceware.org/lvm2/

Management of applications is done by our *Trusted Virtual Application Manager (TVAM)*. It is written in the Ruby programming language and consists of about 3200 lines of code. TVAM is the main management component of the acTvSM platform which glues all parts together. It utilizes the other components to set up disk space, launch virtual applications and manage base system updates. TVAM is an interactive command line tool and provides all necessary management commands to the administrator. It is designed to make the work of the platform operator as easy as possible, so for example the simple command `tvam seal` is sufficient to perform a base system update as described in Section 4.

6   Conclusions

In this paper we describe the interaction of a trusted virtualization platform with services running on top of it. We outline which TPM-measured states occur in the boot process and how structured file systems can help accomplish this task. As our main contribution, we describe the life-cycle of virtual applications on such an integrity-enforcing platform. We cover the installation, execution and removal of application images and also consider how updates can be performed. Finally, we report on our proof-of-concept implementation[5].

In future work we will consider concrete use cases of the architecture such as cloud computing, electronic healthcare or secure key stores.

References

1. Adams, K., Agesen, O.: A comparison of software and hardware techniques for x86 virtualization. In: Proc. of the 12th International Conference on Architectural Support for Programming Languages and Operating Systems. ACM, San Jose (2006)
2. Berger, S., Cáceres, R., Pendarakis, D., Sailer, R., Valdez, E., Perez, R., Schildhauer, W., Srinivasan, D.: TVDc: managing security in the trusted virtual datacenter. SIGOPS Oper. Syst. Rev. 42(1), 40–47 (2008)
3. Catuogno, L., Dmitrienko, A., Eriksson, K., Kuhlmann, D., Ramunno, G., Sadeghi, A.R., Schulz, S., Schunter, M., Winandy, M., Zhan, J.: Trusted virtual domains – design, implementation and lessons learned. In: Chen, L., Yung, M. (eds.) INTRUST 2009. LNCS, vol. 6163, pp. 156–179. Springer, Heidelberg (2010)
4. Coker, G., Guttman, J., Loscocco, P., Sheehy, J., Sniffen, B.: Attestation: Evidence and trust. Information and Communications Security, 1–18 (2008)
5. EMSCB Project Consortium: The European Multilaterally Secure Computing Base (EMSCB) project (2004), http://www.emscb.org/
6. Fruhwirth, C.: New methods in hard disk encryption. Tech. rep., Institute for Computer Languages, Theory and Logic Group. Vienna University of Technology (2005)
7. Garfinkel, T., Pfaff, B., Chow, J., Rosenblum, M., Boneh, D.: Terra: A virtual machine-based platform for trusted computing. In: Proc. SOSP. ACM Press, New York (2003)
8. Grawrock, D.: Dynamics of a Trusted Platform: A Building Block Approach. Intel Press, Richard Bowles (2009) ISBN No. 978-1934053171

---

[5] Prototype available for download from http://trustedjava.sf.net

9. Intel Corporation: Intel Trusted Execution Technology Software Development Guide (December 2009),
   `http://download.intel.com/technology/security/downloads/3151 68.pdf`
10. Kivity, A., Kamay, V., Laor, D., Lublin, U., Liguori, A.: kvm: the Linux Virtual Machine Monitor. In: Proceedings of the Linux Symposium OLS 2007, pp. 225–230 (2007)
11. McCune, J.M., Li, Y., Qu, N., Zhou, Z., Datta, A., Gligor, V., Perrig, A.: TrustVisor: Efficient TCB reduction and attestation. In: Proc. of the IEEE S&P (May 2010)
12. OpenTC Project Consortium: The Open Trusted Computing (OpenTC) project (2005-2009), `http://www.opentc.net/`
13. Pfitzmann, B., Riordan, J., Stueble, C., Waidner, M., Weber, A., Saarlandes, U.D.: The perseus system architecture (2001)
14. Pirker, M., Toegl, R.: Towards a virtual trusted platform. Journal of Universal Computer Science 16(4), 531–542 (2010),
   `http://www.jucs.org/jucs_16_4/towards_a_virtual_trusted`
15. Pirker, M., Toegl, R., Gissing, M.: Dynamic enforcement of platform integrity. In: Acquisti, A., Smith, S.W., Sadeghi, A.-R. (eds.) TRUST 2010. LNCS, vol. 6101, pp. 265–272. Springer, Heidelberg (2010)
16. Schiffman, J., Moyer, T., Shal, C., Jaeger, T., McDaniel, P.: Justifying integrity using a virtual machine verifier. In: Proc. ACSAC 2009, pp. 83–92. IEEE Computer Society, Los Alamitos (2009)
17. Singaravelu, L., Pu, C., Härtig, H., Helmuth, C.: Reducing TCB complexity for security-sensitive applications: three case studies. In: EuroSys 2006: Proceedings of the ACM SIGOPS/EuroSys European Conference on Computer Systems 2006, pp. 161–174. ACM, New York (2006)
18. Toegl, R., Pirker, M., Gissing, M.: acTvSM: A Dynamic Virtualization Platform for Enforcement of Application Integrity. In: Proc. of INTRUST 2010. Springer, Heidelberg (2010) (in print)
19. Trusted Computing Group: TCG TPM specification version 1.2 revision 103 (2007),
   `https://www.trustedcomputinggroup.org/specs/TPM/`
20. Wojtczuk, R., Rutkowska, J.: Attacking intel trusted execution technology. Tech. rep., Invisible Things Lab (2009),
   `http://invisiblethingslab.com/resources/bh09dc/ Attacking%20Intel%20TXT%20-%20paper.pdf`
21. Wojtczuk, R., Rutkowska, J., Tereshkin, A.: Another way to circumvent intel trusted execution technology. Tech. rep., Invisible Things Lab, (2009),
   `http://invisiblethingslab.com/resources/misc09/ Another%20TXT%20Attack.pdf`

Enhancing Accountability in the Cloud via Sticky Policies

Siani Pearson, Marco Casassa Mont, and Gina Kounga

Cloud and Security Research Lab, HP Labs,
Long Down Avenue, Bristol. BS34 8QZ. UK
{Siani.Pearson,Marco.Casassa-Mont}@hp.com

Abstract. This paper introduces and discusses a data management solution to provide accountability within the cloud as well as addressing privacy issues. The central idea is as follows. Customers allow cloud (service) providers to have access to specific data based on agreed policies and by forcing interactions with interchangeable independent third parties called Trust Authorities. The access to data can be as fine-grained as necessary, based on policy definitions, underlying encryption mechanisms (supporting the stickiness of policies to the data) and a related key management approach that allows (sets of) data attribute(s) to be encrypted specifically based on the policy. Access to data is mediated by a Trust Authority that checks for compliance to policies in order to release decryption keys. By these means users can be provided with fine-grained control over access and usage of their data within the cloud, even in public cloud models.

Keywords: accountability, cloud, cloud computing, data management, data tagging, encryption, obligation, policy enforcement, privacy, sticky policies.

1   Introduction

Lack of trust about privacy and security practice is at present a key inhibitor in moving to cloud models [1], and for good reason: European Network and Information Security Agency (ENISA) has identified loss of governance as one of the top risks of cloud computing [2]. The problem solved in this paper is how to ensure that data disclosed within cloud services is used, accessed, processed, stored and shared, etc. based upon agreed (potentially fine-grained) policies and constraints. We define mechanisms using data encryption, driven by policies, to ensure degrees of (fine-grained) data protection; degrees of assurance about compliance to these policies are provided by independent (trusted) third parties called Trust Authorities (TAs). Overall, the challenge is to provide a practical solution to enhancing user control and providing accountability within the cloud.

The term 'accountability' is complex to analyse and has been used in slightly different senses: for example, it is commonly used in computer science with reference to audit and reporting mechanisms. Weitzner *et al* have used the term "information accountability" to refer to checking 'whether the policies that govern data manipulations and inferences were in fact adhered to' [3]. Accountability has been a central principle of much privacy guidance and regulation, including that established

C. Lee et al. (Eds.): STA 2011 Workshops, CCIS 187, pp. 146–155, 2011.
© Springer-Verlag Berlin Heidelberg 2011

by Organisation for Economic Co-operation and Development (OECD), Asia-Pacific Economic Co-operation (APEC) and the Canadian Personal Information Protection and Electronics Documents Act (PIPEDA), with the meaning of placing a legal responsibility upon an organisation that uses Personally Identifiable Information (PII) to ensure that contracted partners to whom it supplies the PII are compliant, wherever in the world they may be. Correspondingly, a definition is "Accountability is the obligation and / or willingness to demonstrate and take responsibility for performance in light of agreed upon expectations. Accountability goes beyond responsibility by obligating an organization to be answerable for its actions" [4]. Such a notion of 'accountability' is increasingly popular in jurisdictions such as Australia, Canada and the US [5], and it is likely that this will form the basis of a new regulatory approach that will help control and enable business in the evolving, dynamic environments that cloud computing is encouraging [6]. Hence approaches such as the one described in this paper could be key to enabling satisfaction of legal and regulatory requirements in the cloud.

2 Our Solution

We define a system and mechanisms to enable the protection of data to be shared by a user (or service) with service providers, based on agreed policies and privacy preferences. The user can be actively involved in the selection of cloud services – multiple, interchangeable services called TAs, as discussed above - that will track and audit for the fulfilment of these policies.

We consider situations, as illustrated for example by Figure 3, which could be common to a number of situations, such as health service provision, access to applications and services in the cloud (storage, computing, etc.), and so on: in all these situations, a customer needs to reveal personal and even sensitive information in order to receive a service, but wishes to control the way in which that information is used.

We aim to enable the user to define policies which are preferences or conditions about how that information should be treated. The policy governs the use of associated data, and may specify the following:

- Purposes of using data (e.g. for research, transaction processing, etc.).
- Data may only be used within a given set of platforms (with certain security characteristics), a given network or a subset of the enterprise
- Other obligations and prohibitions (allowed third parties, people or processes; blacklists; notification of disclosure; deletion of data after a certain time)
- List of trusted TAs (potentially the result of a negotiation process)

The policy may be represented in any convenient format. An example in an XML format is:

```
<Sticky Policy>
    <Purpose>
            Research
    </Purpose>
    <Obligation>
```

```
        <Notification>
              Yes
        </Notification>
        <Deletion>
              After 3 years
        </Deletion>
    </Obligation>
</Sticky Policy>
```

As the data is replicated or shared within the cloud in order to fulfil the service provision request, mechanisms will be in place to ensure that the customer's preferences are respected right along the chain. We illustrate how these mechanisms may be achieved by using cryptographic techniques. We assume that all the stakeholders have, at least, certified public/private key pairs from trusted certification authorities (CAs).

In our approach, personal, private or confidential information that is stored and used in the cloud is associated with machine-readable policies, in such a way that this cannot be compromised. When information is processed, this is done in such a way as to adhere to these constraints.

Policies can be associated with data with various degrees of binding and enforcement. The original 'sticky policy' paradigm was espoused by Karjoth *et al.* [7], and specifies that privacy preferences should flow with personal data to make sure that they can always be enforced. However, no method for strong enforcement was suggested. A variety of techniques for binding data to disclosure policies specifying or constraining how it is to be used are possible, ranging from relatively weak logical bindings (for example, where the personal data is sent in clear and linked to the policies) to strong bindings that use cryptography to encrypt the data, and only provide the decryption key if the conditions specified by the preferences are verified [8]. Furthermore, the personal data and policies can be digitally signed to provide evidence about the conditions under which the data may be used.

One approach to provide a strong binding that enhances integrity is to bind policies to data by encrypting the data under a symmetric key, conditionally shared by sender and receiver (i.e. based on fulfilment of policies), and sticking the data to the policy using public key enveloping techniques similar to Public Key Cryptography Standard (PKCS) 7. An example of this process is shown in Figure 1. The stages are as follows:

1. Generation of the policy by the sender, together with a symmetric key K used to encrypt the data (for efficiency, a symmetric key is used rather than an asymmetric key). If desired, this process may be generalized to allow different attributes to be encrypted separately (i.e. using different symmetric keys generated at this stage), and hence only part of the information revealed when an attribute is decrypted.
2. Generation of the message from the sender to the service provider (SP), which involves using the user's public/private key pair and the signature of the policy using the user's private key. (This makes it possible to verify the integrity of the policy and binds the symmetric key K to the data and the policy). The symmetric key K is encrypted with the TA's public key. In addition, the data is encrypted with the symmetric key K. The resultant 'sticky policy' is sent together with the encrypted data to the SP by using a secure communication channel.

3. Generation of the message from SP to TA, which involves passing on some of the information sent to it by the original sender.
4. The TA carries out policy checking, potentially including challenges to the SP. The SP may have to provide signed statements about its policies.
5. If all checks are fulfilled, the TA will release the shared key: it generates a message from the TA to SP, which involves encrypting the symmetric key K with the SP's public key. By these means SP can get access to K and then decrypt the PII.

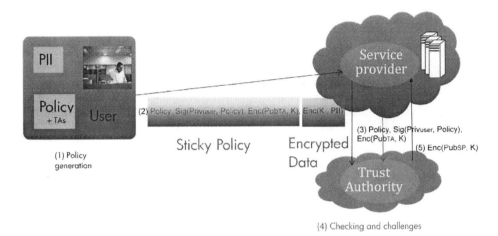

Fig. 1. A sticky policy mechanism using PKI

Further explanation of alternative techniques for sticky policies, including policy-based encryption of data using the policies as identity-based encryption (IBE) keys, is in the related work section. Note also that although an attacker could change the policy and render it illegible, this is detectable as the policy is signed: the mechanisms for handling this are out of scope of this paper.

This technique may be extended to cover the propagation of data along the service provision chain, as shown in Figure 2. It is an analogous process, in which SP1 may add additional policy constraints to form a superset of the previous policy constraints.

The techniques above may be used in any type of environment that supports PKI infrastructure, and not just cloud. Figure 3 illustrates the deployment of our solution in a cloud environment which, as discussed below, may vary slightly according to the way in which data is stored in the cloud. Sticky policies are defined and used in the first engagement between the customer and a Cloud SP (CSP), at the time of disclosing data. These sticky policies dictate the preference conditions and ensure that policy constraints will be audited and degrees of assurance provided. Optionally, sticky policies are also used at the CSP site, at the storage level, dictating constraints on how data can be accessed and used: this involves data access mediation mechanisms and data encryption. Our protocols not only apply to users representing people, but also more broadly to interactions from machine to machine or from service to service provider.

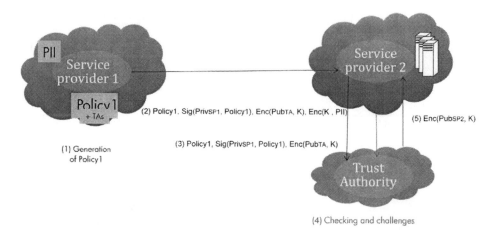

Fig. 2. Propagation of data along the service provision chain

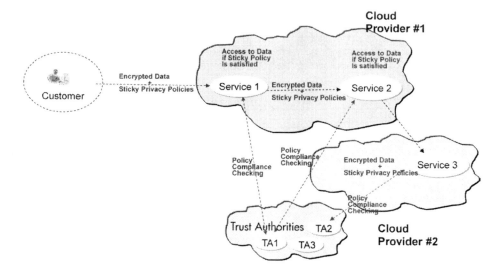

Fig. 3. High-level framework (multi-party cloud interactions)

As shown in Figure 3, the following aspects are part of our solution:

- CSPs publish a "Manifesto" containing the list of supported (macro) policies and Trust Authorities (TAs). Policies relate to access control and obligation behaviours supported by the organisation;
- A user (customer) – interacting with a CSP - can select the granularity of how policies apply to items or specific subsets of personal data to be disclosed (ranging from coarse grained to fine-grained) and customise related preferences (e.g. notification preferences, period of time after deletion, set of agreed purposes, list of parties not to interact with, etc.).

- The user selects a subset of TAs that are to be trusted
- Based on the above selections, a client-side component supports the creation of sticky policies and their association to data, i.e. the bundling of policies, preferences, data and TAs. In other words, the client-side component deals with the packaging of data along with selected parameterised policies and TAs.
- The user can select the option to refer to secured data (e.g. personally identifiable information (PII)) by another third party (this is a cloud storage provider that stores the encrypted data) rather than passing the encrypted data directly to the CSP.
- Encrypted data along with sticky policies is sent to the CSP.
- In order to gain access to the data in clear, the CSP needs to interact with one of the selected TAs (based on availability) in the cloud. During this interaction the CSP has to assert its willingness to fulfil the customised, sticky policies. This creates an audit trail that can be afterward used by the user and TA – in case of policy violations and misbehaviour.
- The CSP will allow for a predefined period of time for connection with the TA. The solution supports the swapping between TAs based on needs.
- Only after satisfying all these requirements (and upon checking additional contextual information), can the TA decide to release the information (decryption keys) that would enable the decryption of data.
- The TA will be able to decrypt and access the data – either in the case where the data was directly disclosed or in the case where just a reference to it was provided (in this latter case, the SP will need to fetch the data).

We have also defined protocols for a variation of the above approach in which a cloud storage provider is used to store the encrypted PII. This entity stores "blobs" of encrypted data associated with a reference to that data. No PII is exposed to this SP as it will not know the encryption key. Instead of the obfuscated data being passed around the cloud, an encrypted reference to that data is used. In addition, we have extended our solution to support degrees of resilience to failure due to communications issues (e.g. delays) between CSPs and TAs.

3 Related Work

Our mechanism is independent of the representation used for the policies. Options include EPAL [9], OASIS XACML [10] and extensions [11,12,13], W3C P3P [14], Ponder [15], PRIME [16], E-P3P [17] and SecPAL4P [18]. Alternatively, a simpler representation for the policies could be used where there is just a specification of certain pre-agreed meta-level tags (with or without using formal ontologies) that could be considered as obligations [19] or might refer to certain attributes of the data that need to be treated or can be exposed in a certain way and could even be just a list of purposes for which the information may be used, with associated obligations that have been agreed in advance off-line.

We can potentially use any encryption mechanism in order to associate policies with data. For example, Voltage [20] and Navajos [21] provide format-preserving encryption and search-enabled encryption respectively [22]; if the operation involves indexing, this could be used when encrypting the different attributes and thereby it would still be possible to do searching and indexing on the encrypted attributes.

The policy can be bound using different mechanisms. For example, we can just associate policies with data or a cryptographic binding could be applied [23]. Both Public Key Infrastructure (PKI) and Identity-Based Encryption (IBE)-based encryption mechanisms have been described as the basis for provision of sticky policies, although not in a cloud context [8, 24]. If IBE is used for this binding then it means that a third party needs to check certain properties at the time of decryption, before a decryption key is released. There are limitations to all these approaches. A logical binding can be easily unbound, but even with a cryptographic binding, after the personal data have been decrypted, the binding is broken, in the sense that the users' data is then fully available to the authorized party and subsequently actions may be taken that contravene the policy. Hence a solution such as the one proposed by Zuo *et al.* [25] needs to be used in combination, to protect data after it has been decrypted, but current options result in stronger protection at the cost of poor scalability, or unrealistic expectations as to the hardware or operating system environment used by service providers. Trusted computing might also be used to try to ensure that receivers act according to associated policies and constraints [26]. Furthermore, the digital signature only proves the authenticity of a binding established in the past by the data subject. If encryption is applied only to text files that adhere to a predefined structure, policies can be relatively easy to corrupt and a skilled hacker can tamper with the file and make the policy illegible. Watermarking schemes [27] and obfuscation techniques [28] can also be used for content protection, but again do not provide support for protecting the data after access.

A technical solution for sticky policies and tracing services is introduced in [8] that leverages Identity-Based Encryption (IBE) and trusted technologies. This solution requires enforcement for third party tracing and auditing parties. One drawback of this approach is that data is bonded with the policy itself, which makes data heavy-weighted and potentially not compatible to the current information systems. However, traceability is provided. An alternative solution, that permits binding of privacy preferences to data and conveying the consent of the individual as well, has been proposed by Pöhls [29]. However, the solution does not avoid the non-consented use of data. Furthermore, IBM [30] has introduced a unified policy model, to provide improved control over suspension and resumption of individuals' personal data, although limited enterprise scenarios were discussed.

There is scope for accountability in the cloud to be provided both in terms of preventive measures such as risk analysis and policy decision and enforcement mechanisms such as the one described in this paper, but also detective measures that include auditing [31], and hence there are a number of other mechanisms that may be used within the cloud that are complementary to our approach (such as transparency protocols for the cloud [32]). In addition, our approach can have a B2C focus, and thus complement other user-centric approaches to information management (e.g. Dataware [33]), but also has B2B applicability, and hence can help organizations transmit and enforce obligations along the service provision chain.

The approach we describe is novel, in particular the way in which we package the data and sticky policies, including: refinement of the notion of sticky policies and their application to the cloud and various options to drive the interaction process between the CSP and TAs. Overall, this is the only system that covers end-to-end data protection from the user, the CSP, TAs and the storage service providers.

4 Current Status and Next Steps

We have worked out the details of how this approach would work, including the underlying cryptographic prototcols both for a classic PKI infrastructure and also for an IBE approach. We have already developed the basic mechanisms for sticky policy management within the EnCoRe project [34]. Next steps are to provide an implementation and investigate enhancements of the protocols, including multiple verification and control.

The deployment of such a system is reasonably straightforward, as it does not require change from existing TAs (apart from dealing with additional policy condition checks) nor from storage providers (if they use the same set of encryption technologies). This would not be the case however for CSPs, as these would need to handle the packaged sticky policies, or use an application to do this locally. Hence it is likely to be most suitable for service provision environments where the increased trust and protection would justify the additional expense, or alternatively to business partners of 'goodwilling' enterprises, who might encourage its use.

5 Conclusions

This solution allows tracing and auditing within the cloud via TAs and enforcement of user preferences by cloud service providers. Our solution differentiates from the state of the art in that it provides an end to end data management solution for the cloud, is scalable, provides different options to drive the interaction process between the CSPs and TAs and allows optional involvement of cloud storage service providers.

The proposed approach will be easy to use and almost transparent to users: user interactions will be mediated by "Privacy Advisors" and/or client applications to mitigate the complexity of creating sticky policies and binding them to data. This solution could be used in a number of different business areas, but would be particularly appropriate where sector-specific legislation or user concerns are strongest – for example in domains relating to defence, healthcare or finance.

Acknowledgements. This work benefitted from input from A. Reed and M. Josephs.

References

1. Pearson, S., Benameur, A.: Privacy, Security and Trust Issues Arising from Cloud Computing. In: CPSRT 2010, CloudCom, IEEE, Los Alamitos (2010)
2. Catteddu, D., Hogben, G. (eds.): ENISA: Cloud Computing: Benefits, Risks and Recommendations for Information Security (2009),
   `http://www.enisa.europa.eu/act/rm/files/deliverables/`
   `cloud-computing-risk-assessment`
3. Weitzner, D., Abelson, H., Berners-Lee, T., Hanson, C., Hendler, J.A., Kagal, L., McGuinness, D.L., Sussman, G.J., Waterman, K.K.: Transparent Accountable Data Mining: New Strategies for Privacy Protection. In: AAAI Spring Symposium on The Semantic Web meets eGovernment, AAAI Press, Menlo Park (2006)
4. Galway Project: Plenary session Introduction, p. 5 (April 28, 2009)

5. Crompton, M., Cowper, C., Jefferis, C.: The Australian Dodo Case: an insight for data protection regulation. World Data Protection Report 9(1), BNA (2009)
6. Galway Project: Data Protection Accountability: The Essential Elements (2009),
   http://www.huntonfiles.com/files/webupload/
   CIPL_Galway_Accountability_Paper.pdf
7. Karjoth, G., Schunter, M., Waidner, M.: Platform for enterprise privacy practices: Privacy-enabled management of customer data. In: Dingledine, R., Syverson, P.F. (eds.) PET 2002. LNCS, vol. 2482, pp. 69–84. Springer, Heidelberg (2003)
8. Casassa Mont, M., Pearson, S., Bramhall, P.: Towards Accountable Management of Identity and Privacy: Sticky Policies and Enforceable Tracing Services. In: DEXA, pp. 377–382. IEEE Computer Society, Los Alamitos (2003)
9. IBM: The Enterprise Privacy Authorization Language (EPAL), EPAL specification, v1.2 (2004),
   http://www.zurich.ibm.com/security/enterprise-privacy/epal/
10. OASIS: XACML,
    http://www.oasis-open.org/committees/
    tc_home.php?wg_abbrev=xacml
11. Ardagna, C., et al.: PrimeLife Policy Language, ACAS, W3C (2009),
    http://www.w3.org/2009/policy-ws/
12. Bussard, L., Becker, M.Y.: Can access control be extended to deal with data handling in privacy scenarios?, ACAS, W3C (2009),
    http://www.w3.org/2009/policy-ws/
13. Papanikolaou, N., Creese, S., Goldsmith, M., Casassa Mont, M., Pearson, S.: ENCORE: Towards a holistic approach to privacy. In: SECRYPT (2010)
14. Cranor, L.: Web Privacy with P3P. O'Reilly & Associates, Sebastopol (2002)
15. Damianou, N., Dulay, N., Lupu, E., Sloman, M.: The Ponder Policy Specification Language (2001),
    http://wwwdse.doc.ic.ac.uk/research/policies/index.shtml
16. Ardagna, C., Vimercati, S., Samarati, P.: Enhancing user privacy through data handling policies. In: Damiani, E., Liu, P. (eds.) Data and Applications Security 2006. LNCS, vol. 4127, pp. 224–236. Springer, Heidelberg (2006)
17. Karjoth, G., Schunter, M., Waidner, M.: Platform for Enterprise Privacy Practices: Privacy-Enabled Management of Customer Data. In: Dingledine, R., Syverson, P.F. (eds.) PET 2002. LNCS, vol. 2482, pp. 69–84. Springer, Heidelberg (2003)
18. Becker, M.Y., Malkis, A., Bussard, L.: A Framework for Privacy Preferences and Data-Handling Policies, MSR-TR-2009-128 (2009),
    http://research.microsoft.com/apps/pubs/
    default.aspx?id=102614
19. Bruening, P., Krasnow Waterman, K.: Data Tagging for New Information Governance Models. IEEE Security and Privacy, 64–68 (September/October 2010)
20. Voltage, http://www.voltage.com/technology/
    Technology_FormatPreservingEncryption.htm
21. Navajos, http://navajosystems.com/technology_encryption.asp
22. Bellare, M., Ristenpart, T., Rogaway, P., Stegers, T.: Format-Preserving Encryption. In: Jacobson Jr., M.J., Rijmen, V., Safavi-Naini, R. (eds.) SAC 2009. LNCS, vol. 5867, pp. 295–312. Springer, Heidelberg (2009)
23. Tang, W.: On using encryption techniques to enhance sticky policies enforcement, TR-CTIT-08-64, Centre for Telematics and Information Technology (2008)

24. Pearson, S., Casassa Mont, M.: A System for Privacy-aware Resource Allocation and Data Processing in Dynamic Environments. In: I-NetSec 2006. IFIP, vol. 201, pp. 471–482. Springer, Heidelberg (2006)

25. Zuo, Y., O'Keefe, T.: Post-release information privacy protection: A framework and next-generation priacy-enhanced operating system. ISF 9(5), 451–467 (2007), http://www.springerlink.com/content/03718003288553u5/

26. Pearson, S., Casassa Mont, M., Novoa, M.: Securing Information Transfer within Distributed Computing Environments. IEEE Security & Privacy Magazine 6(1), 34–42 (2008)

27. Pérez-Freire, L., Comesaña, P., Troncoso-Pastoriza, J.R., Pérez-González, F.: Watermarking security: A survey. In: Shi, Y.Q. (ed.) Transactions on Data Hiding and Multimedia Security I. LNCS, vol. 4300, pp. 41–72. Springer, Heidelberg (2006)

28. Bayardo, R., Agrawal, R.: Data Privacy through Optimal k-Anonymisation. In: International Conference on Data Engineering, pp. 217–228 (2005)

29. Pöhls, H.C.: Verifiable and Revocable Expression of Consent to Processing of Aggregated Personal Data. In: ICICS (2008)

30. Schunter, M., Waidner, M.: Simplified privacy controls for aggregated services — suspend and resume of personal data. In: Borisov, N., Golle, P. (eds.) PET 2007. LNCS, vol. 4776, pp. 218–232. Springer, Heidelberg (2007)

31. Pearson, S., Charlesworth, A.: Accountability as a Way Forward for Privacy Protection in the Cloud. In: Jaatun, M.G., Zhao, G., Rong, C. (eds.) Cloud Computing. LNCS, vol. 5931, pp. 131–144. Springer, Heidelberg (2009)

32. Knode, R., Egan, D.: Digital Trust in the Cloud, CSC (July 2010), http://assets1.csc.com/cloud/downloads/ wp_cloudtrustprotocolprecis_073010.pdf

33. Dataware project, Horizon Digital Economy Research Group, http://www.horizon.ac.uk

34. EnCoRe, Ensuring Consent and Revocation project, http://www.encore-project.info

Enhancement of Critical Financial Infrastructure Protection Using Trust Management

Hisain Elshaafi, Jimmy McGibney, Barry Mulcahy, and Dmitri Botvich

Waterford Institute of Technology, Ireland
{helshaafi,jmcgibney,bmulcahy,dbotvich}@tssg.org

Abstract. Providing protection to the financial infrastructure in the face of faults and malevolent attacks is vital to the stability, availability, and continuity of key financial markets and businesses worldwide. Traditional protection approaches have focused on protecting individual financial institutions (FIs) while ignoring the threats arising from cross-domain interactions as well as those originating from other critical infrastructures. With the growing complexity of inter-organisational boundaries and their increasing interdependence, such isolated approaches are no longer adequate. However, sharing information between FIs relating to critical events and the reliance on others' quality of service attributes such as security requires varying levels of trust between them depending on the requirements of each individual FI and the sensitivity of exchanged information. This paper describes a trust management system developed to allow the evaluation, monitoring, and management of trustworthiness levels of FIs exchanging critical events and information. Trustworthiness levels are used to assure FIs of the reliability of each other and to filter events and data being processed. The system introduces a novel reusable architecture that allows flexibility and extensibility of trust metrics and trust algorithms.

Keywords: financial critical infrastructure, trust management, protection, semantic room.

1 Introduction

A growing amount of sensitive financial and personal data is being carried over, or potentially exposed to, open communication media such as the Internet. This trend subjects financial services and the supporting infrastructure to substantial widespread attacks and fraud attempts that cannot be defended effectively by any organisation on its own. In order to allow detection and proactive response to threats against financial critical infrastructures and thus ensure business continuity, CoMiFin [1], an EU research project, is developing a prototype solution to facilitate information exchange and distributed event processing among groups of federated participants.

These federated groups are called Semantic Rooms (SRs) [2]. The SRs are set up based on common interest, for instance for collaborative protection against Distributed Denial of Service, Intrusion, or Man in the Middle attacks. The SRs are enabled through a common middleware infrastructure (Fig. 1), allowing sharing and processing of information through a secure and trusted environment for the participants to

C. Lee et al. (Eds.): STA 2011 Workshops, CCIS 187, pp. 156–165, 2011.

contribute and analyse data. Exchanged data can include real time security events, historical attack data, and logs that concern other SR participants, for example. Processed data can be used internally by the SR members. In this case, derived events, models, profiles, blacklists, and alerts are made available for the members. Note that in this paper we use the words "member" and "agent" to indicate the SR participants. An agent is a principal whose trust is managed by the Trust Manager and it can be a current, past or future member of the SR.

As illustrated in the figure, members share common resources that in addition to the Trust Manager described in this paper include:

- *Semantic Room Management:* manages the group lifecycle, from creation to disbandment including configuration of the SR and maintaining logs of the SR activities.
- *Event Processing and Data Mining:* provides simple to complex event filtering and processing services to the SR, depending on the SR and the types of events. SR data mining applications mine a large number of events and other data accumulated over time to extract analytical models to be used to assist the online event processing.
- *Metrics Monitoring:* monitors the middleware to assess its status in meeting the requirements specified in the SR contract.
- *Data Store:* supports storage needs of the SR, its events, and knowledge base.
- *SR Contract:* regulates participation and the relationship between members. The contract also governs the services available in the SR, access to those services and requirements in relation to data protection, isolation, trust, security, availability, fault-tolerance, and performance.

Since the members of an SR share potentially sensitive and mission critical information, SR management needs to provide suitable assurance to each of those members indicating their trustworthiness levels. To that end, we developed the CoMiFin Trust Manager. Trust evaluation is based on past behaviour and the reputation of each agent through direct experience, recommendation, and referral. We define trust as a relationship between two entities that indicates the contextual expectations from an entity towards another in relation to reliance in accomplishing a certain action at a certain quality. Trustworthiness level is the level of trust that the trusting entity has in another entity. The trustworthiness level consists of a trust score that is calculated based on weighted ratings given to different types of metrics and events. It also includes a confidence degree which indicates the quantity and variability of the ratings on which the trust score was based. The weighting mechanism of events and metrics allows the enquiring party to determine the context of trust.

A CoMiFin SR member may request information from the Trust Manager regarding the trustworthiness of another member when sending new events and data or when receiving them from other members. This assures each of the SR members of the trustworthiness of other members and provides a mechanism for fine grained access control in the dynamic environment in which the SR membership operates.

This paper is organised as follows: Section 2 describes distributed trust between SRs. Section 3 explains trust events on which trust ratings and scores are based. The reusable core architecture of the CoMiFin Trust Manager is described in section 4,

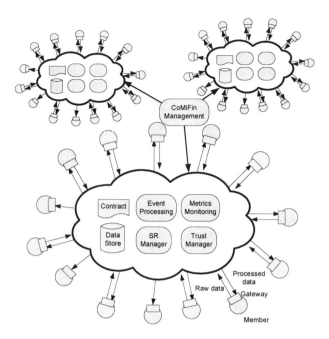

Fig. 1. CoMiFin System

looking at different mechanisms that are used to monitor trust. Section 5 outlines the use of rules in determining the individual trust ratings. Section 6 shows how the Trust Manager calculates the overall agent's trustworthiness levels including the description of the default algorithms. Experiments on the system are then described in section 7. Section 8 provides an overview of the related work that has been done on trust and trust management. The last section concludes the paper and outlines the potential for future work.

2   Distributed Trust: Between Semantic Rooms

In previous work [3], we proposed the overlay of a distributed trust management infrastructure on top of service delivery infrastructure for unstructured networks. This provides a closed loop system where live distributed trust measures are used to modify access control settings in a changing threat environment. This can also be used to assist collaboration *between* SRs. It can be expected that a member of one SR will be a member of other SRs, and the idea is to share information between SRs on the behaviour of common members.

With this architecture, illustrated in Fig. 2, a distributed trust management overlay operates separately from normal SR activity (including local trust management). Two message passing interfaces are defined between the operational layer and the trust management layer and another between the distributed trust managers of individual SRs.

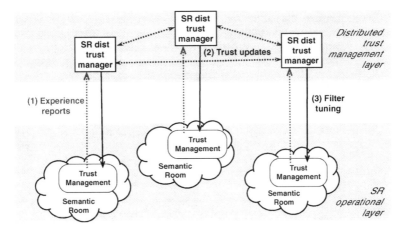

Fig. 2. Distributed Trust Management Overlay

The interfaces are as follows:

- *Experience reports:* SR local trust manager → SR distributed trust manager
- *Trust updates:* SR_i distributed TM ↔ SR_j distributed TM
- *Filter tuning:* SR distributed TM → SR local TM

In a peer to peer network, such as the inter-SR case, information is not stored centrally. In any case, trust by its nature is subjective and thus best managed by the SR doing the trusting. There is no global view: any given SR will be aware of the existence of, and can share information with, zero or more other SRs.

3 Trust Events

Trust events refer to the notifications received by the Trust Manager from the Event Processing and Metrics Monitoring components (Fig. 1). CoMiFin semantic rooms are governed by contracts that define requirements for processing and data sharing services. Trust events received by the Trust Manager indicate violations or adherence to those contracts. Those trust events can be classified into two types:

- *Metrics:* Metrics measure how QoS requirements are adhered to by the SR member. Those metrics are classified into categories including security, performance, and availability. The Trust Manager allows the administrator to customise the weight of each category of metrics in calculating the overall trust. Each category includes one or more metrics. For example, the performance category includes response time metric, and availability includes uptime.
- *Alerts:* Alerts are received from the Event Processing component in relation to events that indicate the level of collaboration of the members in supporting the functioning of the SR such as contributing to blacklists and threat detection.

The alerts are also classified by the Trust Manager into categories including competence, integrity, and willingness of an SR member. These categories can be extended and modified for each SR.

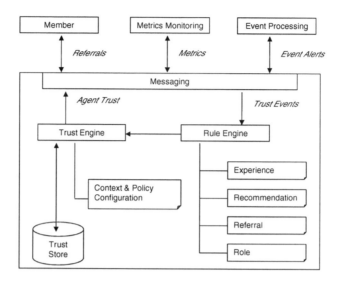

Fig. 3. CoMiFin Trust Manager

4   Trust Evaluation, Monitoring and Management

Fig. 3 illustrates the architecture of the Trust Manager. Each SR shares a common infrastructure that includes a Trust Manager. Agents can dynamically join or leave the membership of an SR. The Trust Manager stores, monitors and updates trust of each of the agents it has knowledge of. It determines the trustworthiness level of an agent using:

- *Direct experience:* It receives alerts (from the Event Processing) and metrics (from the Metrics Monitoring) indicating the level of adherence or violation of a member to the SR's contract.
- *Recommendation:* Requesting recommendations from Trust Managers in other SRs regarding the reputation of an agent.
- *Referral:* A trusted agent can provide another with a reference certifying its reputation. An agent can use the reference to improve its trust; especially useful for new members and those with little or no interactions.

A trust query can be received from a member, Metrics Monitoring system, other CoMiFin SR's Trust Managers, etc. The query invokes the calculation of the trustworthiness level from existing ratings. The SR operations are enhanced by combining classical policy based management with distributed trust management. As illustrated in Fig. 4, incoming events are evaluated by a rules engine within a policy decision point. A filter takes the outcome of these rule evaluations and makes a (binary) decision on whether the event is to be allowed, for example by comparing some function of these rule outcomes with a threshold. This threshold is a function of trust in the event's originator, evaluated by a local trust manager. This local trust manager is influenced by (i) previous experience (hence closed loop feedback in Fig. 4) and (ii) reputation information from third parties.

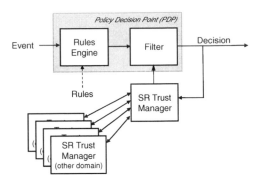

Fig. 4. System combines rule-based filter with trust

5 Ratings Computation

The system utilises the Drools [4] rule engine to specify business rules for processing different categories of trust events and the calculation of resulting ratings. The rules calculate the rating for the event and add other attributes including the recency value (when event happened) and the type of event. Ratings are then stored by the Trust Manager and can be used for calculating the overall trustworthiness level of each agent.

A trust event e can be represented as: $e = (a, g, v_x, v_y, t)$; where a is the agent; g is the category of trust event e.g. performance, security; v_x value agreed in the contract; v_y the actual value measured which may or may not be adhering to the limits in the agreed contract value; and t is the time the event took place.

Additional parameters added to v_x to indicate type of measurement e.g. real number, percentage, and how it is compared to actual value v_y e.g. minimum, maximum, range. For example, the contract may refer to the minimum uptime accepted as 95%.

The rating score s is calculated using the function: $s = f(v_x \circ v_y)$; where $\circ$ is an operator determined by the type of measurements and how they are compared. A simple formula would be v_x / v_y, applicable for example when real numbers are used for measuring the event, v_x is the maximum allowed value in the contract and $v_y \neq 0$. Function f provides the rating score, taking into consideration penalty or reward given as a result of violation or adherence to the contract respectively. Each rating is stored in the database in the form of a tuple $R = (a, g, s, t)$; where s is the rating score.

6 Trust Computation

The trust engine is responsible for providing a snapshot of the current trustworthiness level of an agent. A trust context provides a way to answer the question: "what to trust the agent for?" For instance, an agent may be trusted for its security and integrity but may not be trusted for its competence. Therefore, the Trust Manager can be customised to emphasise certain categories of trust events by giving them higher weights. The trust engine has default algorithms but allows substituting or modifying existing algorithms through plugins. In addition to configuration files, an administrative web interface aims to allow system administrators to access and modify those configurations in a user-friendly manner.

Experience trust is a tuple $T = (a, S, C)$ where S is the score for agent a; and C is the confidence in the score. The default algorithms used to calculate the experience trust are described here. The trust score for agent a, S_a is calculated through a weighted mean of the rating scores:

$$S_a = \sum_{i \in n} \frac{w_i \cdot s_i}{\sum_{i \in n} w_i} \tag{1}$$

where n is the number ratings for agent a; and w is the weighting of the rating score s. The weighting is based on the recency of the rating and the category of event that triggered that rating. w is always between 0 and 1. Recency weight w_t is allowed to decay exponentially.

Category weight w_g is set in the configuration as a value between 0 and 1. The rating score's weight w is calculated as follows:

$$w = \frac{w_t \cdot w_g}{\sum_{i \in n} w_{ti} \cdot w_{gi}} \tag{2}$$

The confidence value of agent a, C_a is calculated using $C_a = c_\eta \cdot c_\delta$; where c_η is the rating quantity confidence; and c_δ is the rating quality confidence. The c_η is calculated as follows:

$$c_\eta = 1 - e^{-\frac{\alpha \cdot n}{10}} \tag{3}$$

where α is a constant parameter that can be used to adjust the slope of the relationship between the total number of ratings and the quantity confidence. The higher the value of α the faster that full confidence (i.e. 1) is reached. It can be set to any positive value but for gradual increase in confidence it should typically be set to a value between 0 and 1.

The quality confidence c_δ is calculated using the following formula:

$$c_\sigma = 1 - \frac{1}{2} \cdot \frac{\sum_{i \in n} \omega_i \cdot |S - s_i|}{\sum_{i \in n} \omega_i} \tag{4}$$

where $|S - s_i|$ is the absolute difference between the agent's trust score and individual rating score. The quality confidence indicates the deviation of the rating scores around the overall trust score and ranges between 0 (highest deviations) and 1 (lowest deviations). The deviations (range between 0 and 2) are weighted to allow varying degrees of confidence based on weight of the deviating rating score.

7   Experiments

The Trust Manager is written in Java and runs as a JBoss Server application with a MySQL database for storing ratings and other trust management data. JBoss clustering is used to support load balancing and scalability and to avoid having a single point of failure. Fig. 5 shows a demonstration of the Trust Manager at work, where it sequentially receives 500 trust events for members A, and B respectively. Member A is set to trigger more negative trust events and hence more frequent negative ratings than those of member B. A request for the trustworthiness level is also received every 10 member events and the trust score and confidence are consequently calculated.

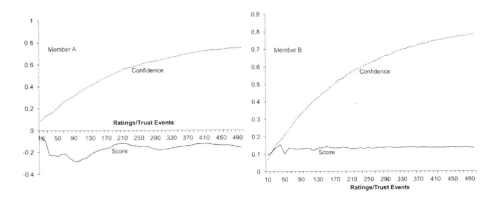

Fig. 5. Ratings and Trust Changes

Trust computation uses the default algorithms that are described in previous section. The trust context is configured to reflect security, reliability, performance and willingness categories. As can be seen in the diagrams, trust scores change according to past ratings including those received after the last trust score calculation. As expected, trust confidence grows as new ratings are made. As the confidence parameter α is set to 0.05, the confidence gradually levels off and its change then becomes more dependent on deviations between the rating scores.

8   Related Work

In the past decade there has been large amount of research on the area of trust in various aspects of multi-agent systems [5, 6], web services [7, 8], e-commerce [9], and information filtering [3]. The concept of trust varies, with those works frequently interpreting trust in the context of security as a way of achieving authentication and access control, as in [10]. The CoMiFin Trust Manager on the other hand allows its administrator to customise the system to measure trust based on reputation for an adaptable context and therefore the trustworthiness levels can reflect security, integrity, competence, predictability, etc., of the agents based on weights. However, the Trust Manager builds upon, and extends from, the results of previous research particularly systems and algorithms developed in ReGreT [11], and FIRE [5] and TOPAS [3]. The Trust Manager prototype is developed to suit the requirements of a set of nodes collaborating in information exchange in relation to security threats to their assets and infrastructure. Another important feature of the Trust Manager that is not supported in existing research is that future and existing trust models and algorithms, such as those mentioned above, can be made as add-ons to the Trust Manager, consequently changing how the trustworthiness is calculated and what trust means. The Trust Manager therefore introduces novel ideas that allow flexibility and extensibility of the trust metrics and trust algorithms based on the requirements.

9 Conclusion and Future Work

This paper has presented a trust management system that can monitor and evaluate trustworthiness levels of members of groups of financial institutions, sharing critical events and data relating to financial infrastructure protection within Semantic Rooms. The aim of this collaboration is to protect those institutions against threats and attacks that would otherwise be unavoidable using existing isolated protection mechanisms.

The Trust Manager has a reusable architecture that is highly flexible and extensible, allowing for composition and modification of rules, algorithms, and trust contexts. The rules engine receives trust events and, based on the customisation of the categories of events, it fires specific extensible rules. Those rules then generate the rating including a new score resulting from the event. The trust engine allows choosing between multiple algorithms for calculating the overall trustworthiness level. This paper has discussed a default set of algorithms.

Since trust means different things for different requirements, the Trust Manager allows composition of the trust context which indicates the focus of the trust semantics, for instance; integrity, security, or competence. The Trust Manager is developed as part of a research project focusing on financial infrastructure protection. However, the solution is generic and is applicable to other business and technical domains. Future research and development work will advance the functionality and the features of the Trust Manager, including a user interface to allow the system administrator to intuitively control and formulate the rules, algorithm, and contexts at runtime.

Acknowledgments. The work described in this paper was partially funded by the EU FP7 project CoMiFin [1]. We would like to thank our partners in CoMiFin for providing feedback on the system.

References

1. CoMiFin (Communication Middleware for Monitoring Financial Critical Infrastructures), http://www.comifin.eu
2. Lodi, G., Querzoni, L., Baldoni, R., Marchetti, M., Colajanni, M., Bortnikov, V., Chockler, G., Dekel, E., Laventman, G., Roytman, A.: Defending Financial Infrastructures Through Early Warning Systems: The Intelligence Cloud Approach. In: Proc. 5th Annual Workshop on Cyber Security and Information Intelligence Research, Knoxville, TN, USA (2009)

3. McGibney, J., Botvich, D.: A Trust Overlay Architecture and Protocol for Enhanced Protection against Spam. In: Proc. 2nd Int. Conf. on Availability, Reliability, and Security (ARES), Vienna, pp. 749–756 (2007)
4. Drools, http://www.jboss.org/drools
5. Huynh, T., Jennings, N., Shadbolt, N.: An integrated trust and reputation model for open multi-agent systems. Journal of Autonomous Agents and Multi-Agent Systems 13(2), 119–154 (2006)
6. Xiong, L., Liu, L.: PeerTrust: Supporting Reputation-based Trust for Peer-to-Peer Electronic Communities. IEEE Transactions on Knowledge and Data Engineering (TKDE) 16(7), 843–857 (2004)
7. Singh, M.P.: Trustworthy service composition: Challenges and research questions. In: Proc. of the Autonomous Agents and Multi-Agent Systems, Workshop on Deception, Fraud and Trust in Agent Societies, pp. 117–135 (2002)
8. Malik, Z., Bouguettaya, A.: RATEWeb: Reputation Assessment for Trust Establishment among Web services. The Int. Journal on Very Large Data Bases 18(4), 885–911 (2009)
9. Reiley, D., Bryan, D., Prasad, N., Reeves, D.: Pennies from Ebay: The Determinants of Price in Online Auctions. Journal of Industrial Economics 55(2), 223–233 (2007)
10. Blaze, M., Feigenbaum, J., Keromytis, Λ.: KeyNote: Trust Management for Public-Key Infrastructures. In: Security Protocols Int. Workshop, Cambridge, England, pp. 56–63 (1998)
11. Sabater, J.: Trust and reputation for agent societies. Departament d'Informática, Universitat Autónoma de Barcelona (UAB), Ph.D. Thesis (2002)

Towards Natural-Language Understanding and Automated Enforcement of Privacy Rules and Regulations in the Cloud: Survey and Bibliography

Nick Papanikolaou, Siani Pearson, and Marco Casassa Mont

Cloud and Security Lab
Hewlett-Packard Laboratories
{nick.papanikolaou,siani.pearson,marco.casassa-mont}@hp.com

Abstract. In this paper we survey existing work on automatically processing legal, regulatory and other policy texts for the extraction and representation of privacy knowledge and rules. Our objective is to link and apply some of these techniques to policy enforcement and compliance, to provide a core means of achieving and maintaining customer privacy in an enterprise context, particularly where data is stored and processed in cloud data centres. We sketch our thoughts on how this might be done given the many different, but so far strictly distinct from one another, approaches to natural-language analysis of legal and other prescriptive texts, approaches to knowledge extraction, semantic representation, and automated enforcement of privacy rules.

Keywords: natural-language processing, privacy policies, policy enforcement, cloud computing.

1 Introduction

Privacy is a central concern of growing importance in our society, especially with the continuing growth and popularity of online services that require the sharing of personal data. There have been numerous accounts of the notion of privacy and several attempts at formulating an adequate definition, but due to its complexity and dependence on context, this notion is highly elusive and difficult to pin down in such a way that satisfies the needs of customers and suppliers alike. In order to tackle citizens' privacy demands, numerous privacy laws and regulations have been enacted, and enterprises - which administer and manage huge databases of personally identifiable information as part of normal business practice - are required to demonstrate compliance with these laws and regulations. The consequences of failing to comply can be severe, not only for an enterprise but for its customers, whose ensuing loss of privacy could be very damaging to their reputations and finances (cf. identity theft). For this reason, there is a significant business need for tools and techniques to (automatically and efficiently) analyze privacy texts, extract rules and subsequently enforce them throughout the supply chain.

Clearly it is unreasonable to expect a computer program to fully understand a legal or other policy text. However there are a variety of techniques and programs for

C. Lee et al. (Eds.): STA 2011 Workshops, CCIS 187, pp. 166–173, 2011.

analyzing, annotating and extracting information from texts, and there have been various attempts at applying such techniques in the context of privacy. Furthermore there is much work on formalizing privacy and representing privacy-related properties in unambiguous logical form, which lends itself better to automated analysis. As for the enforcement of privacy rules and requirements, there exist rule-based systems that distil privacy knowledge into a form that can be executed directly by a machine. Of course, such systems have their limitations, but there are numerous practical benefits, especially as they reduce the effort required to ensure compliance significantly.

In the literature there is a tendency for the tasks and objectives in the previous paragraph (parsing and analysis of source texts, knowledge extraction, semantic representation, and enforcement of privacy rules) to be considered each in isolation. However these tasks may be seen as essentially interlinked processes in a privacy compliance lifecycle, so that the output of one task is the input of the next. This is a lifecycle because the processes need to be continually repeated in order to account for new privacy rules that emerge as societal needs, laws and regulations change. It should be noted here that there is some work being done in the European research project CONSEQUENCE to automate the full lifecycle involved in managing data sharing agreements, from capturing agreements in a pseudo-language to translating them into enforceable policies; however the mapping from legal texts to this pseudo-language representation is a human process and does not seem to involve automated natural-language analysis.

This paper attempts to survey work on natural language processing and semantic representation of legal and regulatory privacy-related knowledge. We have divided this survey into four principal groupings of papers:

1. Work on parsing and basic natural-language processing of legal and regulatory texts,
2. Work on knowledge extraction from texts,
3. Work on semantic representations of privacy and privacy-related knowledge, and
4. Work on automating compliance with privacy legislation and regulation.

It is our interest to see how these techniques can be combined and cross-linked in order to build a platform for automatically recognizing and enforcing privacy rules.

2   Parsing and Basic Analysis of Source Texts

First we consider practical approaches – namely, tools and techniques - to the task of natural-language processing of legal and regulatory texts. It is worthwhile to note that the main techniques for analysis of such texts tend to have many similarities across different domains, whether the texts refer to healthcare regulations, business best practice, or privacy rules: the common element is the prescriptive nature of the texts. In particular, texts that consist exclusively of detailed descriptions of rules often use standard sentence structures and patterns, which can be identified and formalized to a significant degree. What changes with different application domains, naturally, is the vocabulary, and the frequency of particular word clusters (see [11] for statistical results regarding the vocabulary and phrases common to privacy policies in particular). The papers [1], [2], [14], [15] all describe different tools for analysis of prescriptive texts, and we review these next. Also of note is work in the IBM REALM project [24].

Moulin and Rousseau [1] describe a "knowledge acquisition system" known as SACD, implemented in Prolog, which has been developed for the analysis of regulatory texts. SACD was used to process the National Building Code of Canada, so that its stipulations could be represented in a machine-readable, indexable and searchable form. What is particularly interesting about SACD is that it can adapt the knowledge representation structures it uses automatically, as it processes input. Furthermore it provides a graphical user interface during the process of syntactic analysis, which allows for user intervention when a particular text fragment has been decomposed incorrectly or inaccurately. SACD makes use of chart-parsing algorithms and Prolog definite-clause grammars, which are ideally suited to the low-level analysis of sentence structure and meaning. The authors do mention the fundamental limitation of their approach, namely that the built-in grammars need to be repeatedly revised and extended to be able to parse new language elements, vocabulary and usage patterns. However, the system is capable of adapting its representations of knowledge, as text is parsed. Moulin and Rousseau's paper describes work that falls into almost all of the categories in our classification, including knowledge representation and learning; the link to compliance is mentioned, but the authors do not explain how it might be automatically achieved using their tool.

Michael, Ong and Rowe [2] and Ong [15] develop an architecture and concrete tool for analyzing texts with prescriptive rules. Their approach alludes to knowledge extraction and logical representation of rules, but the tool they present is specifically an extractor which turns a prescriptive sentence into a 'meaning list'; how this meaning list can be used by a handler or enforcement mechanism is beyond the scope of their work. In terms of textual analysis, their approach is to use an off-the-shelf part of speech (POS) tagger and to process its output to determine whether the input sentence describes an obligation, permission or interdiction; the meaning list resulting from analysis of the sentence identifies the different actors involved and their interrelationships.

Brodie et al. [14] present a tool, SPARCLE, designed for authoring technically enforceable privacy policies using natural language. The tool is designed to parse and interpret English text describing privacy rules, and generate from that text appropriate XACML policies. In particular, the tool provides a structured policy authoring environment. What is appealing about SPARCLE is the ability to link access control statements to the original natural language requirements; this aids both understanding and transparency.

3 Knowledge Extraction from Texts and Learning

Antón and a number of different collaborators (see [3,5,6,7,8]) have used textual mining techniques to analyze privacy policies and a number of different privacy and privacy-related regulations. For example, in [3] the authors focus on privacy policies from financial institutions which claim to be compliant with the Gramm-Leach-Bliley Act (GLBA). Papers [3] and [5] refer to the use of a tool called PGMT (Privacy Goal Management Tool), which is a tool for representing and analyzing rules arising in privacy regulations as restricted natural-language statements. In [6] the authors discuss the extraction of structured rules from source texts using an NLP platform called *Cerno*.

In [7] Breaux, Anton and Vail use their approach of *semantic parameterization* to represent the US HIPAA (Health Insurance Portability and Accountability Act) Privacy Rule as a set of restricted natural-language statements, classified as rights, constraints or obligations. They identify standard phrases appearing in the legislative document, and note the frequency of their occurrence and the corresponding modality (right/obligation/interdiction etc.). They also discuss how to handle ambiguities. This work is extended further in [8], where the authors develop a detailed classification of constraints and introduce means of handling complex cross-references arising in the legal text of the HIPAA.

Delannoy et al. [9] combine a template-matching technique with machine learning in order to match rules from the Canadian 1991 tax guide with text describing case studies of particular individuals; this approach in principle allows one to see which tax rules apply in a given situation. The paper describes an architecture and tool called MaLTe, which is capable of learning how to apply rules to different input texts.

Delisle et al. [10] describe in detail a framework for extracting meaning from the structure of technical documents. Their approach is relevant to the analysis of prescriptive texts in that they assume that input documents are highly structured and somewhat predictable. The authors propose a number of techniques for identifying patterns in texts and converting sentences to Horn clauses. The Horn clauses represent knowledge about the domain in question; through the use of machine learning techniques, this knowledge is extended and refined as more documents are supplied.

Stamey and Rossi [11] use singular-value decomposition and latent semantic analysis techniques to analyze privacy policy texts. They identify commonly occurring topics and key terms and their relations. They are also able to detect similar word meanings; the strength of their approach is that they are able to pick out ambiguities in privacy policies and make them visible to the user. The tool *Hermes* developed by the authors allows automated analysis of an entire privacy policy text, outputting an overall ranking of the policy (when compared to a reference text).

We are also aware of much work on knowledge extraction from legislation [16-20]. Due to space limitations we will not expand on this further.

4 Semantic Models and Representations

Waterman [4] develops a simple table-based representation of particular laws. This author demonstrates a so-called 'intermediate isomorphic representation' of a rule from the US Privacy Act, and similarly for a rule from the Massachusetts Criminal Offender Records Law. The key idea here is to use a structured representation that can be mapped directly back to the original legal text and to corresponding computer code. The representation still uses natural language, but with additional logical structure. The additional structure helps to separate out actors, verbs, context and particular constraints that exist in the legal text (and which are often implied or included indirectly with the use of cross-references).

The framework proposed by Barth, Datta, Mitchell and Nissenbaum [12] comprises a formal model which is used to express and reason about norms of transmission of personal information. This work does not involve automatically analyzing text, but does provide a formalism for manually representing notions of privacy found in legislation – particularly in the texts of HIPAA, COPPA and GLBA. The formal model provides notations for defining sets of agents communicating via messages, with particular roles, in specified contexts; linear temporal logic, with a past operator, allows one to express properties that the agent behaviours should satisfy. Policy compliance is formally defined in terms of this model. Although the authors assume that their formalism is for a human user, we envisage the possibility that using natural-language analysis it should be possible to extract from texts some privacy rules expressed in this formalism.

May, Gunter and Lee [13] define a semantic model for expressing privacy properties, and apply it to the HIPAA Privacy Rule; it is based on a classical access control model used in operating system design. The authors translate the legal text into a structured format that uses the commands in the proposed access control model to express rules. The paper does not restrict itself to representation; once the legal rules have been formally expressed, the authors use the SPIN model checker [23] to automatically reason about the consistency of the generated rules; they demonstrate subtle differences between the year 2000 and year 2003 versions of the HIPAA Privacy Rule.

It is clear that a uniform, consistent, formal representation of privacy knowledge and privacy rules in particular is useful for automated reasoning about privacy issues. We are keen to make use of existing formal representations of privacy rules when performing natural-language analysis of privacy-related texts, since the usefulness of such representations has already been demonstrated for complex texts, particularly American privacy legislation.

5   Policy Enforcement and Compliance

We are not aware of any previous work that addresses the whole lifecycle of natural-language analysis of privacy texts with the goal of enforcing suitable rules, e.g. in an enterprise setting (although the EU CONSEQUENCE project mentioned before does take an holistic approach it does not involve natural-language analysis). As stated in the Introduction, achieving compliance with privacy legislation and regulations is a central concern in enterprises, and means of automating compliance are highly desirable. Since new privacy rules are almost exclusively expressed using natural-language, means of automatically analyzing the appropriate texts and extracting rules from them necessary – the resulting rules can then be incorporated into existing enterprise rule-bases, such as those used in compliance checkers or information governance (GRC) platforms. We mention here some work on automated policy enforcement and compliance, which has so far been developed separately and independently of any consideration of automated knowledge and rule extraction.

The EnCoRe research project [24] is developing a platform for expressing and enforcing privacy preferences for personal data; recent case studies include a system for managing data held within an enterprise's HR systems, and health data stored about individuals and tissue samples in a biobank. Through the use of a suitable policy enforcement architecture, legal and regulatory privacy rules, along with individuals' privacy preferences, can be automatically enforced so that unauthorized and/or unsuitable access to data is prevented. In [21] we proposed a simple conceptual model for representing privacy rules, which can be directly mapped to technically enforceable access control policies (expressed e.g. using XACML).

In [22] Pearson et al. propose a tool for providing decision support with regards to privacy-sensitive projects that arise in an enterprise. Decision support systems are built on knowledge bases with rich sets of rules, and the process of translating legal texts, regulations and corporate guidelines into technically enforceable rules is complex and laborious. For this reason a conceptual model is a useful aid.

There is much work on aspect-oriented access control for privacy [25,26]. Also, Peleg et al. [27] have proposed a framework for situation-based access control that is useful for handling the privacy of patients' health records. Bussard and Becker have extended their previous work on formalising access control policies to privacy-related scenarios in [28].

We believe there is scope for integration of several of the different approaches described so far into a natural-language processing pipeline, which can be integrated with technical enforcement mechanisms to achieve compliance for privacy: this starts with the initial task of analyzing natural-language privacy texts, to the extraction of formalized rules and their automatic enforcement.

We are working on developing tools for automating privacy in cloud computing and, for this, natural-language analysis of provider SLAs, international laws and regulations will need to be combined with suitable enforcement methods such as distributed access control [29], sticky policies and policy-based obfuscation [30].

6 Review and Future Work

We have in this paper surveyed a number of existing works related to the analysis of privacy and privacy-related texts, with the goal of representing the knowledge and rules therein in a logical form that is machine readable and automatically enforceable. We presented a grouping of these works in four classes, which may be seen as constituting essential steps in a natural-language processing pipeline; such a pipeline may be seen as a workflow that would be included as part of the compliance lifecycle for an enterprise.

We have focused specifically on research in the privacy space, due to its growing significance as a societal concern and the critical consequences faced by enterprises that fail to meet compliance with privacy law and regulations.

References

1. Moulin, B., Rousseau, D.: Automated Knowledge Acquisition from Regulatory Texts. IEEE Expert 7(5), 27–35 (2002)
2. Bret Michael, J., Ong, V., Rowe, N.C.: Natural-Language Processing Support for Developing Policy-Governed Software Systems. In: Proceedings of 39th International Conference and Exhibition on Technology of Object-Oriented Languages and Systems (TOOLS 39), pp. 263–274 (2001)
3. Antón, A.I., Earp, J.B., He, Q., Stufflebeam, W., Bolchini, D., Jensen, C.: Financial Privacy Policies and the Need for Standardization. IEEE Security and Privacy 2(2), 36–45 (2004)

4. Krasnow Waterman, K.: Pre-processing Legal Text: Policy Parsing and Isomorphic Intermediate Representation. In: Proceedings of PRIVACY 2010 - Intelligent Information Privacy Management AAAI Spring Symposium. Stanford Center for Computers and Law, Palo Alto (2010)
5. Breaux, T.D., Antón, A.I.: Deriving Semantic Models from Privacy Policies. In: Proceedings of the Sixth International Workshop on Policies for Distributed Systems and Networks, POLICY 2005 (2005)
6. Kiyavitskaya, N., Zeni, N., Breaux, T.D., Antón, A.I., Cordy, J.R., Mich, L., Mylopoulos, J.: Extracting Rights and Obligations from Regulations: Toward a Tool-Supported Process. In: Proceedings of ASE 2007 (2007)
7. Breaux, T.D., Vail, M.W., Antón, A.I.: Towards Regulatory Compliance: Extracting Rights and Obligations to Align Requirements with Regulations. In: Proceedings of 14th IEEE International Requirements Engineering Conference, RE 2006 (2006)
8. Breaux, T.D., Antón, A.I.: Analyzing Regulatory Rules for Privacy and Security Requirements. IEEE Transactions on Software Engineering 34(1), 5–20 (2008)
9. Delannoy, J.F., Feng, C., Matwin, S., Szpakowicz, S.: Knowledge Extraction from Text: Machine Learning for Text-to-rule Translation. In: Brazdil, P.B. (ed.) ECML 1993. LNCS, vol. 667. Springer, Heidelberg (1993)
10. Delisle, S., Barker, K., Delannoy, J., Matwin, S., Szpakowicz, S.: From Text to Horn Clauses: Combining Linguistic Analysis and Machine Learning. In: Proceedings of Canadian AI Conference, AI/GI/CV 1994 (1994)
11. Stamey, J.W., Rossi, R.A.: Automatically Identifying Relations in Privacy Policies. In: Proceedings of SIGDOC 2009 (2009)
12. Barth, A., Datta, A., Mitchell, J.C., Nissenbaum, H.: Privacy and Contextual Integrity: Framework and Applications. In: Proceedings of IEEE Symposium on Security and Privacy (2006)
13. May, M.J., Gunter, C.A., Lee, I.: Privacy APIs: Access Control Techniques to Analyze and Verify Legal Privacy Policies. In: Proceedings of Computer Security Foundations Workshop, CSFW 2006 (2006)
14. Brodie, C.A., Karat, C., Karat, J.: An Empirical Study of Natural Language Parsing of Privacy Policy Rules Using the SPARCLE Policy Workbench. In: Proceedings of Symposium on Usable Privacy and Security, SOUPS (2006)
15. Ong, V.L.: An Architecture and Prototype System for Automatically Processing Natural-Language Statements of Policy. Master's thesis, Naval Postgraduate School, Monterey, California (2001)
16. Davies, J., Grobelnik, M., Mladenic, D. (eds.): Semantic Knowledge Management. Springer, Heidelberg (2009)
17. Breuker, J., Casanovas, P., Klein, M.C.A., Francesconi, E. (eds.): Law, Ontologies and the Semantic Web. IOS Press, Amsterdam (2009)
18. Casanovas, P., Sartor, G., Casellas, N., Rubino, R. (eds.): Computable Models of the Law. Springer, Heidelberg (2008)
19. Benjamins, V.R., Casanovas, P., Breuker, J., Gangemi, A. (eds.): Law and the Semantic Web. Springer, Heidelberg (2005)
20. Bourcier, D.: Legal Knowledge and Information Systems. IOS Press, Amsterdam (2003)
21. Mont, M.C., Pearson, S., Creese, S., Goldsmith, M., Papanikolaou, N.: A Conceptual Model for Privacy Policies with Consent and Revocation Requirements. In: Proceedings of PrimeLife/IFIP Summer School 2010: Privacy and Identity Management for Life. LNCS. Springer, Heidelberg (2010)

22. Pearson, S., Rao, P., Sander, T., Parry, A., Paull, A., Patruni, S., Dandamudi-Ratnakar, V., Sharma, P.: Scalable, accountable privacy management for large organizations. In: Proceedings of 13th Enterprise Distributed Object Computing Conference Workshop (EDOCW 2009), pp. 168–175 (2009)
23. SPIN, http://www.spinroot.org
24. IBM REALM Project,
    http://www.zurich.ibm.com/security/publications/2006/
    REALM-atIRIS2006-20060217.pdf
25. Chen, K., Wang, D.: An aspect-oriented approach to privacy-aware access control. In: Proceedings of the Sixth International Conference on Machine Learning and Cybernetics, Hong Kong, August 19-22 (2007)
26. Berghe, C.V., Schunter, M.: Privacy Injector - Automated Privacy Enforcement through Aspects. In: Danezis, G., Golle, P. (eds.) PET 2006. LNCS, vol. 4258, pp. 99–117. Springer, Heidelberg (2006)
27. Peleg, M., Beimel, D., Dori, D., Denekamp, Y.: Situation-Based Access Control: privacy management via modeling of patient data access scenarios. Journal of Biomedical Informatics (to appear)
28. Bussard, L., Becker, M.Y.: Can Access Control be Extended to Deal with Data Handling in Privacy Scenarios?. In: Proceedings of W3C Workshop on Access Control Application Scenarios (2009)
29. Becker, M.Y., Sewell, P.: Cassandra: Distributed Access Control Policies with Tunable Expressiveness. In: Proceedings of 5th IEEE International Workshop on Policies for Distributed Systems and Networks (POLICY 2004), Yorktown Heights, NY, USA, June 7-9, pp. 159–168. IEEE Computer Society, Los Alamitos (2004)
30. Mowbray, M., Pearson, S., Shen, Y.: Enhancing privacy in cloud computing via policy-based obfuscation. Journal of Supercomputing, doi:10.1007/s11227-010-0425-z

Secure Workstation for Special Applications

Adam Kozakiewicz[1], Anna Felkner[1], Janusz Furtak[2], Zbigniew Zieliński[2],
Marek Brudka[3], and Marek Małowidzki[4]

[1] NASK – Research and Academic Computer Network,
Wąwozowa 18, 02-796 Warsaw, Poland
{adam.kozakiewicz,anna.felkner}@nask.pl
[2] Military University of Technology, Faculty of Cybernetics,
Institute of Teleinformatics and Automation, gen. S. Kaliskiego 2, 00-908 Warsaw, Poland
{jfurtak,zzielinski}@wat.edu.pl
[3] Filbico Sp. z o.o., Prymasa S. Wyszyńskiego 7, 05-220 Zielonka, Poland
mbrudka@filbico.pl
[4] Military Communication Institute, ul. Warszawska 22A, 05-130 Zegrze, Poland
m.malowidzki@wil.waw.pl

Abstract. The paper presents the recently started project which aims to develop a secure environment for processing of restricted information. The solution being developed by the consortium employs virtualization to allow data from different security domains to be processed on the same physical machine. The system can host Windows and Linux systems as secured guest operating systems. The proposed implementation offers advanced user authentication techniques and cryptographic protection. The project is expected to reach technology demonstrator phase in late 2012.

Keywords: operating systems, virtual machines, multiple independent levels of security, encryption, authentication.

1 Introduction

The paper presents an overview of a project called "Secure Workstation for Special Applications"[1], developed by a consortium led by the Military University of Technology in Warsaw. The aim of the project is to develop a secure environment for processing of sensitive (or even classified) information from different security domains (either data from separate administrative domains or data with different classification levels; in both cases data that should be processed separately) on the same physical machine. This goal will be achieved through application of virtualization technology to provide different virtual machines with either Linux or Windows systems for each security level.

While the application of virtual machines for various information domains is not new in mainframe world[1], full hardware assisted virtualization in x86 architectures was impossible [2] until advances in PC chipsets made by Intel (VT, vPro) and AMD

---

[1] Project funded by the Polish Ministry of Science and Higher Education under grant OR00014011 (Polish project title: "Bezpieczna stacja do zastosowań specjalnych").

C. Lee et al. (Eds.): STA 2011 Workshops, CCIS 187, pp. 174–181, 2011.

(AMD-V). These trusted extensions enable not only to support virtualization in hardware, but also to create separated partitions for processing information in different security domains.

The existing virtualization packages, both commercial (such as VMWare[3]) and open-source (VirtualBox[4], Xen[5], KVM[6]) can already take full advantage of hardware virtualization. However, our goal is to deliver a complete technology demonstrator with augmented security, complying with legal and certification requirements. We believe that the results of our project may be a basis for an integrated solution for public administration, military, or commercial users.

The paper is organized as follows: Section 2 presents in detail the goals of the project. Section 3 gives an overview of the planned activities and Section 4 attempts to envision the effects of application of the designed solution. Section 5 contains related work. In Section 6 we present the project's current status and conclude with a short summary in Section 7. Appendix A presents the project consortium.

2 Project Goals

The essence of the project is the development of a secure workstation for processing of multilevel sensitive information (MLS, multiple levels of security) through integration of:

- existing virtualization technology (software and hardware, e.g. [5, 6]),
- formal methods ensuring confidentiality and integrity of data,
- cryptographic methods of securing removable and non-removable media, both on the host machine and in the virtualized environments, with keys (and – if it proves possible – algorithms) stored in external hardware,
- advanced authentication and access control,
- advanced audit measures.

Note that we are going to leverage an existing virtualization package, as the development of yet another is not a project goal. We focus on a higher-level solution, i.e., a virtualization-based workstation. Moreover, using a well-tested codebase as a starting point allows to save time and concentrate on novel aspects of the project.

The main goal of the project, apart from research work, is to develop an advanced technology demonstrator, which will potentially be a basis for certified COTS (commercial off-the-shelf) computer systems. The demonstrator will include:

1. secure system platform – software component integrating a secure host operating system and virtual machine management tools,
2. special versions of guest operating systems – secure configurations of Windows and Linux systems, prepared to run under control of the secure system platform,
3. technical and operational documentation of the system, recommendations, procedures and templates,
4. examples of cryptographic data protection and authentication mechanisms.

The resulting system will be able to simultaneously run several instances of guest operating systems, providing strict access control, cryptographic security and data transfer restrictions. Each instance will be a separate security domain, processing data with different security levels (e.g., a "public" and a "classified" virtual machine running simultaneously) or data that should be separated because of law or company's policy requirements (e.g., two "classified" virtual machines, connected to two systems serving different purposes).

The basic configuration of such a system is a relatively simple task. The added value of the project lies mainly in three areas:

- proper separation of different security domains
- numerous security-focused enhancements – cryptographic protection, advanced access control, advanced authentication techniques;
- enhancements preparing the system for potential future certification – advanced audit mechanisms for all parts of the system.

3 Planned Activities

The project is split into nine interrelated tasks, organized into four rough phases: initial, modeling, implementation and closing.

3.1 Initial Phase

The goal of this phase is to define the detailed scope of the project. This includes research on the current state of the art, basic design decisions and the formulation of requirements. The two tasks comprising this phase are as follows:

Task 1. Analysis of the state of the art of existing virtualization solutions; analysis of the relevant legal acts.

Apart from overview of the current technology and law, this task joins both aspects by finding the ways in which the legal regulations constrain technical decisions regarding the architecture of the system and different aspects of its functionality. Among the main goals of this task is also the choice of the virtualization platform to be used as a basis for development in later phases of the project. For obvious reasons this choice is mostly restricted to open source solutions, however selection of one of the options is not a trivial task, as the solutions differ in several aspects, influencing the architecture of the system (e.g. type of hypervisor) and amount of work necessary to implement expected functionality.

Task 2. Requirements and architectural concept of the secure system platform.

This task includes specification of the functional and nonfunctional requirements and high-level design of the system. While work on this task can proceed in parallel with Task 1, it is partially dependent on its results, especially the legal restrictions and technology choices.

3.2 Modeling Phase

This phase includes the theoretical analysis of the system, facilitating possible future certification of the whole system or its parts. Two tasks form this phase:

Task 3. Development of a formal model of the MLS-type secure workstation for special applications.

In this task formal models of the system should be developed, focusing on the secure system platform. The goal is to enable a formal verification of integrity and secrecy of the processed data. We propose an approach to the construction of the secure workstation software by specializing MDA (Model Driven Architecture) [7] to model driven security [8]. Namely, we would integrate security models (expressed in languages for modeling security) with UML process models. Modeling will be performed using languages including, but not limited to UML, OCL (Object Constraint Language) and SecureUML, as well as tools such as RSA (Rational Software Architect). Simulation with the use of RSA would be used already when the models are constructed. This approach helps finding and fixing integrity and secrecy problems early.

Task 4. Development of techniques for authentication of users and cryptographic data protection solutions.

The beginning of this task is theoretical and clearly a part of the modeling phase, but it continues through the next phas, ending in implementation of the analyzed solutions. The topics of this task are access control methods, authentication using biometric and non-biometric methods and cryptographic protection of removable and non-removable media. While legal regulations enforce only using mandatory access control (MAC [9, 10]), this system will be based on a trust management language from the RT (Role-based Trust Management [11]) family, enabling more detailed specification of access rules. The language is capable of implementing MAC, while also enabling specification of complex, time constrained "need to know" rules.

3.3 Implementation Phase

In this – longest – phase the secure workstation will be developed and documented. This phase also includes basic verification and quality control of the created code (unit tests, integration tests, regression tests). There are three main tasks in this phase, although, as previously mentioned, Task 4 is also partially included.

Task 5. Development of the secure system platform.

This task is the heart of the entire project. The main part of the system will be implemented on the basis of the results of all previous tasks. This includes:

- specification of detailed requirements for this part of the workstation,
- preparation of a secure configuration of the host operating system,
- creation of the virtual machine management mechanisms, including modification and development of an existing virtual machine monitor,
- modification of the host operating system's setup to ensure that the virtual machine monitor is the only interface to the host system accessible by users,
- integration of the mechanisms developed in Task 4,
- development of advanced verification, integrity monitoring, backup and audit mechanisms for the platform.

The most important part of this task is securing virtualization to prevent attacks against one of the guest systems from propagating to the host system, hypervisor or other guest systems. With growing popularity of cloud technology, virtual environments are becoming a target for specialized malware [12, 13, 14] – the secure system platform must deal with this threat to prevent compromising the security of other data in the system when one of the guest systems falls victim to that type of threat.

Task 6&7. Development of a special version of a Linux/UNIX (Task 6) and Windows (Task 7) operating system.

Each of these tasks should result in a complete, secure default configuration of a guest (virtualized) operating system (either from Windows or Linux/UNIX family), to be used under control of the secure system platform. The tasks concentrate on adaptation and/or creation of recommendations and templates for a secure configuration. Currently we are not sure whether source code modifications will be required (and whether they would prove feasible, especially in case of Windows). We also plan to implement advanced and fault-tolerant audit mechanisms.

3.4 Closing Phase

In this phase the system will be thoroughly tested and verified. Apart from that, it is crucial to document all the lessons learned during development works. These goals make it natural to split this phase into two tasks:

Task 8. Development of a test plan and validation of security of the workstation.

This task should empirically verify the quality of the developed system, concentrating on the security of processed data. This will involve preparation of test plans, implementation of tests and actual testing. The tests will focus on various forms of attacks, both against the secure system platform and the guest systems.

Task 9. Preparation of conclusions and recommendations regarding deployment and exploitation of the secure workstation in military and government institutions.

This task concludes the project by summarizing the project's findings. The reports should specify, whether the product can be certified as is and – if not – what should be done to make it possible. They should also present recommendations on using the secure workstation in production environments. There are two aspects to the recommendations. One is the workstation itself – analysis of its features and capabilities. This includes both proposed deployment procedures and possible future work – functionalities not envisaged in the original project, which became apparent during development and could make the solution more useful. The other focuses on the legal, organizational and physical environment. This includes deployment guidelines, specifying the technical and organizational issues that must be addressed, but also recommendations showing the possible ways in which law could be adapted to better support this type of solutions.

4   Effects and Applications of the System

MLS information processing is currently possible using existing tools. However, due to strict administrative regulations (at least in Poland), physical data separation is required – i.e., data from different security levels *must* be processed using separate, disconnected systems, certified for this particular security level. The predominant approach – physical isolation or air gap – is the most secure scenario, but it is inconvenient and expensive.

We do not expect that "mixing" top secret and unclassified data on a single hardware will ever be allowed by security regulations. However, an appropriately verified solution *could* enable simultaneous processing of data with "similar" ("neighboring") clauses (e.g., unclassified and restricted). Moreover, even if this will never be allowed, our solution will still be useful for separating data that belong to different security domains and, due to law or local security policy, should be isolated. Due to increasing processing performance of modern computer systems, this is technically feasible, and would limit the amount of required hardware and related costs, bringing in the inherent advantages of virtualization (failure protection, fast recovery, etc).

We expect that our workstation could be deployed by the police, the military sector, public administration, and all other potential users demanding higher security.

5   Related Work

There are a number of solutions marketed as "virtualization-based secure workstation" available; however, due to lack of technical details, it is usually difficult to assess whether a particular product is just virtualization software pre-installed (and, possibly, pre-configured) on particular hardware or an important extension to existing technology. We believe that our project has similar goals to the NSA High Assurance Platform initiative [15] (hardware key storage, disk encryption) or products based on the former NetTop project [16] (such as HP NetTop [17], offering advanced logging, networking separation and VPN end-to-end encryption).

6   Current Status of the Project

The project started on November 17th, 2010 and is currently entering the modeling phase. State of the art analysis and basic requirements are completed.

After some initial research, we selected three candidates for the base virtualization solution: VirtualBox [4], Xen [5] and KVM [6]. During subsequent works, consisting of legal analysis (e.g., licensing rules), analysis of offered functionality, project and code reviews, stability and performance tests, etc., we have excluded VirtualBox (mainly due to fact that VB is a type 2 supervisor – harder to separate from the host operating system; additionally it proved less stable in tests). The two other packages differ in many aspects but we estimate that their overall usefulness is similar (at the time of writing, the final decision is being made).

7   Summary

The paper contains an overview of a project aiming at development of an integrated, virtualization-based workstation for simultaneous processing of data from different security domains. The anticipated solution will combine existing virtual technology, advanced, mostly hardware-based security mechanisms, and, finally, formal security modeling, taking legal and certification aspects in mind.

The project started in the end of 2010. A finished technology demonstrator will be available in the second half of 2012.

References

1. Goldberg, R.P., Popek, G.J.: Formal Requirements for Virtualizable Third Generation Architectures. Communication of the ACM 17(7) (1974)
2. Robin, J.S., Irvine, C.E.: Analysis of the Intel Pentium's Ability to Support a Secure Virtual Machine Monitor. In: Proceedings of the 9th USENIX Security Symposium, Denver, Colorado, USA, August 14-17 (2000)
3. VMWare, Virtualization Overview
4. Oracle VM VirtualBox – User Manual,
   http://www.virtualbox.org/manual/UserManual.html
5. Barham, P., Dragovic, B., Fraser, K., Hand, S., Harris, T., Ho, A., Neugebauer, R., Pratt, I., Wareld, A.: Xen and the Art of Virtualization. University of Cambridge Computer Laboratory, CGF Brussels (2004)
6. Warnke, R., Ritzau, T.: QEMU, Kernel-based Virtual Machine (KVM) & libvirt (2010), http://qemu-buch.de
7. Frankel, D.S.: Model Driven Architecture: Applying MDA to Enterprise Computing. John Wiley & Sons, Chichester (2003)
8. Lodderstedt, T., Basin, D.A., Doser, J.: SecureUML: A UML-based modeling language for model-driven security. In: Jézéquel, J.-M., Hussmann, H., Cook, S. (eds.) UML 2002. LNCS, vol. 2460, pp. 426–441. Springer, Heidelberg (2002)
9. Bell, D.D., La Padula, L.J.: Secure Computer System: Unified Exposition and Multics Interpretation. ESDTR-75-306. ESD/AFSC, Bedford, MA, Hanscom AFB (1974), http://csrc.nist.gov/publications/history/bell76.pdf
10. Bell, D.E.: Looking Back at the Bell-La Padula Model, Reston, VA, 20191 (2005)
11. Li, N., Mitchell, J.C.: RT: A Role-Based Trust Management Framework. In: 3rd DARPA Information Survivability Conference and Exposition (DISCEX III), pp. 201–212 (2003)
12. King, S.T., Chen, P.M., Wang, Y., Verbowski, C., Wang, H.J., Lorch, J.R.: SubVirt: Implementing Malware with Virtual Machines. In: IEEE Symp. on Security and Privacy (the Oakland Conference) (2006)
13. Ferrie, P.: Attacks on Virtual Machine Emulators. In: Association of Anti Virus Asia Researchers Conference, Auckland, New Zealand (2006)
14. Rutkowska, J.: Subverting Vista Kernel for Fun and Profit. In: SyScan 2006, Singapore (2006)
15. NSA High Assurance Platform,
    http://www.nsa.gov/ia/programs/h_a_p/index.shtml
16. NetTop,
    http://www.nsa.gov/research/tech_transfer/fact_sheets/nettop.shtml
17. HP NetTop,
    http://h71028.www7.hp.com/enterprise/downloads/HP_NetTop_Whitepaper2.pdf

Appendix: Consortium Members

Military University of Technology, the leader of the consortium is well known of being the leading in Poland technical university offering 14 specializations of education on the 7 faculties for both military and civil group of students. MUT conducts research, development, implementation and modernization of technical sciences, chemical, physical, economic and military. The primary areas of scientific and research activities leading in the Faculty of Cybernetics are as follows: simulation and artificial intelligence, computer vision and image analysis, computer networks security, dependability and diagnosing as well as designing of cryptosystems based on the hard computational problems (differential and linear cryptanalysis of ciphers, application of elliptic curves in cryptography, implementation of ciphers in programmable devices).

Filbico Sp. z o.o., the industrial partner in the consortium, is the IT company, which develops dedicated information systems for military forces and uniformed services. Filbico experience encloses command and control systems, fire control software, crisis management and data security solutions.

Military Telecommunications Institute is a public research institute integrating scientific research, development and production in the areas of command systems, telecommunications and national security. MCI is a leading communications systems integrator, handling the entire process from system design to deployment and maintenance, and a provider of military communication and information security solutions. The scope of research activities includes network planning and management, radiocommunications, electronic warfare, net-centric systems, electromagnetic compatibility, and cryptology.

Research and Academic Computer Network (NASK). NASK is the Polish national registry of Internet names in the .pl domain and a leading data networks operator offering telecommunications and data solutions to business, administration and academic customers. From 1 October 2010 NASK has a status of Research Institute. A part of the NASK organization, CERT Polska is Poland's first Computer Emergency Response Team. NASK Research Division conducts research in several areas, including network modeling, auction theory, simulation, optimization methods, network security and biometrics. NASK efforts in this project are led by the Network and Information Security Methods Team in the Research Division.

Dynamic Security Monitoring and Accounting for Virtualized Environments

Antonio Muñoz[1], Rajesh Harjani[1], Antonio Maña[1], and Rodrigo Díaz[2]

[1] Escuela Técnica Superior de Ingeniería Informática
Universidad de Málaga, Spain
{amunoz,rajesh,amg}@lcc.uma.es
[2] ATOS OriginRodrigo Diaz Rodriguez
rodrigo.diaz@atosresearch.eu

Abstract. In this paper we present the design of an architecture for dynamic security monitoring and enforcement, based on software protection scheme, for client software running in Virtualized Environments. Monitoring mechanisms check a set of policy-defined conditions at runtime to detect threats or anomalous behaviour. Enforcement will be achieved using secure software execution methods that comply with the policies defined. The architecture presented allows for context adaptation of the policies defined using the language defined in PASSIVE[1]. The automatic runtime enforcement of these policies is crucial to achieve real security in virtualized platforms.

Keywords: Monitoring rules, Accounting, Dynamic Monitoring, Security Monitoring.

1 Introduction

The emergence of highly distributed systems operating in Virtualized Environments poses significant challenges for system security and dependability (S&D) and makes it necessary to develop mechanisms supporting the dynamic monitoring and evolution of applications running on it. In these settings, seamless and dynamic evolution of software becomes a central element for ensuring the security and dependability of systems by maintaining applications up to date and ensuring that they are used correctly. This problem increases in Virtualized Environments in which sets of applications run over several virtualized environments that in turn run in parallel over the same physical layer.

The approach presented in this paper is based on NOVA OS Virtualization Architecture (NOVA) [1], but a description of NOVA is out of the scope of this paper. However if the reader is interested, a further description of NOVA can be found at [1]. Regarding NOVA architecture, several threats have been identified in the instrumentation of Virtualized Environments. Some of them are performed through the x86 interface. Malicious guest operating systems may attack the Virtual Machine Monitor (VMM) by exploiting any security breach of the x86 interface. But

---

[1] ICT PASSIVE project (http://ict-passive.eu/).

C. Lee et al. (Eds.): STA 2011 Workshops, CCIS 187, pp. 182–189, 2011.

this will not affect the hypervisor or the rest of Virtual Machines (VMs) as the NOVA architecture has been designed isolating each VM by associating a single VMM to each VM. As VMMs cannot attack themselves since they are not directly communicated, alternatively, a malicious VMM would need to attack any other component that is shared by different VMMs, for instance a device driver. But as the communication channel between the driver and different VMMs is separated, an attack to the driver can be avoided by simply shutting this communication point. Other types of attacks are related with device drivers. Any driver that performs Direct Memory Access (DMA) has access to the entire memory of the system, and therefore could handle completely the guest. By using an Input/Output Memory Management Unit (IOMMU) the hypervisor restricts DMA transfers to its own memory avoiding this situation. Attacks to device drivers may also be performed remotely through a network card, but due to the nature of the NOVA architecture, this would only compromise the driver.

The PASSIVE monitoring model focuses on runtime supervision of applications, allowing the detection of problems in the operation of individual instances of applications and supporting the automated reconfiguration of these applications. However, in order to enhance trust in applications, it is necessary to analyse their behaviour when used in different Virtualized environments. A high-level dynamic analysis can detect situations that are not possible with static or local dynamic analysis, such as problems in the implementations, in the models describing them or even problems caused by the interaction of different solutions. The results of this analysis provide a basis for taking actions that can support the evolution of applications in response to the identified problems. This paper describes the PASSIVE monitoring framework that addresses this target. The remaining paper is organized as follows, Section 2 is dedicated to describe the background and related work, Section 3 describes the accounting, in Section 4 the Monitoring Architecture of PASSIVE is explained and we conclude with Section 5 describing the ongoing work and the conclusions obtained.

2   Background and Related Work

This infrastructure has been recently designed as part of the PASSIVE project. To the best of our knowledge, there is not any other infrastructure providing the same features as the one we present in this paper. For this reason, not much directly related previous work is found in the literature. Thus, this section gives an account of some partially related approaches.

Software evolution is related to the changes that need to be introduced on a software system following its release for operational use. This evolution may happen because (i) the system needs to adapt to new contexts, (ii) some requirements have changed or (ii) new errors, attacks or vulnerabilities have been found. Surveys have shown that, for many projects, software maintenance and evolution consumes the majority of the overall software life-cycle costs, and there are indications that these costs are proportionally increasing. The detection of violations from expected properties has been proposed as the initial point of maintenance and evolution activities in software development [2]. Work on maintenance architectures is of narrow scope and obsolete [3]. Maintenance technologies [4, 5] tend to ignore the very first phase of this activity, which is error detection. In fact, detection of a malfunction with the objective of facilitating evolution is not supported at all.

Furthermore, as in any form of dynamic software deployment, trust in the applications that are available and can be deployed through the PASSIVE framework is a fundamental prerequisite. Despite the recognition of the importance and necessity of trust in human interactions and exchanges and, as a consequence, the recent increase of the volume of the literature on this topic (e.g. [6-9]), trust is currently poorly assessed for the purposes of dynamic deployment of software. More specifically, none of these strands of work addresses effectively some important aspects of software service trust, most notably the need to assess it for dynamically composed and deployed software services, as in the case of the PASSIVE applications, and ground it not only on subjective opinions but also on dynamically acquired information about the behaviour and quality of a software service in diverse deployment contexts. Furthermore, each trust assessment should be accompanied by an evaluation of its accuracy and risk [10].

3 Accounting

With the growing use of virtualized environments, data center administrators are demanding more and more accurate methods of the accounting models used to track the usage of virtualized resources and services utilization and to the linking of the resource consumption with the users. Accounting resources consumption is always a challenging task, especially, when you are working in virtualized environments. One example of this challenge is the accounting of Central Processing Unit (CPU) time that is traditionally based on timer interrupt handler since timer interrupt is periodically delivered to OS. Nevertheless, in virtualized systems CPU time is shared among multiple virtual CPUs and the timer interrupt is paused on the CPUs that are scheduled out. This operation results in an inaccurate accounting. The key point of accurate CPU time accounting is to distinguish the time allocated to "this Virtual CPU (VCPU)" and "other VCPUs". Para-virtualization achieves this goal by modifying the timer handling routines and offering better performance by a virtual machine abstraction that is similar but not identical to the underlying hardware. This is the approach we have adopted in PASSIVE to get the time accounting right. Measurement of resource consumption (CPU, storage, network utilization) can be done with existing system tools when following a per-virtual machine basis approach, but, in the case of per-process/application basis approach or in paravirtualized environments this solution is not feasible. When measuring the resources consumed by a certain process/application in a virtualized environment, both, the resources consumed directly by application together with the resources consumed by the Operating System (OS) virtualization (hypervisor, virtual machine monitor) should be accounted.

Modern VM environments, such as the one used in the context of PASSIVE (NOVA), consist of a distributed and multi-layered software stack including a hypervisor, multiple VMs and guest OSes, device driver modules, and other service infrastructure. The functionality of the NOVA hypervisor is similar to that of an operating system kernel: abstracting from the underlying hardware platform and isolating the components running on top of it. In this architecture, a centralized accounting management is unfeasible, as device control and accounting information are distributed across the whole system. Consequently, a two-level accounting approach is needed, at host-level and guest-level, to correctly measure the real resource consumption. At the lowest-level of the virtual machine, the privileged hypervisor and host driver modules have direct control over hardware devices and can measure their consumption. At the highest-level, the guest OS has knowledge about the resource consumption of the application that are running on it. However, the VM is running on unpriviledge virtualized devices without direct access to the physical devices. The accounting challenge in PASSIVE is not only limited to resources consumption tracking, it should take also into account specific privacy constraints that may impose restrictions on the type of the user data to be collected. For this reason, the PASSIVE Accounting component will be strongly connected with the PASSIVE identity management and access control systems.

4 Monitoring Architecture

Monitoring security and dependability properties during the operation of software systems is widely accepted as a measure of runtime verification that increases system resilience to dependability failures and security attacks. PASSIVE monitoring advocates the need for this form of system verification and has developed a monitoring framework, to support the monitoring of these properties during the operation of a system. It should be noted, however, that whilst monitoring is able to detect violations of S&D properties at runtime, it can not always provide information that is necessary for understanding the reasons that underpin the violation of an S&D property and making decisions about what would be an appropriate reaction to it.

Furthermore, it is often necessary to try to predict the possibility of violation using information about the current state of a system rather than wait until all the information that would enable a definite decision about the violation becomes available. This is because an accurate early prediction can widen the scope of possible reactions to the violation or even provide scope for taking pre-emptive action that prevents the violation.

In our monitoring system, the absence of a signal after the elapse of a given signalling period can be detected by specifying a monitoring rule, requiring that the time between two consecutive signals from the same device should not exceed the given period. Detecting, however, the occurrence of a violation of this rule is not in itself sufficient for establishing the reasons why some device has failed to send the expected signals. In such cases, a further search for possible causes of the violation could be useful for deciding how to react to the violation.

The aim of the PASSIVE monitoring framework is to analyse problems detected in the operation of applications from a high-level point of view in order to support automated reaction and evolution of applications operating in Virtualized environments. In achieving this goal, we have designed PASSIVE dynamic security monitoring and enforcement model. As shown in Figure1, this infrastructure is composed by: Local Application Surveillance (LAS), Intra Platform Surveillance (IPS) and Global Application Surveillance (GAS). The IPS collects information related to violations of monitoring rules in the context of different virtualized environments in order to analyze them and come up with the expected reactions to be performed by the monitoring administrators. Usually, these reactions are materialized by means of changes in the virtualized environment configuration.

Our goal is to provide new capabilities to the Virtual Environment (VE) increasing its security and reliability. The key point of this approach is an architecture based on the PASSIVE Monitoring infrastructure including a three dimension monitoring mechanism. This mechanism has to be able to provide ease of identification of origin of errors, capturing precise and specific information about attacks, errors and malfunctioning, lowering the time required to identify and fix errors, provides an early detection, an increased protection of the VE code during the monitoring process and the increased ability to assess the integrity and compliance of the VE after.

Local Application Surveillance (LAS) and Intra Platform Surveillance (IPS) components are integrated in every Virtual Machine Monitor (VMM)[2] in the Virtualized Environment. Every IPS has responsibility for collecting information related to the violation of monitoring rules expressing properties that need to be satisfied at runtime and underpin the trustworthiness of the application. Violations are detected by every LAS as an additional functionality of these. Thus, LAS forwards this information to the IPS, which is responsible to perform an analysis on this data.

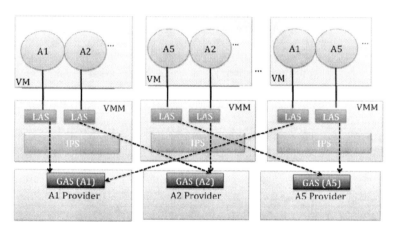

Fig. 1. Monitoring Architecture

Global Application Surveillance (GAS) is the component that performs an analysis based on both the monitoring rules violations and the LAS and IPS analysis rules. For instance, this analysis gives the IPS Administrator information about a specific monitoring rule that is frequently violated. This component retrieves the monitoring rules violations from the MR reader component. It also retrieves the local analyser rules from the IPS rules data bank component. IPS analyser rules express abnormal situations in terms of monitoring rules violations. The IPS analyser is in charge of matching analysis rules with violations of monitoring rules happened in the associated application.

---

[2] Nova Architecture.

MR reader: This component reads and stores monitoring rules violations from the monitoring results log file created by the LAS.

IPS rules Data Bank: This component stores analysis rules. It is managed by the IPS Administrator through the IPS GUI.

IPS GUI: This component is a graphical interface through which the IPS Administrator interacts with the IPS. It has three main functionalities: (i) it displays the analysis report from the IPS Analyser, (ii) it manages the IPS rules in the IPS rules Data Bank, and (iii) it inspects the contents of the MR reader. It is important to take into account that the integration of an IPS into a PASSIVE virtualized environment does not affect the operation of the Virtualized Environment. The purpose of the IPS is to provide more information to the IPS administrator about the operation of applications. Using this information the IPS administrator can modify the application or Virtualized Environment configuration in order to adapt the system behaviour.

Global Application Surveillance (GAS) is a component that operates outside the Virtualized Environment. The purpose of the GAS is to receive and analyse information provided from different IPSs in order to make a secondary form of analysis. This analysis is enabled by the input of information about analysis results from different IPSs. Thus, GAS is able to detect whether certain monitoring rules are violated in the context of different VEs (IPSs). GAS is composed of the following four components: GAS Analyser: This component is in charge of evaluating monitoring rules violations from different applications that are running in different Virtualized Environments. The global analysis is based on the IPS analysis results, and on the GAS Rules (GASMR). The IPS analysis results are expressed in terms of IPS analyser rules violations. These results can include monitoring rules violations detected by VMMs. GASRs express particular conditions in terms of IPS analyser rules violations occurred in different IPSs. Consequently, the global analysis depends on the IPS analyser rules violations found in the IPS analysis results. IPSA results reader: This component stores the results produced by the different IPS that are connected to a particular GAS. GASR Data Bank: This component keeps a record of the GASRs. GAS Administrators manage this data bank in order to express their GAS analysis preferences. GAS GUI: This Component is the interface used by the GAS Administrator to access to the GAS. Through this GUI GAS Administrators receive the analysis result reports from the GAS Analyser. This component is also used in order to update or inspect the contents of the GASR Data Bank, and to inspect the contents of the IPSA results reader.

The LAS records violations of the monitoring rules to a log file. The IPS reads the information about these violations from the log file (through the IPS Reader component). The communication between IPS and GAS is based on a specific interface that is offered by the IPS and is used by GAS to access the analyser results.

Figure2 is a deployment diagram that illustrates how each GAS receives analysis results from several IPS. The first node in the diagram has a VMM and a IPS. The second node has a GAS. Two different strategies are designed according to the initial version of the architecture. Figure3 shows the basic dynamic security monitoring architecture model that includes an IPS placed out of the Virtualized Environment. This model provides a possible complete analysis of the violated monitoring rules, but these rules are very complex and hard to be analyzed since they are not filtered, and this can produce overloads in the monitoring system. One appeal of this architecture is that it is designed to reduce these overloads that include one IPS in the Virtualized Environment located between VMM and User layer as we show in Figure1. This model also includes a GAS per application running in the set of Virtualized Environments. This GAS is placed outside of the Virtualized Environment. This model allows collecting the monitoring data organized in such a way that its analysis is estimated more efficient than the basic model.

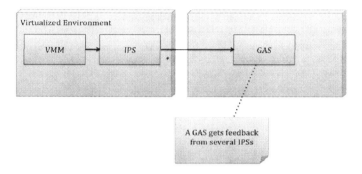

Fig. 2. IPS and GAS relationship

The IPS will store violated monitoring rules in a log file. Initially these rules will be expressed in EC-Assertion [1]. EC-Assertion is a first order temporal logic language based on Event Calculus. Monitoring rules in this language have the generic form B → H stating that when B is True, H must also be True. Both B (Body) and H (Head) are defined as conjunctions of Event Calculus predicates. The predicates used in monitoring rules express the occurrence of an event (Happens predicate), the initiation or termination of a fluent (i.e. condition) by the occurrence of an event (Initiates and Terminates predicates respectively), or the validity of fluent (HoldsAt predicate). Predicates are associated with time variables that indicate the time point at which the predicate is True. Events in EC-Assertion may represent operation invocations and responses or signals and messages generated during the operation of a system and are associated with a time variable. A detailed account of EC-Assertion is beyond the scope of this paper and can be found in [1]. The monitoring rules must be designed to provide the information required by the application, which uses the VE in order to assess its correct functioning. When an event is received by the IPS that is managed by the core monitoring mechanism, the event is forwarded to the appropriate monitoring service, which evaluates the state of the application by applying the monitoring rules defined for that application. If a violation of one of these rules is detected, this violation is reported to the GAS, which registers it and takes appropriate actions. These actions can be: stop running the application, pause it, reset it, etc.

5   Conclusion and Ongoing Work

This paper has presented the PASSIVE infrastructure for monitoring applications deployed in Virtualized Environments. This infrastructure adds two monitoring layers on top of the given NOVA monitoring model in order to provide support for evolution of applications.

Currently, the results of the analysis performed by the PASSIVE monitoring subsystem are reflected on the system behaviour by means of changes done by a human administrator. As future work we are targeting the automated reaction of the system according to the analysis resulting from the PASSIVE monitoring subsystem. Another interesting strand of research currently initiated is the identification of the changes that must be applied to a component when a problem is detected. We are working on studying the feasibility of using instead of a first order temporal logic language based on Event Calculus a High order temporal logic although it is more complex or even an intermediate step as the Event Calculus and the Alternating Time Epistemic Logic (ATEL).

Acknowledgements

The work in this paper was partly sponsored by the EC Framework Programme as part of the ICT PASSIVE project (http://ict-passive.eu/).

References

1. Steinberg, U., Kauer, B.: NOVA: a microhypervisor-based secure virtualization architecture. In: Proceedings of the 5th European Conference on Computer systems (EuroSys 2010), pp. 209–222. ACM, New York (2010)
2. Chowdhury, A., Meyers, S.: Facilitating Software Maintenance by Automated Detection of Constraint Violations, Tech. Rep. CS-93-37 Brown Univ. (1993)
3. Sellink, A., Verhoef, C.: An Architecture for Automated Software Maintenance. In: Proceedings of the 7th Intl. Workshop on Program Comprehension (1999)
4. Verhoef, C.: Towards automated modification of legacy assets. Annals of Software Engineering 9(1-4), 315–336 (2000)
5. van den Brand, M.G.J., Sellink, M.P.A., Verhoef, C.: Control flow normalization for COBOL/CICS legacy system. In: Proceedings of the 2nd Euromicro Conf. on Maintenance and Reengineering
6. Corritore, L., et al.: On-line trust: concepts, evolving themes, a model. Int. J. of Human-Computer Studies 58(6), 737–758 (2003)
7. Jøsang, A.: Trust and Reputation Systems. In: Aldini, A., Gorrieri, R. (eds.) FOSAD 2007. LNCS, vol. 4677, pp. 209–245. Springer, Heidelberg (2007)
8. McKnight, D.H., Chervany, N.L.: The Meanings of Trust. Technical Report MISRC Working Paper Series 96-04, University of Minnesota (1996)
9. Resnick, P., et al.: Reputation systems. Communications of the ACM 43(12), 45–48 (2000)
10. Spanoudakis, G.: Dynamic Trust Assessment of Software Services. In: Proc. of 2nd International Workshop on Service Oriented Software Engineering, IW-SOSE 2007 (2007)

Cryptography Goes to the Cloud

Isaac Agudo[1], David Nuñez[1], Gabriele Giammatteo[2],
Panagiotis Rizomiliotis[3], and Costas Lambrinoudakis[4]

[1] Department of Computer Science, E.T.S. Ingeniería Informática,
University of Málaga, E-29071 Málaga, Spain
[2] Research and Development Laboratory, Engineering Ingegneria Informatica S.p.A.
Via Riccardo Morandi, 32 00148 Roma - Italy
[3] Laboratory of Information and Communication Systems Security,
Department of Information and Communication Systems Engineering,
University of the Aegean Samos, GR-83200, Greece
[4] Department of Digital Systems, University of Piraeus,
Piraeus, Greece
{isaac,dnunez}@lcc.uma.es, gabriele.giammatteo@eng.it,
prizomil@aegean.gr, clam@unipi.gr

Abstract. In this paper we identify some areas where cryptography can help a rapid adoption of cloud computing. Although secure storage has already captured the attention of many cloud providers, offering a higher level of protection for their customer's data, we think that more advanced techniques such as searchable encryption and secure outsourced computation will become popular in the near future, opening the doors of the Cloud to customers with higher security requirements.

Keywords: Cloud Computing, Searchable Encryption, Secure Storage.

1 Introduction

The wide adoption of cloud computing is raising several concerns about treatment of data in the cloud. Advantages of cloud storage are enormous: I) ubiquitous access: anywhere, anyhow, anytime access to your data, ii) high reliability, iii) resilience and iv) scalability, v) cost efficiency. But, unfortunately, to date, also several security and legal risks should be considered: i) unauthorized access, ii) sensitive data disclosure, iii) IPR protection, iv) communication threats and loads in transferring data, v) data integrity. As stated in [17][18], cloud data security is the most worrying issue of cloud technology and before enterprises or public authorities will fully outsource their data management to cloud vendors replacing their internal facilities, security has to improve to acceptable levels. This is also the opinion of the European Commission [16].

Cryptography could help increasing adoption of Cloud Computing by skeptic or more security concerned companies. The first level of security where cryptography can help Cloud computing is secure storage and this is the focus of Section 2. There are already some cloud providers that have started providing secure storage services but offering different levels of protection.

C. Lee et al. (Eds.): STA 2011 Workshops, CCIS 187, pp. 190–197, 2011.
© Springer-Verlag Berlin Heidelberg 2011

The major handicap of secure storage is that we cannot outsource the processing of this data without decrypting it before or without revealing the keys used for encryption. If we want companies to use the full potential of Cloud Computing we cannot restrict our effort to secure storage but also to secure processing or computation. The first steps in this direction are directed to enable search on encrypted data, see Section 2.2. This allows companies to store confidential information in the cloud whilst still being able to access it partially without having to decrypt it. In this model many companies could share a dataset, update and query it without leaking any information to the cloud provider. By using these techniques, governments could store their citizen databases in the Cloud and access individual records without worrying about disclosure of personal information.

The last measure we discuss in this paper is Secure Computation (Section 3). By secure computation we understand not only that the Cloud Provider cannot get any confidential data used in the computation but also that the output of the computation is verifiable.

2 Secure Storage

The main concern around data storage is the protection of information from unauthorized access. In several usage scenarios the risk of data being disclosed, lost, corrupted or stolen is unacceptable. Until data is stored on resources owned, controlled and maintained by the data owner, the possibility of unauthorised access is reduced by any physical countermeasure or trust in authentication/authorisation mechanism put in place by him/her self (e.g. physically located in room at the establishment, behind closed doors and installing network firewalls and ACLs at software level).

Things radically change when moving from resources fully controlled by the data owner to resources administrated by third party entities like public clouds. Resources that sit outside the user's domain are resources not owned and not controlled by the user and even trusting the resources' provider, the risk that someone (e.g. an employee of the resources' vendor) can access and disclose/corrupt data is considerable. In the literature this risk is usually known as insider abuse or insider threat [18][19][20]. This is the major risk that, presently, is preventing the large adoption of cloud-based solutions by enterprises. Before companies move their data to the cloud, benefitting from the cloud storage advantages, all issues deriving from storing data on un-owned and un-trusted resources must be addressed, including the inconsistencies with this new model, put there by the legal frameworks.

The secure storage approach aims to avoid insider threats using encryption techniques to protect data from unauthorised access. The core concept of secure storage is the encryption of data in the trusted environment before sending it outside to the un-trusted cloud storage resource. There are a wide range of encryption algorithms at the cutting edge which have been proved to be secure that can be used to perform encryption/decryption operations (e.g. AES, Serpent, Blowfish). Theoretically both symmetric and asymmetric algorithms can be used, but, since the latter are much slower than the former, for performance reasons symmetric algorithms are preferred. The usage of encryption as a technique to secure data guarantees the confidentiality of data and helps to detect any corruption in data.

The main issue in the secure storage approach is the management of encryption keys. In fact, once data is encrypted, keys become the true bits to protect! If keys were stored in the un-trusted environment along with data, an attacker could have at his/her disposal both data and the keys to decrypt the data, with disastrous consequences. Keys are stored on a *keystore* that can be implemented either on a i) portable device (e.g., an usb pen-drive) owned by the user who can plug it anywhere (within the trusted environment) or ii) in a specialised server which sits somewhere in the trusted environment. The last solution is the most flexible schema which would allow the user to access data from any location within the trusted environment and would also enable scenarios in which keys could be shared by multiple users (e.g. see Adi Shamir's *How to share a secret* [21] work on the sharing of keys).

A basic architecture of a secure storage system is presented in fig. 1: when the user wants to store data on an un-trusted resource: i) encrypts data at an encryption point (it may be either the user's machine or a service offered within the trusted environment), ii) encrypted data is sent to the storage service and iii) keys are stored on the keystore. Inverse procedure is applied when data must be accessed: it is transferred from the un-trusted storage to the encryption point, here keys are retrieved, the decryption takes place and original data is sent back to the user.

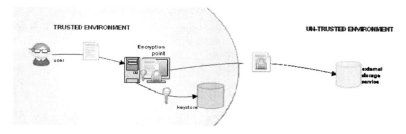

Fig. 1. Basic architecture of a secure storage system

Starting from this basic architecture a more complex one can be developed, for instance to replicate data on multiple storage services (even coming from different vendors) to augment data integrity and reliability in case of failure or corruption of one of the storages.

2.1 Cloud Storage Offerings

All commercial cloud providers offer to their customers at least one cloud storage service: Amazon' S3 and SimpleDB, Microsoft Windows Azure Storage services, Google App Engine Datastore, just to cite the most popular. All these products are very powerful for their scalability and storage capacity, but their security mechanisms are based on authentication of users and the ACLs attached to the data stored. That said, these security mechanisms are too weak in a distributed and un-trusted environment since the risk of data disclosure and corruption still exists. In order to fill the gap between common storage services offered by cloud vendors and security requirements, a secure storage system can be built on top of bare cloud storage.

Implementing such a system, all data stored on the cloud is encrypted and illegible, addressing, in this way, security requirements while still keeping the advantages of cloud storage.

Two good examples of commercial secure storage services which encrypt data client-side before transmitting it outside the user's machine (reasonably considered trusted) are: i) *Spideroak*, that is a cloud based backup and file synchronisation service which uses client-side encryption and implements a so called zero knowledge system where keys (neither the master passwords nor encryption keys) are never transmitted to the service's provider and ii) *GoldKey – Cloud Storage Security Key* with the peculiarity of storing keys on the GoldKey Token: a portable device very similar to a usb pen-drive instead of the user's machine. In contrast, an example of an ineffective secure storage service is *Dropbox*. It offers its users an online space to store data using Amazon's S3 as a back-end storage service. Users' data is encrypted before being stored on S3, but it has to be considered that Dropbox encrypts data in its servers keeping the keys in its servers. This, in fact, nullifies the added value of encryption since, unless for particular use cases, users consider Dropbox' servers as trusted as S3 servers.

Looking at the open source panorama, a promising project released under GNU License named Tahoe-LAFS aims to provide components to build a distributed secure storage system. Besides the encryption mechanism, it also implements an algorithm [22] that splits data in n chunks storing them on different nodes. At retrieval time only $m<n$ nodes are needed to rebuild the original data. This algorithm makes the system more resistant to server failures and/or attacks, by increasing data integrity assurance. A similar approach is used by EncryptMe: a proof of concept secure storage system realised for grid infrastructures [23].

2.2 Searchable Encryption

Searchable encryption is a broad concept that deals with searches in encrypted data. The goal is to outsource encrypted data and be able to conditionally retrieve or query data without having to decrypt all the data.

An interesting problem related with searchable encryption is Private Information Retrieval (PIR) [8][9]. The problem here is for the user to retrieve information from a database without revealing any information about the requested data to the server. Searchable encryption goes one step further by allowing the user not only to retrieve information privately but also to search it.

The first searchable encryption scheme was defined in 2000 [10]. It makes use of symmetric encryption and provides:

- query isolation for searches
- controlled searching
- hidden queries

Those three properties guarantee that the server is not able to learn anything more about the plaintext than the search result, it needs the user's authorisation to search for an arbitrary word and the user need not reveal the word they are searching for. There are some other symmetric schemes for searchable encryption that enhance security and efficiency [11].

Another approach for searchable encryption is to use asymmetric encryption. The first scheme for searchable encryption that makes use of public key cryptography is the Public-Key Encryption with keyword Search (PEKS) scheme, proposed by Boneh et al. [12]. By using public key cryptography it is possible for multiple persons to encrypt data but only the owner of the private key will be able to search for a keyword. This scheme has been enhanced in [13][14]

More advanced solutions also allow searching with wildcards [15]. Most of those schemes use *hidden vector encryption* (HVE). We can see HVE as an identity-based encryption where both the encryption and the decryption key are derived from a vector.

3   Secure Outsourcing of Computation

Computation outsourcing is applied when an entity has to perform a task that requires computation power and resources that the entity cannot dispose and the delegation of this task to an external provider is the only option. Secure outsourcing refers to such an outsourcing in which security requirements, and sometimes privacy requirements can be met. The main challenge of a secure outsourcing is to delegate a computation to a set of service providers that are either distrusted or partially trusted without exposing and revealing either the input data or the computed output. Moreover, the client wants to be able to verify the correctness of the result in order to trust the new data that they possess.

The concept of computation outsourcing can be seen as the core of the cloud computing model. However, such a model of outsourcing, i.e. a distribution of computations under rather loose restrictions cannot be applied in all cases. Indeed, there is a plethora of applications for which there are strong security and privacy requirements and there are companies and research institutes that avoid at any cost a Cloud infrastructure due to security scepticism. Hospitals and health service providers, clinical research institutes, stockbrokers and capital investment companies are just a few examples. It is clear that the design of secure outsourcing computation schemes is a very challenging research area.

3.1   Technical Solutions

Several secure computation outsourcing techniques have been proposed and there are classic results for the problems of secure two-party and multi-party computation. In most cases, the main idea is that the client performs some pre-processing over the input data before sending it to the entity in charge of the computation. This pre-processing adds some structured randomness. After the computation some post-processing is required to remove the added randomness and reveal the final computation output. These technical solutions can be divided into two main categories. The first that a third trusted party (TTP) plays a vital role in the security and solutions so the presence of the TTP is not necessary. We will concentrate on the second category. The computing can be performed either by using special encrypted functions, called garbled circuits, or by using encrypted input data, with a special form of encryption, called homomorphic encryption.

The notion of garbled circuits was introduced by Yao [1]. Initially, the function to be computed is first encrypted by an entity, called the constructor, with symmetric cryptography. Then, another party, called the evaluator, decrypts the function using the keys that correspond to the input data. The use of symmetric encryption algorithms endows efficiency in terms of implementation to the garbled circuits. However, this procedure is one-time-pad like. That means that the garbled circuits can be used only once and their size is proportional to the size of the function to be computed. Several hardware implementations have been proposed to accelerate the procedure.

Homomorphic encryption has several applications including e-voting systems. It allows the computation of encrypted data with requiring any additional information. The first homomorphic encryption schemes were designed to perform specific operations (e.g., multiplications for RSA, additions for Paillier, or additions and one multiplication [4]), allowing the outsourcing of encryption or digital signing. These schemes are very useful for another critical cryptography related secure cloud challenge, the secure storage (see next section). However, over the last few years, fully homomorphic encryption schemes that have been proposed allow for arbitrary computations on encrypted data [5, 6]. However, these schemes are not yet practical, as shown in fully homomorphic encryption which is not yet efficient enough to be used in practical applications.

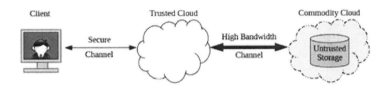

Fig. 2. The Trusted/Commodity Cloud Architecture [7]

Several of the existing solutions have been adapted to the cloud model. The majority of these solutions are lacking either in generality or practicality and scalability [3]. As a general architecture, a multi-cloud approach has been proposed, i.e. two or more clouds that can be used for securing the outsource computation. More precisely, in one of proposals, a trusted cloud is responsible for the security critical operations, i.e. the pre-processing and post-processing encryption and decryption (see Fig. 2). Then, the main operations can be performed by any untrusted cloud. In this approach, any existing MPC solution can be used, but there is no guarantee concerning the correctness of the result.

The second architecture aims to fill this gap. It is based on the cheap computational power that cloud offers, and it uses the core of error correction codes theory, i.e. redundancy. Instead of using only one cloud provider to perform a given computation, two or more different clouds are used. If at least one of them is honest, then the user can either verify the correctness of the result or identify an incorrect output.

As a direct generalisation of the problem of secure outsourcing one can look at the case where a group of clients, that trust each other, want to use a cloud based computation service that they do not fully trust. In this scenario, the proposed fully homomorphic encryption schemes do not apply [2] and additional assumptions are required.

4 Conclusions

We have reviewed in this paper the recent advances in crypto that we foresee will add a new layer of security to Cloud Computing and boost its adoption. As we have shown in the paper, most cryptographic primitives are ready to be used. We only need to convince Cloud Providers to implement them or produce efficient implementations that could ease its inclusion in open source Cloud Computing platforms.

We think that Europe is in a good position to lead this activity. There are many EC funding projects working on Cloud Computing and we expect that collaboration between them can produce the drive needed for this development.

Acknowledgements

The work in this paper was partly sponsored by the EC Framework Programme as part of the ICT PASSIVE project (http://ict-passive.eu/) and by the Ministry of Science and Innovation through the ARES (CSD2007-00004) project.

References

[1] Yao, A.C.-C.: How to generate and exchange secrets. In: Foundations of Computer Science (FOCS 1986), pp. 162–167 (1986)

[2] van Dijk, M., Juels, A.: On the impossibility of cryptography alone for privacy-preserving cloud computing. In: Hot Topics in Security (HotSec 2010), pp. 1–8. USENIX Association (2010)

[3] Gentry, C., Halevi, S.: Implementing Gentry's fully-homomorphic encryption scheme. Cryptology ePrint Archive, Report 2010/520 (2010),
http://eprint.iacr.org/2010/520

[4] Boneh, D., Goh, E.-J., Nissim, K.: Evaluating 2-DNF formulas on ciphertexts. In: Kilian, J. (ed.) TCC 2005. LNCS, vol. 3378, pp. 325–341. Springer, Heidelberg (2005)

[5] Smart, N., Vercauteren, F.: Fully homomorphic encryption with relatively small key and ciphertext sizes. In: Nguyen, P.Q., Pointcheval, D. (eds.) PKC 2010. LNCS, vol. 6056, pp. 420–443. Springer, Heidelberg (2010)

[6] van Dijk, M., Gentry, C., Halevi, S., Vaikuntanathan, V.: Fully homomorphic encryption over the integers. In: Gilbert, H. (ed.) EUROCRYPT 2010. LNCS, vol. 6110, pp. 24–43. Springer, Heidelberg (2010)

[7] Bugiel, S., Nurnberger, S., Sadeghi, A.R., Schneide, T.: Twin Clouds: An Architecture for Secure Cloud Computing. In: Workshop on Cryptography and Security in Clouds, Zurich, March 15-16 (2011)

[8] Chor, B., Kushilevitz, E., Goldreich, O., Sudan, M.: Private information retrieval. J. ACM 45(6), 965–981 (1998)

[9] Kushilevitz, E., Ostrovsky, R.: Replication is not needed: single database, computationally-private information retrieval. In: Proceedings of 38th Annual Symposium on Foundations of Computer Science, pp. 364–373 (1997)

[10] Song, D.X., Wagner, D., Perrig, A.: Practical techniques for searches on encrypted data. In: 21st Symp. on Security and Privacy (S&P), Berkeley, California, pp. 44–55. IEEE Computer Society, Los Alamitos (2000)

[11] Curtmola, R., Garay, J.A., Kamara, S., Ostrovsky, R.: Searchable symmetric encryption: improved definitions and efficient constructions. In: 13th ACM Conference on Computer and Communications Security (CCS 2006), pp. 79–88 (2006)

[12] Boneh, D., Di Crescenzo, G., Ostrovsky, R., Persiano, G.: Public key encryption with keyword search. In: Cachin, C., Camenisch, J.L. (eds.) EUROCRYPT 2004. LNCS, vol. 3027, pp. 506–522. Springer, Heidelberg (2004)

[13] Di Crescenzo, G., Saraswat, V.: Public Key Encryption with Searchable Keywords Based on Jacobi Symbols. In: Srinathan, K., Rangan, C.P., Yung, M. (eds.) INDOCRYPT 2007. LNCS, vol. 4859, pp. 282–296. Springer, Heidelberg (2007)

[14] Rhee, H.S., Park, J.H., Susilo, W., Lee, D.H.: Improved searchable public key encryption with designated tester. In: ASIACCS, pp. 376–379. ACM, New York (2009)

[15] Boneh, D., Waters, B.: Conjunctive, subset, and range queries on encrypted data. In: Vadhan, S.P. (ed.) TCC 2007. LNCS, vol. 4392, pp. 535–554. Springer, Heidelberg (2007)

[16] Jeffery, K., Neidecker-Lutz, B.: The Future Of Cloud Computing, Opportunities For European Cloud Computing Beyond (2010),
http://cordis.europa.eu/fp7/ict/ssai/docs/
cloud-report-final.pdf

[17] Chen, Y., Paxson, V., Katz, R.H.: What's New About Cloud Computing Security? Technical Report No. UCB/EECS-2010-5, (January 20, 2010),
http://www.eecs.berkeley.edu/Pubs/TechRpts/2010/
EECS-2010-5.html

[18] RSA, The Role of Security in Trustworthy Cloud Computing

[19] Oladimeji, E.A.: Security threat Modeling and Analysis: A goal-oriented approach (2006)

[20] Ristenpart, T., Tromer, E., Shacham, H., Savage, S.: Hey, you, get off of my cloud: exploring information leakage in third-party compute clouds (2009)

[21] Shamir, A.: How to share a secret. Commun. ACM, 612–613 (1979)

[22] Plank, J.S., Luo, J., Schuman, C.D., Xu, L., Wilcox-O'Hearn, Z.: A Performance Evaluation and Examination of Open-Source Erasure Coding Libraries For Storage (2009)

[23] Galiero, G., Giammatteo, G.: Trusting third-party storage providers for holding personal information. A Context-based Approach to Protect Identity-related Data in Untrusted Domains, Identity in the Information Society 2(2), 99–114

Identity Management Challenges for Intercloud Applications

David Núñez[1], Isaac Agudo[1], Prokopios Drogkaris[2], and Stefanos Gritzalis[2]

[1] Department of Computer Science, E.T.S. de Ingeniería Informática,
University of Málaga, E-29071 Málaga, Spain
{dnunez,isaac}@lcc.uma.es
[2] Laboratory of Information and Communication Systems Security,
Department of Information and Communication Systems Engineering,
University of the Aegean Samos, GR-83200, Greece
{pdrogk,sgritz}@aegean.gr

Abstract. Intercloud notion is gaining a lot of attention lately from both enterprise and academia, not only because of its benefits and expected results but also due to the challenges that it introduces regarding interoperability and standardisation. Identity management services are one of the main candidates to be outsourced into the Intercloud, since they are one of the most common services needed by companies and organisations. This paper addresses emerging identity management challenges that arise in intercloud formations, such as naming, identification, interoperability, identity life cycle management and single sign-on.

Keywords: Cloud computing, identity management, intercloud, interoperability.

1 Introduction

The adoption of the cloud computing design pattern is rapidly evolving as more and more organisations reach out for the benefits of distributed datacenters. One of the main advantages of cloud computing is that it provides a model of *"utility computing"*; that is, it is capable of offering on-demand provisioning of computing resources, such as storage, computation and networking. This provision of resources is metered for billing and accounting purposes, making possible a *"pay-as-you-go"* model, which could be beneficial for companies. This paradigm can be put in contrast with previous models, based on the acquisition of equipment and software licences. The main benefits that companies and organisations expect from adopting the cloud computing paradigm are the improved flexibility and scalability of their IT services, as well as the resulting cost savings from the outsourcing of such services [1].

Cloud computing infrastructures combine virtualisation and Service Oriented Architecture (SOA) technologies in order to deliver services through shared computing and storage resources, software, applications, and defined business processes. Depending of the level of abstraction, these services are referred to as *Infrastructure as a Service* (IaaS), *Platform as a Service* (PaaS), and *Software as a Service* (SaaS). However, as the resource capability of a single cloud is generally

C. Lee et al. (Eds.): STA 2011 Workshops, CCIS 187, pp. 198–204, 2011.

finite, we are moving towards the *Intercloud* perspective, where clouds cooperate with each other in an attempt to evolve their computing and storage capabilities. For such cooperation to be feasible and efficient, this federation of clouds should be established on common semantics regarding addressing, messaging, naming and identification.

Digital identity management services in cloud computing environments are mainly responsible for authenticating users and supporting access control to services based on user attributes. Such services should preserve the users' privacy while supporting interoperability across multiple domains and simplifying management of identity validation. However, as they evolve to Intercloud mouldings, identity management systems should not only be capable of identifying users but also resources that originate from different clouds.

This paper addresses the challenges that arise in the Intercloud mouldings regarding identity management systems that will not only allow for users' and resource's identification but also support and improve interoperability across multiple domains. The rest of the paper is structured as follows: Section 2 provides an overview of the existing identity management approaches in distributed systems while Section 3 addresses the challenges in Intercloud formations. Finally, Section 4 concludes this paper and provides pointers for future work.

2 Identity Management in Distributed Systems

Identity management service provision in traditional IT environments can be performed either through something possessed by user, traits or attributes that constitute a user's real world identity, by something assigned to the user by a third party entity or by something the derives from a user's earlier conduct and attainments. According to [2][3], these functionalities can be classified into the following four categories:

- *Credential identity service*, where the user is identified through pre- assigned credentials such as a digital certificate,
- *Identifier identity service*, where the user is identified through the allocation of specific identifiers, such as an email account or Identification Card number,
- *Attribute identity service*, where the user is identified through specific attributes that correspond to her real world entity and finally
- *Pattern identity service*, where the user is identified through reputation, honour, trust records and history access records.

As we move on to distributed systems deployment and grid computing, where computing resources and services are shared within virtual organisations, identity management services must provide seamless and secure access to eligible users regardless of the requested resource location [4][5]. Based on their architecture, such identity management systems can be classified into two categories: i) centralised and ii) federated. In the centralised model, user identification is performed by a central entity, which is responsible for both user identification and authentication. Prior to accessing the requested resource or service, users must first receive authorisation from this entity. This obligatory interaction brings up the disadvantages of this approach regarding administration and privacy weaknesses together with the deficiency of privilege delegation and cross-domain access control. The most renowned systems based on this approach are PKI [6] and Kerberos [7]. The federated model, on the other hand, is based on the establishment of trust relationships between the participating parties. After all participants mutually consent on agreements, standards and technologies they form trust relationships and are then obliged to provide legitimate information about their users whenever another trusted participant requests it. Each relying party can still retain its preferred identification service however once a user is successfully authenticated to a domain, he/she is able to receive personalised services across the federated domains, through the portability of his/her identity. Identity management systems based on this approach include WS-Federation [8], Liberty Alliance Project [9] and Shibboleth [10].

3   Challenges for Identity Management in the Intercloud

This section addresses the challenges associated with the Intercloud scenario that a complete identity management solution must overcome to leverage the impending advantages of Intercloud applications.

3.1   Naming and Identification of Intercloud Resources

The nature of the resources involved in the cloud computing paradigm is varied; it ranges from physical components (servers, storage units, etc.) to abstract elements (virtual machines, data repositories, applications, etc.). All these components can be seen as resources of the cloud that are offered to the users. Furthermore, in the Intercloud scenario even clouds themselves could be seen as potential resources to be exploited, as a high-level component capable of offering computation, storage and networking.

Due to this plethora of different kinds of resources, users of cloud computing infrastructures need to be sure of the identity of the resources that they request; that is, they need to know for certain *which* resource is the one they want to request. There is a strong need for appropriate naming and identification mechanisms that enable univocality of resources' identity and permits unambiguous requests. *Naming* is the process of creating a linguistic expression that designates an object [11], while *identification* is the process of distinguishing such an object from the rest in a specific context. Both concepts are closely related, so they are usually grouped together and referred as *identification*. However, we distinguish between the two concepts and treat them separately. These mechanisms are very important, since in most cases they are the basis for advanced functionalities like service discovery, as well as for important security properties, such as authenticity and integrity.

A current approach for the naming and identification of cloud resources is presented in [12], based on the use of XRI [13] and XRDS [14], which are both developed by OASIS. XRI is an extensible scheme for resource naming and identification of resources, while XRDS is an XML-based generic format for resource description and service discovery; XRDS enables the description of resources as well as their associated services, which are called *service endpoints* (SEPs). However, OASIS has recently released XRD 1.0 [15], a new standard for the description and discovery of resources, which supersedes XRDS. The main difference between XRD and XRDS is that, while XRDS describes the services associated to a resource (*endpoints*) in a single document, XRD opts to describe each endpoint in a separate document and to link them all in the resource document. As a consequence, XRDS documents need to be kept up to date with respect with its associated services' attributes, which is something manageable in a private environment where the control of all services is held by the same administrator; however, this is not the case in the Intercloud scenario, so it is essential that each service is described independently, for example, using separate XRD description documents.

3.2 Interoperability of Identity Information in the Intercloud

As we mentioned before, the outsourcing of internal services is one of the main reasons for the enterprise to adopt the cloud computing paradigm. Some companies are eager to embrace this paradigm because of the cost savings that they expect to achieve as the result of this outsourcing. However, the applications and services within a company are not isolated, and they usually form a network of dependencies, with complex relations among them; some of these services may not be outsourced, so special care must be taken with respect to interoperability, which must be preserved.

Some of the most common services rendered by current IT departments within companies are the ones related with identity management, such as access control, privilege management, authentication and user provisioning. For this reason, identity management solutions for the Intercloud should be interoperable with current identity management systems in the enterprise, in order to enable the outsourcing of such advanced services.

One of the main problems related with the interoperability of identity management systems is the use of different "*languages*" to express the identity information, such as X.509 certificates, SAML assertions or WS-Federation security tokens [10]. That is, there is a *syntactic* obstacle that a complete solution has to deal with. Furthermore, even if the involved parties agree at the syntactic level, the use of different formats, names and meanings for identity attributes also produces incompatibilities. This problem represents a *semantic* obstacle that has to be resolved as well.

The syntactic level problems are tackled through the use of encapsulation and translation mechanisms. In order to achieve real interoperability, it is really important to focus both research and industry effort on the definition and application of standard technologies to facilitate these tasks. For example, WS-Federation includes profiles that enable the use of different formats for expresing the security tokens, like SAML assertions and X.509 certificates; more profiles for other formats can be defined so that it is extensible. Furthermore, it introduces a special entity called Security Token Service (STS) that is responsible for issuing, managing and validating security tokens; it is also capable of encapsulating and translating between different formats in order to achieve interoperability between different security domains.

Regarding the interoperability issues between different attribute schemes at the semantic level, standards like the X.520 and X.521 ITU-T Recommendations [17][18] and the RFCs 4519 and 4524 [19][20] have tried to solve the problem by identifying common attributes associated to the identity of people and organizations. There exist other initiatives like eduPerson and eduOrg [21], focused in the solving the same problem for educational organizations. However, in the context of the Intercloud, these initiatives are not enough; there is a strong need for solutions that include more types of subjects, resources and services. Another approach to tackle the interoperability problems at the semantic level is the use of ontologies [22][23], which may enable the integration of heteregenous attribute schemes.

As we have seen, the interoperability problems of traditional identity management systems also appear in the Intercloud and they can be classified as syntactic and semantic; both aspects have to be resolved by a complete solution, which should be standard-based.

3.3   Identity Life Cycle Management in the Intercloud

Throughout the life cycle of an entity's digital identity, numerous alternations regarding attributes, authorisation, provision or entitlement can occur depending on an organisation's policy and entity's availability or behaviour. A swift synchronisation of these alternations, to all concerned parties within the Intercloud, seems imperative in order for each entity to have a similar confrontation. Such synchronisation delays could only lead to ineffective resource sharing but also to security vulnerabilities. Depending on the identity management infrastructures deployed within the Intercloud, a common "language" for performing this synchronisation must be adopted. Alternatively, similar to the Certificate Revocation List (CRL) method in PKI, a common repository could be introduced, where every alternation would be announced. In this direction, OASIS has proposed Service Provisioning Markup Language (SPML), an XML framework for managing the provisioning and allocation of identity information and system resources within and between organisations [24].

3.4   Single Sign-on for Interactions on the Intercloud

The scenario introduced by the Intercloud increases the number of possible interactions that could occur between different actors that participate in the formation. In such interactions, the parties involved are required to mutually exchange identity information, identification and authentication purposes regardless of having previous knowledge of each others identity information or not. From an identity management point of view, the main actors that participate in these interactions are:

- *Intercloud users*, which are the actors that request resources and services, such as human users, external applications (e.g., an IT application from a company), internal applications or cloud providers.
- *Intercloud service providers*, which are cloud providers that are able to offer services or resources to Intercloud users.
- *Intercloud identity providers*, which are cloud providers that are able to authenticate Intercloud users and to share the result of this authentication to Intercloud service providers. They are also responsible for issuing, certifying and managing the identity information of their associated Intercloud users.

In typical cloud environments which support single sign-on functionality, users are able to use the whole spectrum of services and applications without logging-in each time they request a different application or service within the cloud. Similarly, in the Intercloud scenario, users should also be able to access various resources and services offered by different Intercloud service providers, once an Intercloud identity provider has successfully authenticated them. However, as the requested resource could belong to a different cloud, a user's identity information or an equivalent assurance should be transferred to the corresponding Intercloud service provider, without any further actions on the user's part. Consequently, the user's home cloud should be able to perform a single sign-on in order to gain access to the resources offered by another cloud that participates in an Intercloud formation. In this direction, an identity management infrastructure able to support authentication among federated clouds, based on SAML assertions, is proposed in [25].

4 Conclusions

The evolution of cloud computing and the emergence of the Intercloud notion has brought up several challenges regarding interoperability, coherence and standardisation in an attempt to support a dynamic expansion of capabilities. Identity management is an early challenge that must be resolved since identification and authentication must be performed not only for users but for resources as well, within heterogeneous cloud environments. Apart from that, identity management solutions for the Intercloud should be interoperable with current identity management systems in the enterprise, in order to enable the outsourcing of advanced services such as access control, authentication and user provisioning. This paper has addressed emerging identity management challenges regarding interoperability, identity life cycle management and single sign-on that arise in Intercloud formations in an attempt to outline the required characteristics of an efficient identity management system for Intercloud applications. Currently, we are focusing on the interoperability problem, at both syntactic and semantic levels. However, as we have seen throughout this paper, there are several key issues that must be treated and overcome to fully realise the potential of the Intercloud.

Acknowledgements

The work in this paper was partly sponsored by the EC Framework Programme as part of the ICT PASSIVE project (grant agreeement no. 257644) and the ICT NESSoS project (grant agreement number no. 256980).

References

1. Chung, M., Hermans, J.: KPMG's 2010 Cloud Computing Survey (2010)
2. El Maliki, T., Seigneur, J.M.: A Survey of User-centric Identity Management Technologies. In: International Conference on Emerging Security Information, Systems and Technologies, pp. 12–17 (2007)
3. Cao, Y., Yang, L.: A survey of Identity Management technology. In: Information Theory and Information Security, pp. 287–293 (2010)

4. Privacy and Identity Management for Community Services (PICOS),
   http://www.picos-project.eu/
5. Future of Identity in the Information Society (FIDIS), http://www.fidis.net/
6. Kuhn, R., Hu, V.C., Polk, W., Chang, S.: Introduction to Public Key Technology and the Federal PKI. National Institute of Standards and Technology (2001)
7. Kerberos: The Network Authentication Protocol,
   http://web.mit.edu/kerberos/
8. WS-Federation, Web Services Federation (2007),
   http://www.ibm.com/developerworks/library/specification/ws-fed
9. Liberty Alliance Project, http://www.projectliberty.org
10. Shibboleth, http://shibboleth.internet2.edu/
11. International Organization of Standardization. Information technologies: Metadata Registries (ISO/IEC 11179-5), http://metadata-standard.org/
12. Celesti, A., Villari, M., Puliafito, A.: A naming system applied to a RESERVOIR cloud. In: Sixth International Conference on Information Assurance and Security (2010)
13. OASIS: Extensible Resource Identifier (XRI) Syntax V2.0,
   http://docs.oasis-open.org/xri/xri-syntax/2.0/specs/cs01/xri-syntax-V2.0-cs.html
14. OASIS: Extensible Resource Identifier (XRI) Resolution V2.0,
   http://docs.oasis-open.org/xri/2.0/specs/xri-resolution-V2.0.html
15. OASIS: Extensible Resource Descriptor (XRD) V1.0,
   http://docs.oasis-open.org/xri/xrd/v1.0/xrd-1.0.html
16. Bertino, E., Paci, F., Ferrini, R., Shang, N.: Privacy-preserving Digital Identity Management for Cloud Computing. Data Engineering 32(1) (2009)
17. ITU-T Recommendation X.520 (November 2008): The Directory - Selected attribute types (2008)
18. ITU-T Recommendation X.521 (November 2008): The Directory - Selected object classes (2008)
19. Sciberras, A.: RFC 4519 – Lightweight Directory Access Protocol (LDAP): Schema for User Applications. Internet Engineering Task Force (2006)
20. Zeilenga, K.: RFC 4524 – COSINE LDAP/X.500 Schema. Internet Engineering Task Force (2006)
21. Internet2 MACE: eduPerson & eduOrg Object Classes,
   http://middleware.internet2.edu/eduperson/
22. Wache, H., Voegele, T., Visser, U., Stuckenschmidt, H., Schuster, G., Neumann, H., Hübner, S.: Ontology-based integration of information-a survey of existing approaches. In: IJCAI 2001 Workshop: Ontologies and Information Sharing, pp. 108–117 (2001)
23. Priebe, T., Dobmeier, W., Kamprath, N.: Supporting Attribute-based Access Control with Ontologies. In: Proceedings of the First International Conference on Availability, Reliability and Security, pp. 465–472. IEEE Computer Society, Washington (2006)
24. Service Provisioning Markup Language (SPML),
   http://xml.coverpages.org/ni2003-06-05-a.html
25. Celesti, A., Tusa, F., Villari, M., Puliafito, A.: Security and Cloud Computing: InterCloud Identity Management Infrastructure. In: 19th IEEE International Workshop on Enabling Technologies: Infrastructures for Collaborative Enterprises, pp. 263–265 (2010)

Author Index

Agudo, Isaac   190, 198
Aivaloglou, Efthimia   130

Botvich, Dmitri   156
Brudka, Marek   174

Casassa Mont, Marco   146, 166
Chabanne, Hervé   16
Cheng, Hongbing   116
Chevalier, Céline   16
Cho, Kyung Soo   25, 50
Chu, Hai-Cheng   41

Díaz, Rodrigo   182
Drogkaris, Prokopios   198
Duan, Huiying   31

Ech-Cherif El Kettani, Mohamed
    Dafir   56
Eggen, Skjalg   116
Elshaafi, Hisain   156
En-Nasry, Brahim   56

Felkner, Anna   7, 174
Furtak, Janusz   174

Giammatteo, Gabriele   190
Gissing, Michael   138
Gritzalis, Stefanos   198

Han, Jong Wook   103
Harjani, Rajesh   182
Hong, Bonghee   71, 77

Jeon, Seungwoo   71
Jin, Ling   25
Joo, Hyung-Ju   64

Kim, Gihong   71
Kim, Goo   77
Kim, Iee Joon   25
Kim, Seung Kwan   25, 50
Kim, Ung Mo   25, 50
Kim, Young Hee   50

Kounga, Gina   146
Kozakiewicz, Adam   1, 7, 174
Kwon, Joonho   71, 77

Lambrinoudakis, Costas   190
Lasota, Krzysztof   1
Lee, Deok Gyu   103
Lee, Eunjung   64
Lim, Ji Yeon   25, 50

Małowidzki, Marek   174
Maña, Antonio   130, 182
McGibney, Jimmy   156
Mulcahy, Barry   156
Muñoz, Antonio   130, 182

Núñez, David   190, 198

Papanikolaou, Nick   166
Park, Dong-Hwa   94
Park, Hyo-Dal   94
Park, Jong Hyuk   41
Park, Woon Jeung   84
Pearson, Siani   146, 166
Pirker, Martin   138
Power, Eamonn   130

Rizomiliotis, Panagiotis   190
Rong, Chunming   116
Ryu, Wooseok   77

Sandy, Ian   130
Seo, Kyong-Jin   64
Skianis, Charalampos   130

Toegl, Ronald   138

Waller, Adrian   130
Wu, Li-Wei   41

Yoon, Jae Yeol   50
Yu, Hsiang-Ming   41

Zieliński, Zbigniew   174